Spelling Workout

Phillip K. Trocki

MODERN CURRICULUM PRESS

COVER DESIGN: Pronk & Associates

ILLUSTRATIONS: Rick Ewigleben. 32: Jim Steck. 33: Chris Knowles. 48: Jim Steck. 49: Eric Larsen. 64: Jim Steck.. 80: Jim Steck. 81: Chris Knowles. 96: Jim Steck.. 112: Jim Steck. 113: Chris Knowles. 113: penguin: Rick Ewigleben. 166: Jim Steck.

PHOTOGRAPHS: All photos © Pearson Learning unless otherwise noted.

Cover: Artbase Inc.
6: Darrell Gulin/Corbis. 9, 10: Stephen Frink/Corbis. 13: Bob Daemmrich/Stock Boston/PictureQuest. 14: Joseph Sohm/Chromosohm/Stock Connection/PictureQuest. 17: David Buffington/PhotoDisc, Inc. 18: Paul Kaye/Corbis. 21: David Young-Wolff/PictureQuest. 23: Laura Dwight/Corbis. 29: Joseph Sohm; Chromosohm Inc./Corbis. 30: AFP/Corbis. 33: Jonathan Nourok/PhotoEdit. 38: CMCD/PhotoDisc, Inc. 40: Will Hart Photography. 41: Roger Ressmeyer/Corbis. 45: The Purcell Team/Corbis. 46: Gale Zucker/Stock Boston. 51: Pictor International/Pictor International Ltd./PictureQuest. 53: Walter Choroszewski/PictureQuest. 54: Robert Holmes/Corbis. 57: Martin B. Withers/Frank Lane Picture Agency/Corbis. 58: Michael & Patricia Fogden/Corbis. 61: Robert Brenner/PhotoEdit. 62: AFP/Corbis. 65: T. Arruza/Bruce Coleman Incorporated. 67: Westlight Stock-OZ Productions/Corbis. 69: IFA Bilderteam/Stock Photography/PictureQuest. 75: C Squared Studios/PhotoDisc, Inc. 77: Bettmann/Corbis. 79: Culver Pictures/PictureQuest. 81: Peter Johnson/Corbis. 82: Galto Images/Corbis. 83: Picture Finders Ltd./PictureQuest. 86: Brian Cosgrove/Dorling Kindersley. 89: Will Hart Photography. 90: Morton Beebe, S.F./Corbis. 95: Kevin R. Morris/Corbis. 101: Gunter Marx/Corbis. 102: Ewing Galloway/Index Stock Imagery. 105: Ecoscene/Corbis. 106: Paul A. Saunders/Corbis. 108: Corbis. 109: Richard Hutchings/PhotoEdit. 113: Ted Spiegel/Corbis. 114: Pioneer Publications, Inc. 117: David A. Northcott/Corbis. 119: Lynda Richardson/Corbis. 125, 126: Jeffrey L. Rotman/Corbis. 133: Richard Nowitz Photography. 134: U.S. Space & Rocket Center/NASA. 138: Kim Taylor/Dorling Kindersley. 141: Bob Krist/Corbis. 142: Richard Bickel/Corbis.

Acknowledgments
ZB Font Method Copyright © 1996 Zaner-Bloser.

Some content in this product is based upon *Webster's New World Dictionary for Young Adults.* © 2001 Hungry Minds, Inc. All rights reserved. Webster's New World is a trademark or registered trademark of Hungry Minds, Inc.

NOTE: Every effort has been made to locate the copyright owner of material reprinted in this book. Omissions brought to our attention will be corrected in subsequent editions.

Modern Curriculum Press
An imprint of Pearson Learning
299 Jefferson Road, P.O. Box 480
Parsippany, NJ 07054-0480

www.pearsonlearning.com
1-800-321-3106

ISBN 0-7652-2489-5

3 4 5 6 7 8 9 10 DBH 07 06

Modern Curriculum Press

Table of Contents

Spelling Workout—Our Philosophy

Integration of Spelling with Reading and Writing

In each core lesson for *Spelling Workout*, students read spelling words in context in a variety of fiction and nonfiction selections. The reading selections provide opportunities for reading across the curriculum, focusing on the subject areas of science, social studies, health, language arts, music, and art.

After students read the selection and practice writing their spelling words, they use list words to help them write about a related topic in a variety of forms such as descriptive paragraphs, stories, news articles, poems, letters, advertisements, and posters. A proofreading exercise is also provided for each lesson to help students apply the writing process to their own writing and reinforce the use of spelling words in context.

The study of spelling should not be limited to a specific time in the school day. Use opportunities throughout the day to reinforce and maintain spelling skills by integrating spelling with other curriculum areas. Point out spelling words in books, texts, and the student's own writing. Encourage students to write, as they practice spelling through writing. Provide opportunities for writing with a purpose.

Phonics-Based Instructional Design

Spelling Workout takes a solid phonic and structural analysis approach to encoding. The close tie between spelling and phonics allows each to reinforce the other. *Spelling Workout* correlates closely to *MCP Phonics*, although both programs are complete within themselves and can be used independently.

Research-Based Teaching Strategies

Spelling Workout utilizes a test-study-test method of teaching spelling. The student first takes a pretest of words that have not yet been introduced. Under the direction of the teacher, the student then self-corrects the test, rewriting correctly any word that has been missed. This approach not only provides an opportunity to determine how many words a student can already spell but also allows students to analyze spelling mistakes. In the process students also discover patterns that make it easier to spell list words. Students study the words as they work through practice exercises, and then reassess their spelling by taking a final test.

High-Utility List Words

The words used in *Spelling Workout* have been chosen for their frequency in students' written and oral vocabularies, their relationships to subject areas, and for structural as well as phonetic generalizations. Each list word has been cross-referenced with one or more of the following:

Carroll, Davies, and Richman. *The American Heritage Word Frequency Book*

Dale and O'Rourke. *The Living Word Vocabulary*

Dolch. *220 Basic Sight Words*

Fry, Polk, and Fountoukidis. *Spelling Demons—197 Words Frequently Misspelled by Elementary Students*

Green and Loomer. *The New Iowa Spelling Scale*

Hanna. *Phoneme Grapheme Correspondences as Cues to Spelling Improvement*

Harris and Jacobson. *Basic Elementary Reading Vocabularies*

Hillerich. *A Written Vocabulary of Elementary Children*

Kucera and Francis. *Computational Analysis of Present-Day American English*

Rinsland. *A Basic Vocabulary of Elementary Children*

Sakiey and Fry. *3000 Instant Words*

Thomas. *3000 Words Most Frequently Written*

Thomas. *200 Words Most Frequently Misspelled*

A Format That Results in Success

Spelling Workout treats spelling as a developmental process. Students progress in stages, much as they learn to speak and read. In *Spelling Workout*, they move gradually from simple sound/letter relationships to strategies involving more complex word-structure patterns.

Sample Core Lesson

- **Spelling Words in Action** presents an engaging and informative reading selection in each lesson that illustrates the spelling words in context.

- The activity in the box at the end of the reading selection helps students focus on the spelling patterns of the list words presented in the lesson.

Blends with **l** and **r**

Lesson 13

Spelling Words in Action

How tall is General Sherman?

Wooden Soldier

The day of the **class** trip was finally here. The students followed their teacher across the **grass**. A bird flew overhead. They all looked up. Then they saw it. The tree was huge. Its **trunk** was as wide as a **truck** is long.

The students were visiting Sequoia National Park in California. They were looking at the tallest tree in the world. It is a sequoia named General Sherman. It is 272 feet tall. The students looked up **from** the **flat** land around the tree. It was like looking at a 20-story building.

General Sherman is still growing in Sequoia National Park. Maybe you will visit it someday.

Look back at the words in dark print. What do you notice about their spelling? Say each word. What consonant sounds do you hear?

53

- The **Tip** explains the spelling patterns, providing a focus for the lesson.

- The **List Words** box contains the spelling words for each lesson.

- **Spelling Practice** exercises give students an opportunity to practice writing new words while reinforcing the spelling patterns.

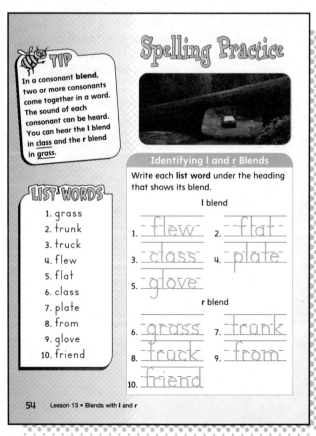

TIP

In a consonant **blend**, two or more consonants come together in a word. The sound of each consonant can be heard. You can hear the l blend in <u>class</u> and the r blend in <u>grass</u>.

Spelling Practice

Identifying l and r Blends

Write each **list word** under the heading that shows its blend.

LIST WORDS

1. grass
2. trunk
3. truck
4. flew
5. flat
6. class
7. plate
8. from
9. glove
10. friend

l blend

1. flew
2. flat
3. class
4. plate
5. glove

r blend

6. grass
7. trunk
8. truck
9. from
10. friend

54 Lesson 13 • Blends with **l** and **r**

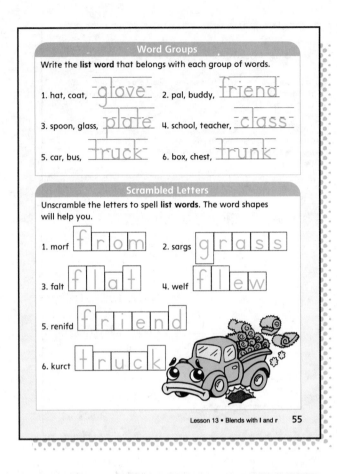

Word Groups

Write the **list word** that belongs with each group of words.

1. hat, coat, **glove**
2. pal, buddy, **friend**
3. spoon, glass, **plate**
4. school, teacher, **class**
5. car, bus, **truck**
6. box, chest, **trunk**

Scrambled Letters

Unscramble the letters to spell **list words**. The word shapes will help you.

1. morf **from**
2. sargs **grass**
3. falt **flat**
4. welf **flew**
5. renifd **friend**
6. kurct **truck**

- Word meaning activities provide opportunities to practice list words while helping students develop their vocabularies.

- Activities such as crossword puzzles, riddles, and games help motivate students by making learning fun.

Spelling and Writing

Proofreading

Each sentence has two mistakes. Use the proofreading marks to fix each mistake. Write the misspelled **list words** correctly on the lines.

Proofreading Marks

◯ spelling mistake
≡ capital letter

1. Jackie bought a flate piece of land in oregon.
2. it has lots of green grase.
3. My frend jackie likes it there.

1. **flat**
2. **grass**
3. **friend**

Writing a Poem

Trees give us shade, fruit, and branches to climb. Write a poem about a tree. Proofread your poem and fix any mistakes.

_____
_____
_____
_____
_____
_____
_____

BONUS WORDS

growl
fresh
plan
blanket
crown

- **Spelling and Writing** reinforces the connection between spelling and everyday writing, and encourages students to apply the list words in different contexts.

- **Proofreading** practice builds proofreading proficiency and encourages students to check their own writing.

- **Writing** activities provide opportunities for students to use their spelling words in a variety of writing forms and genres. Write-on lines are provided. Students may also wish to use separate sheets of paper.

- **Bonus Words** offer more challenging words with similar spelling patterns. Activities in the *Teacher's Edition* give students the opportunity to practice the words with a partner.

Sample Review Lesson

- The **Review** lesson allows students to practice what they've learned.

- The spelling patterns used in the previous five lessons are reviewed at the beginning of the lesson.

- **Check Your Spelling Notebook** suggests that students look at their spelling notebooks to review any words that give them trouble. A partner activity provides practice for those words in a variety of learning modalities—kinesthetic, visual, and auditory.

- A variety of activities provides practice and review of selected list words from the previous lessons.

- **Show What You Know** is a cumulative review of the words in the five previous lessons using a standardized-test format.

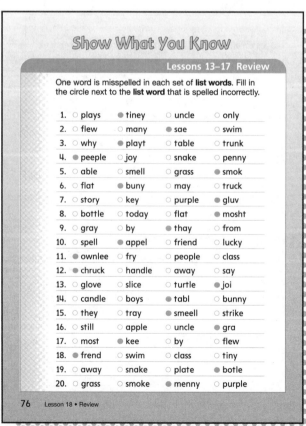

Spelling Workout in the Classroom

Classroom Management

Spelling Workout is designed as a flexible instructional program. The following plans are two ways the program can be taught.

The 5-day Plan
Day 1 – Spelling Words in Action and Warm-Up Test
Days 2 and 3 – Spelling Practice
Day 4 – Spelling and Writing
Day 5 – Final Test

The 3-day Plan
Day 1 – Spelling Words in Action and Warm-Up Test/Spelling Practice
Day 2 – Spelling Practice/Spelling and Writing
Day 3 – Final Test

Testing

Testing is accomplished in several ways. A **Warm-Up Test** is administered after reading the **Spelling Words in Action** selection and a **Final Test** is given at the end of each lesson. Dictation sentences for each **Warm-Up Test** and **Final Test** are provided.

Research suggests that students benefit from correcting their own **Warm-Up Tests**. After the test has been administered, have students self-correct their tests by checking the words against the list words. You may also want to guide students by reading each letter of the word, asking students to point to each letter and circle any incorrect letters. Then, have students rewrite each word correctly.

Tests for review lessons are provided in the *Teacher's Edition* as reproducibles following each lesson. These tests provide not only an evaluation tool for teachers, but also added practice in taking standardized tests for students.

Individualizing Instruction

Bonus Words are included in every core lesson as a challenge for better spellers and to provide extension and enrichment for all students.

Review lessons reinforce correct spelling of difficult words from previous lessons.

Spelling Notebook allows each student to analyze spelling errors and practice writing troublesome words independently. Notebook pages appear as reproducibles in the *Teacher's Edition.*

A reproducible individual **Student Record Chart** provided in the *Teacher's Edition* allows students to record their test scores.

Ideas for meeting the needs of ESL students are provided.

Dictionary

In the back of each student book is a comprehensive dictionary with definitions of all list words and bonus words. Students will have this resource at their fingertips for any assignment.

The Teacher's Edition —Everything You Need!

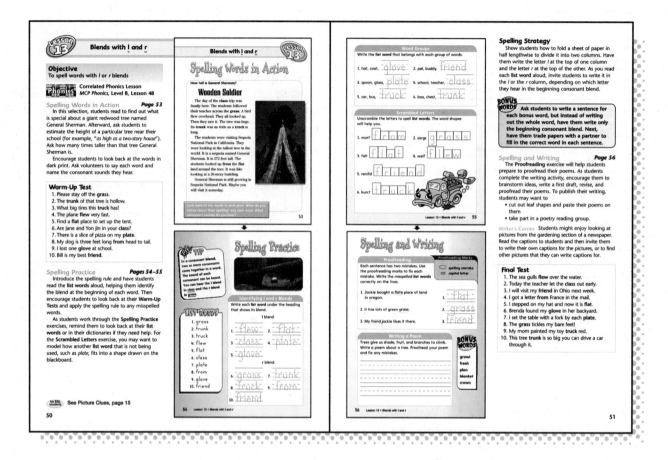

- The **Objective** clearly states the goals of each core lesson.

- Spelling lessons are correlated to *MCP Phonics*.

- Ideas for introducing and setting a purpose for reading are given for each reading selection.

- A **Warm-Up Test**, or pretest, is administered before the start of each lesson. Dictation sentences are provided.

- Concise teaching notes give guidance for working through the lesson.

- Ideas for meeting the needs of ESL students are highlighted.

- **Spelling Strategy** activities provide additional support for reinforcing and analyzing spelling patterns.

- Activities for using the **Bonus Words** listed in the student books are provided.

- **Spelling and Writing** includes suggestions for helping students use proofreading marks to correct their work. Suggestions for using the writing process to complete the writing activity are also offered.

- **Writer's Corner** extends the content of each reading selection by suggesting ways in which students can explore real-world writing.

- A **Final Test** is administered at the end of the lesson. Dictation sentences are provided.

Lesson Review Test (Side A)

Read each set of words. Fill in the circle next to the word that is spelled correctly.

1. ⓐ frum   ⓑ from
   ⓒ frome   ⓓ fromm

2. ⓐ todae   ⓑ tooday
   ⓒ tuday   ⓓ today

3. ⓐ joye   ⓑ joi
   ⓒ joy   ⓓ jooy

4. ⓐ slise   ⓑ sliec
   ⓒ slies   ⓓ slice

5. ⓐ tiney   ⓑ tiny
   ⓒ tinnie   ⓓ tinney

6. ⓐ turdle   ⓑ tertle
   ⓒ turtle   ⓓ turtel

7. ⓐ friend   ⓑ freind
   ⓒ frend   ⓓ frennd

8. ⓐ smoak   ⓑ smook
   ⓒ smoek   ⓓ smoke

9. ⓐ key   ⓑ kee
   ⓒ kea   ⓓ keye

- **Review** lessons review spelling objectives, give guidance for further practice of list words, and provide dictation sentences for a **Final Test**. Reproducible two-page standardized tests to help prepare students for test-taking are supplied for assessment purposes after each **review** lesson.

Take It Home 3

Your child has learned to spell many new spelling words and would enjoy sharing them with you and your family. Here are some ways to help your child review the words in Lessons 13–17 and have some family fun too!

Slice of Life
Best friend, why not, slice of pizza—these are just some of the everyday phrases that contain your child's spelling words. Help your child come up with and list even more. Encourage your child to share the list at school.

Lesson 13
1. class
2. flat
3. flew
4. friend
5. from
6. glove
7. grass
8. plate
9. truck
10. trunk

Lesson 14
1. snake
2. smell
3. still
4. smoke
5. spell
6. swim
7. slice
8. most
9. strike
10. story

Lesson 15
1. away
2. boys
3. gray
4. joy
5. may
6. plays
7. say
8. they
9. today
10. tray

Lesson 16
1. bunny
2. by
3. fry
4. key
5. lucky
6. many
7. only
8. penny
9. tiny
10. why

Lesson 17
1. apple

Spelling Enrichment

Dictionary Activities

Around the World Designate the first person in the first row to be the traveler. The traveler must stand next to the student seated behind him or her. Then, dictate any letter of the alphabet at random. Instruct the two students to quickly name the letter of the alphabet that precedes the given letter. The student who is first to respond with the correct answer becomes the traveler while the other student sits at that desk. The traveler then moves to compete with the next person in the row. The game continues with the traveler moving up and down the rows as the teacher dictates various alphabet letters. See who can be the traveler who has moved the farthest around the classroom. For variety, you may want to require students to state the letter that follows the given letter. You may also want to dictate pairs of list words and have students name which word comes first.

Stand-Up While the teacher pronounces a word from the spelling dictionary, students look up the entry word and point to it. Tell students to stand up when they have located the entry. See who is the first student to stand up.

This game can be played using the following variations:

1. Have students stand when they have located the guide words for a given word.

2. Have students stand when they are able to tell on what page a given list word appears in the dictionary.

Alphabetical Scramble Prepare tagboard cards with spelling words written on them in large letters. Distribute the cards to students. Call on three students to come to the front of the room and arrange themselves so that their word cards are in alphabetical order.

Cut-Off Distribute a strip of paper to each student. Instruct students to write any four spelling words on the strip. All but one of the words should be in alphabetical order. Then have students exchange their strip with a partner. Students use scissors to cut off the word that is not in alphabetical sequence and tape the remaining word strips together. If students find this activity too difficult, you might have them cut all four words off the strip and arrange them alphabetically on their desks.

Applied Spelling

Journal Allow time each day for students to write in a journal. A spiral bound notebook can be used for this purpose. Encourage students to express their feelings about events that are happening in their lives at home or at school, or they could write about what their plans are for the day. To get them started, you may have to provide starter phrases. Allow them to use "invented" spelling for words they can't spell.

Collect the journals periodically to write comments that echo what the student has written. For example, a student's entry might read, "I'm hape I gt to plae bazball todae." The teacher's response could be "Baseball is my favorite game, too. I'd be happy to watch you play baseball today at recess." This method allows students to learn correct spelling and sentence structure without emphasizing their errors in a negative way.

Letter to the Teacher On a regular basis, invite students to write a note to you. At first you may have to suggest topics or provide a starter sentence. It may be possible to suggest a topic that includes words from the spelling list. Write a response at the bottom of each letter that provides the student with a model of any spelling or sentence structure that apparently needs improvement.

Daily Edit Each day, provide a brief writing sample on the board that contains errors in spelling, capitalization, or punctuation. Have students rewrite the sample correctly. Provide time later in the day to have the class correct the errors on the board. Discuss why the spelling is as it is while students self-correct their work.

Acrostic Poems Have students write a word from the spelling list vertically. Then instruct them to join a word horizontally to each letter of the list word. The horizontal words must begin with the letters in the list word. They also should be words that describe or relate feelings about the list word. Encourage students to refer to a dictionary for help in finding appropriate words. Here is a sample acrostic poem:

   Zebras
   Otters
   Ostriches

- Reproducible **Take It Home Masters** also follow each **Review** lesson and strengthen the school–home connection by providing ideas for parents and students for additional practice at home. Plus, they provide the complete set of spelling words for that group of lessons.

- Suggested games and group activities make spelling more fun.

Spelling Strategies for Your ESL Students

You may want to try some of these suggestions to help you promote successful language learning for ESL students.

* Prompt use of spelling words by showing pictures or objects that relate to the topic of each selection. Invite students to discuss the picture or object.

* Demonstrate actions or act out words. Encourage students to do the same.

* Read each selection aloud before asking students to read it independently.

* Define words in context and allow students to offer their own meanings of words.

* Make the meanings of words concrete by naming objects or pictures, role-playing, or pantomiming.

Spelling is the relationship between sounds and letters. Learning to spell words in English is an interesting challenge for English First Language speakers as well as English as a Second Language speakers. You may want to adapt some of the following activities to accommodate the needs of your students—both native and non-English speakers.

Rhymes and Songs

Use rhymes, songs, poems, or chants to introduce new letter sounds and spelling words. Repeat the rhyme or song several times during the day or week, having students listen to you first, then repeat back to you line by line. To enhance learning for visual learners in your classroom and provide opportunities for pointing out letter combinations and their sounds, you may want to write the rhyme, song, poem, or chant on the board. As you examine the words, students can easily see similarities and differences among them. Encourage volunteers to select and recite a rhyme or sing a song for the class. Students may enjoy some of the selections in *Miss Mary Mack and Other Children's Street Rhymes* by Joanna Cole and Stephanie Calmenson or *And the Green Grass Grew All Around* by Alvin Schwartz.

Student Dictation

To take advantage of individual students' known vocabulary, suggest that students build their own sentences incorporating the list words. For example:

Mary ran.

Mary ran away.

Mary ran away quickly.

Sentence building can expand students' knowledge of how to spell words and of how to notice language patterns, learn descriptive words, and so on.

Words in Context

Using words in context sentences will aid students' mastery of new vocabulary.

* Say several sentences using the list words in context and have students repeat after you. Encourage more proficient students to make up sentences using list words that you suggest.

* Write cloze sentences on the board and have students help you complete them with the list words.

Point out the spelling patterns in the words, using colored chalk to underline or circle the elements.

Oral Drills

Use oral drills to help students make associations among sounds and the letters that represent them. You might use oral drills at listening stations to reinforce the language, allowing ESL students to listen to the drills at their own pace.

Spelling Aloud Say each list word and have students repeat the word. Next, write it on the board as you name each letter, then say the word again as you track the letters and sound by sweeping your hand under the word. Call attention to spelling changes for words to which endings or suffixes were added. For words with more than one syllable, emphasize each syllable as you write, encouraging students to clap out the syllables. Ask volunteers to repeat the procedure.

Variant Spellings For a group of words that contain the same vowel sound, but variant spellings, write an example on the board, say the word, and then present other words in that word family (*cake: rake, bake, lake*). Point out the sound and the letter(s) that stand for the sound. Then, add words to the list that have the same vowel sound (*play, say, day*). Say pairs of words (*cake, play*) as you point to them, and identify the vowel sound and the different letters that represent the sound (long *a: a_e, ay*). Ask volunteers to select a different pair of words and repeat the procedure.

Vary this activity by drawing a chart on the board that shows the variant spellings for a sound. Invite students to add words under the correct spelling pattern. Provide a list of words for students to choose from to help those ESL students with limited vocabularies.

Categorizing To help students discriminate among consonant sounds and spellings, have them help you categorize words with single consonant sounds and consonant blends or digraphs. For example, ask students to close their eyes so that they may focus solely on the sounds in the words, and then pronounce *smart, smile, spend*, and *special*. Next, pronounce the words as you write them on the board. After spelling each word, create two columns—one for *sm*, one for *sp*. Have volunteers pronounce each word, decide which column it fits under, and then write the word in the correct column. Encourage students to add to the columns any other words they know that have those consonant blends.

To focus on initial, medial, or final consonant sounds, point out the position of the consonant blends or digraphs in the list words. Have students find and list the words under columns labeled *Beginning, Middle,* and *End.*

Tape Recording Encourage students to work with a partner or their group to practice their spelling words. If a tape recorder is available, students can practice at their own pace by taking turns recording the words, playing back the tape, and writing each word they hear. Students can then help each other check their spelling against their *Spelling Workout* books. Observe as needed to be sure students are spelling the words correctly.

Comparing/Contrasting To help students focus on word parts, write list words with prefixes or suffixes on the board and have volunteers circle, underline, or draw a line between the prefix or suffix and its base word. Review the meaning of each base word, then invite students to work with their group to write two sentences: one using just the base word; the other using the base word with its prefix or suffix. For example: *My favorite mystery was due at the library Monday afternoon. By Tuesday afternoon the book was overdue!* Or, *You can depend on Jen to arrive for softball practice on time. She is dependable.* Have students contrast the two sentences, encouraging them to tell how the prefix or suffix changed the meaning of the base word.

Questions/Answers Write list words on the board and ask pairs of students to brainstorm questions or answers about the words, such as "Which word names more than one? How do you know?" (*foxes,* an *es* was added at the end) or, "Which word tells that something belongs to the children? How do you know?" (*children's* is spelled with an *'s*)

Games

You may want to invite students to participate in these activities.

Picture Clues Students can work with a partner to draw pictures or cut pictures out of magazines that represent the list words, then trade papers and label each other's pictures. Encourage students to check each other's spelling against their *Spelling Workout* books.

Or, you can present magazine cutouts or items that picture the list words. As you display each picture or item, say the word clearly and then write it on the board as you spell it aloud. Non-English speakers may wish to know the translation of the word in their native language so that they can mentally connect the new word with a familiar one. Students may also find similarities in the spellings of the words.

Letter Cards Have students create letter cards for vowels, vowel digraphs, consonants, consonant blends and digraphs, and so on. Then, say a list word and have students show the card that has the letters representing the sound for the vowels or consonants in that word as they repeat and spell the word after you. You may wish to have students use their cards independently as they work with their group.

Charades/Pantomime Students can use gestures and actions to act out the list words. To receive credit for a correctly guessed word, players must spell the word correctly. Such activities can be played in pairs so that beginning English speakers will not feel pressured. If necessary, translate the words into students' native languages so that they understand the meanings of the words before attempting to act them out.

Change or No Change Have students make flash cards for base words and endings. One student holds up a base word; another holds up an ending. The class says "Change" or "No Change" to describe what happens when the base word and ending are combined. Encourage students to spell the word with its ending added.

Scope and Sequence for MCP Spelling Workout

Skills	Level A	Level B	Level C	Level D	Level E	Level F	Level G	Level H
Consonants	1–12	1–2	1–2	1	1	1, 7, 9	RC	3
Short Vowels	14–18	3–5	3	2	RC	RC	RC	RC
Long Vowels	20–23	7–11, 15	4–5, 7–8	3	RC	RC	RC	RC
Consonant Blends/Clusters	26–28	13–14	9–10, 17	5, 7	RC	RC	RC	RC
y as a Vowel	30	16	11–13	RC	RC	RC	27	RC
Consonant Digraphs—th, ch, sh, wh, ck	32–33	19–21	14–16	9	RC	RC	RC	RC
Vowel Digraphs		33	6–7, 9	19–21, 23	8–10	11, 14–17	25	RC
Vowel Pairs	29		26	20, 22	7–8, 10	14	25	
r-Controlled Vowels		22, 25	19–20	8	RC	RC	RC	4
Diphthongs	24	32	31	22–23	11	17	RC	RC
Silent Consonants			8	11	4	8–9	RC	RC
Hard and Soft c and g		21	2	4	2	2	RC	
Plurals			21–22	25–27, 29	33–34	33	RC	RC
Prefixes		34	32–33	31–32	13–17	20–23, 25	7–8, 33	7–11, 19–20
Suffixes/Endings	34–35	26–28	21–23, 25, 33	13–17	25–29, 31–32	26–29, 31–32	5, 9, 13–14, 16, 26	5, 25–27
Contractions		23	34	28	20	RC	RC	RC
Possessives				28–29	20	RC	RC	RC
Compound Words				33	19	RC	34	RC
Synonyms/Antonyms				34	RC	RC	RC	RC
Homonyms		35	35	35	RC	34	RC	RC
Spellings of /f/: f, ff, ph, gh				10	3	3	RC	RC
Syllables					21–23	RC	RC	1
Commonly Misspelled Words					35	34	17, 35	17, 29, 35
Abbreviations						35	RC	RC
Latin Roots							11, 15, 31	13–16

Skills	Level A	Level B	Level C	Level D	Level E	Level F	Level G	Level H
Words with French or Spanish Derivations							10, 29	RC 28
Words of Latin/French/Greek Origin								21–23, 28
List Words Related to Specific Curriculum Areas							31–34, 28, 32	
Vocabulary Development	●	●	●	●	●	●	●	●
Dictionary	●	●	●	●	●	●	●	●
Writing	●	●	●	●	●	●	●	●
Proofreading	●	●	●	●	●	●	●	●
Reading Selections	●	●	●	●	●	●	●	●
Bonus Words	●	●	●	●	●	●	●	●
Review Tests in Standardized Format	●	●	●	●	●	●	●	●
Spelling Through Writing								
Poetry	●	●	●	●	●	●	●	●
Narrative Writings	●	●	●	●	●	●	●	●
Descriptive Writings	●	●	●	●	●	●	●	●
Expository Writings	●	●	●	●	●	●	●	●
Persuasive Writings			●	●	●	●	●	●
Notes/Letters	●	●	●		●	●	●	●
Riddles/Jokes	●	●	●					
Recipes/Menus	●	●	●			●	●	
News Stories		●	●	●	●	●	●	●
Conversations/Dialogues	●	●		●	●	●		●
Stories	●	●	●	●	●	●		●
Interviews/Surveys		●			●	●	●	RC
Logs/Journals	●	●	●	●	●	●	●	
Ads/Brochures		●	●	●	●	●	●	●
Reports					●	●	●	●
Literary Devices							●	●
Scripts		●					●	●
Speeches					●	●		●
Directions/Instructions	●	●		●				●

Numbers in chart indicate lesson numbers

RC = reinforced in other contexts

● = found throughout

Consonants

Objective
To use consonants to spell words

 Phonics
Correlated Phonics Lessons
MCP Phonics, Level B, Lessons 1–3

Spelling Words in Action   *Page 5*

In this selection, students read to find out how difficult it is to use all 26 letters in one sentence. You may wish to read the passage aloud with them. Afterward, students may enjoy working in small groups to try to write a sentence using as many of the letters as possible.

Encourage students to look back at the words in dark print. Ask volunteers to say each word and identify the consonant sounds.

Warm-Up Test
1. The red **fox** is a beautiful animal.
2. **Cut** out the shapes.
3. Who climbed the **hill**?
4. I love my **new** puppy!
5. Please **put** your books away.
6. Did you eat **all** of your lunch?
7. The **moon** lit up the night sky.
8. Please **tell** me about your trip.
9. We **saw** a great movie!
10. The **wind** blew the kite up high.

Spelling Practice   *Pages 6–7*

Introduce the spelling rule and have students read the **list words** aloud. Encourage students to look back at their **Warm-Up Tests** and apply the spelling rule to any misspelled words.

As students work through the **Spelling Practice** exercises, remind them to look back at their **list words** or in their dictionaries if they need help. For the **Word Puzzle**, you may need to explain the meanings of Across and Down as well as the relationship between the numbers preceding clues and those in the puzzle. If necessary, help students complete the first item.

 for ESL students   See Rhymes and Songs, page 14.

18

Spelling Words in Action

How many letters are in the alphabet?

Alphabet Acrobat

There are 26 letters in the alphabet. Not long ago someone **saw** a way to use all 26 letters in one sentence. Here it is:

"The quick brown **fox** jumps over a lazy dog."

The sentence uses **all** 26 letters of the alphabet. See if you can find them all.

No one has been able to write a sentence using each letter just once. Can you **put** all the letters of the alphabet into one sentence? If your sentence has fewer than 33 letters, **tell** everyone you know. You may have set a **new** world record!

Look back at the words in dark print. Say each word. What consonant sounds do you hear?

5

Spelling Practice

TIP
Consonants are all the letters of the alphabet except a, e, i, o, u, and sometimes y. Each consonant spells its own sound. Listen for each sound in the **list words**.

LIST WORDS
1. fox
2. cut
3. hill
4. wind
5. put
6. all
7. moon
8. saw
9. tell
10. new

Writing Consonants
Write the missing consonants for each word. Trace the letters to spell **list words**.

1. wind   2. put
3. saw   4. fox
5. new   6. all
7. tell   8. hill
9. moon   10. cut

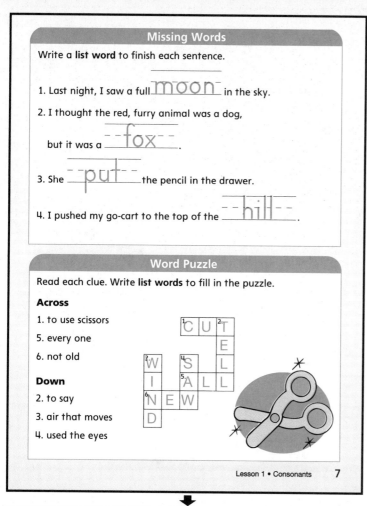

Missing Words

Write a **list word** to finish each sentence.

1. Last night, I saw a full ‾‾moon‾‾ in the sky.

2. I thought the red, furry animal was a dog,

   but it was a ‾‾fox‾‾.

3. She ‾‾put‾‾ the pencil in the drawer.

4. I pushed my go-cart to the top of the ‾‾hill‾‾.

Word Puzzle

Read each clue. Write **list words** to fill in the puzzle.

Across
1. to use scissors
5. every one
6. not old

Down
2. to say
3. air that moves
4. used the eyes

¹C	U	T	²T
			E
³W		⁴S	L
I		⁵A	L
⁶N	E	W	
D			

Lesson 1 • Consonants   7

Spelling and Writing

Proofreading

Each sentence has two mistakes. Use the proofreading marks to fix each mistake. Write the misspelled **list words** correctly on the lines.

Proofreading Marks
- ⬭ spelling mistake
- ⊙ add period

1. Carl made a nue alphabet⊙

2. He wrote down al the letters⊙

3. Then he putt a picture next to each letter⊙

1. ‾‾new‾‾

2. ‾‾all‾‾

3. ‾‾put‾‾

Writing a Sentence

It's not easy to use every letter of the alphabet in one sentence. Try this instead. Write one sentence using as many **list words** as you can. Proofread your sentence. Fix any mistakes.

BONUS WORDS

bad
ball
fix
ear
trip

8   Lesson 1 • Consonants

Spelling Strategy

Write one-syllable words on the board that begin with the same single consonants as the **list words**. Say each word as you write it and ask students to name a **list word** that begins with the same consonant sound. Invite volunteers to write the **list word** on the board and circle the beginning consonants in both words.

BONUS WORDS Pair the students into teams of partners. Each team should think of a word that rhymes with each bonus word, and write it down. Suggest that they use the rhyming words to write a poem.

Spelling and Writing   *Page 8*

The **Proofreading** exercise will help the students prepare to proofread their writing. As students complete the writing activity, encourage them to share ideas, write a first draft, revise, and proofread their work. To publish their writing, students may want to
- count the number of different letters they used
- mark that number on their papers
- display their sentences on the bulletin board.

Writer's Corner The class may enjoy learning more about world records. Read selected entries from the *Guinness Book of World Records* aloud, and have students make up and write their own entries for a class book of records.

Final Test
1. We are **all** in the play.
2. Please **cut** the pizza in slices.
3. A **fox** lives in the forest.
4. I rode my bike down the **hill**.
5. The **wind** took my hat!
6. The **moon** is bright tonight.
7. I **put** my backpack on the hook.
8. I **saw** a robin in the park.
9. Please **tell** me your name.
10. My **new** coat is warm.

Objective
To use consonants to spell words

 Correlated Phonics Lessons
MCP Phonics, Level B,
Lessons 1–3

Spelling Words in Action   *Page 9*
Students can read this selection to find out about a manatee's unusual teeth. You may wish to read the passage aloud with them. After reading, invite students to talk about what is special about other animals' teeth.

Encourage students to look back at the words in dark print. Ask volunteers to say each word and identify the consonant sounds.

Warm-Up Test
1. Will you **let** me ride your bike?
2. My brother played a song on **his** guitar.
3. I **had** a hamburger for lunch.
4. I will **ask** my mother if you can stay for dinner.
5. How **old** is your little sister?
6. She **took** her umbrella with her.
7. Today is Sunday, and it is **also** my birthday.
8. Grandpa **sat** at the head of the table.
9. The glass **fell** to the floor and broke.
10. I will **get** a broom to sweep up the glass.

Spelling Practice   *Pages 10–11*
Introduce the spelling rule and have students read the **list words** aloud. Encourage students to look back at their **Warm-Up Tests** and apply the spelling rule to any misspelled words.

As students work through the **Spelling Practice** exercises, remind them to look back at their **list words** or in their dictionaries if they need help. Tell students that although some words may fit more than one blank, each word should be used only one time as an answer. For the **Story**, have students read the entire sentence before choosing a word. If the word they choose doesn't make sense in the sentence, encourage them to try another word.

 for ESL students See Picture Clues, page 15

20

Spelling Words in Action

What are "marching molars"?

Did You Ever See a Manatee?

Manatees are big animals that live in water. They are gentle giants and love to play.

Manatees eat sea grasses and weeds. They **also** eat tree branches hanging close to the water.

Scientists studied manatees and discovered something special. When a manatee's front teeth wore out, they **fell** out! Then the teeth in the back moved toward the front. New teeth grew in the back. Scientists **had** never seen this before. They called these teeth "marching molars" because they are always "marching" from the back of the manatee's mouth to the front.

A manatee can live to be about 60 years **old**. **His** teeth are not nearly that old, though!

Look back at the words in dark print. Say each word. What consonant sounds do you hear?

9

Spelling Practice

TIP
Consonants are the building blocks of all words. Any letter that is not a vowel is a **consonant**. Listen for the sounds of the consonants in these words.
get   had   took

LIST WORDS
1. let
2. his
3. had
4. ask
5. old
6. took
7. also
8. sat
9. fell
10. get

Writing Consonants
Write the missing consonants for each word. Trace the letters to spell **list words**.

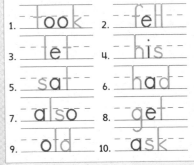

1. took   2. fell
3. let   4. his
5. sat   6. had
7. also   8. get
9. old   10. ask

Word Clues

Read each clue. Then write the **list word** that rhymes with the underlined word.

1. It means **allowed**.
   It rhymes with <u>pet</u>. let

2. It means **got hold of**.
   It rhymes with <u>look</u>. took

3. It means **used a chair**.
   It rhymes with <u>cat</u>. sat

4. It means **go and bring something**.
   It rhymes with <u>net</u>. get

Story

Write **list words** to finish the story.

The Lion House

I saw a big lion at the zoo. When he opened his

mouth, I saw no teeth! I decided to ask about the

lion. I was sure he had teeth once. The zookeeper told

me, "His teeth fell out. He is a very old

lion. We also have some baby lions." I looked at the

baby lions. They did not have teeth either!

Spelling and Writing

Proofreading

Each sentence has two mistakes. Use the proofreading marks to fix each mistake. Write the misspelled **list words** correctly on the lines.

Proofreading Marks
◯ spelling mistake
☰ capital letter

1. sally, the olt giraffe, was crying.

2. Doctor allen tuk a look at Sally's eyes.

3. the giraffe hed an eyelash in its eye.

1. old

2. took

3. had

Writing a Story

Write a story about a visit to the dentist. Tell what the dentist did to your teeth. Use as many **list words** as you can. Proofread your story. Fix any mistakes.

_____

_____

_____

_____

_____

_____

_____

BONUS WORDS
look
cold
blue
ship
mask

Spelling Strategy

To reinforce consonant sounds in the **list words**, have students work with a partner and take turns

- saying each word, emphasizing the consonant sounds
- writing the **list word** or words that have the consonant sounds they hear
- spelling each word aloud, and then naming the consonants and the vowels.

BONUS WORDS
Have students draw a picture for each bonus word, and then trade papers with a partner. Each partner should write sentences using the correct bonus word for each of the pictures.

Spelling and Writing   Page 12

The **Proofreading** exercise will help the students prepare to proofread their writing. As students complete the writing activity, encourage them to share ideas, write a first draft, revise, and proofread their work. To publish their writing, students may want to

- create a class book of "Visits to the Dentist"
- role-play their experiences in the dentist's office.

Writer's Corner Invite a local veterinarian to talk to the class about caring for animals' teeth. Before the visit, students can write one or two questions they want to ask the doctor. Encourage students who have pets of their own to ask about preventive dental care for their particular animals.

Final Test

1. Tina is **also** going with us.
2. I **had** a toy bear when I was a baby.
3. I'll **ask** Mike to help me.
4. Tim left **his** jacket in the car.
5. I **let** my sister wear my scarf.
6. Did you remember to **get** milk?
7. My **old** boots are too small.
8. It really hurt when I **fell** on the ice!
9. I **took** off my hat when I came inside.
10. Mom and Dad **sat** on the couch.

Lesson 3 — Short Vowels a and i

Objective
To spell words with short *a* and short *i*

 Correlated Phonics Lessons
MCP Phonics, Level B,
Lessons 8–12

Spelling Words in Action   Page 13

In this selection, students learn about sports equipment. You may wish to read the passage aloud with them. After reading, invite students to come up with sentences using the different meanings of hand.

Encourage students to look back at the words in dark print. Ask volunteers to say each word and identify the short-vowel sound.

Warm-Up Test
1. The **band** played a happy song.
2. Does this glove **fit** your hand?
3. I let **him** borrow my pen.
4. I need a **tack** to hang the map.
5. I felt **sad** when my friend moved away.
6. I made a **list** of school supplies.
7. Is this a catcher's **mitt**?
8. I **have** a dog named Buster.
9. It **will** rain tomorrow.
10. **Skin** is what covers our bodies.

Spelling Practice   Pages 14–15

Introduce the spelling rule and have students read the **list words** aloud. Encourage students to look back at their **Warm-Up Tests** and apply the spelling rule to any misspelled words.

As students work through the **Spelling Practice** exercises, remind them to look back at their **list words** or in their dictionaries if they need help. For the **Opposites** exercise, you might want to review antonym pairs, asking students to name the opposites of words, such as new (*old*), up (*down*), large (*small* or *little*), hot (*cold*), and do (*don't*).

 See Student Dictation, page 14

22

Short Vowels a and i — Lesson 3

Spelling Words in Action

Why is it important to have the right equipment?

Be Prepared

It is important to **have** the right sports equipment. Is your baseball **mitt** the right size? You **will** find it hard to catch those fly balls if your mitt is too big.

If your sneakers do not **fit** right, you might fall and **skin** your knee. That would make you **sad**.

On hot days, you might use a sweat **band**. This cloth band fits around the top of your head. It keeps sweat from running down your face or into your eyes.

When a sports season starts, make a **list** of what you will need. Make sure you always have the right equipment.

Say each word in dark print in the paragraphs. What vowel sounds do you hear?

13

Spelling Practice

 TIP
Each **list word** has the short **a** sound or the short **i** sound. You hear the short i sound in <u>fit</u>. You hear the short **a** sound in <u>sad</u> and in <u>have</u>, even though <u>have</u> has more than one vowel.

LIST WORDS
1. band
2. fit
3. him
4. tack
5. sad
6. list
7. mitt
8. have
9. will
10. skin

Identifying Short Vowel Sounds
Write each **list word** under the heading that shows its short vowel sound.

a as in cat
1. band   2. tack
3. sad   4. have

i as in sit
5. fit   6. him
7. list   8. mitt
9. will   10. skin

14   Lesson 3 • Short Vowels **a** and **i**

Opposites

Write a **list word** that means the opposite of each word.

1. won't   will   2. happy   sad

3. her   him   4. haven't   have

Rhyming

Write a **list word** to match each clue.

1. These two **list words** rhyme with each other.   fit   mitt

2. This word rhymes with <u>thin</u>.   skin

3. This word rhymes with <u>back</u>.   tack

4. This word rhymes with <u>fist</u>.   list

5. This word rhymes with <u>hand</u>.   band

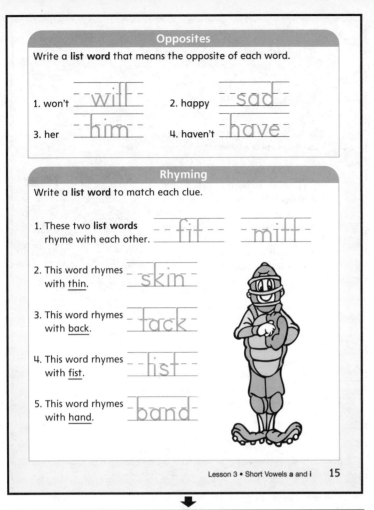

Spelling and Writing

Proofreading

Each sentence has two mistakes. Use the proofreading marks to fix each mistake. Write the misspelled **list words** correctly on the lines.

Proofreading Marks

◯ spelling mistake
⊙ add period

1. I ⟨hav⟩ gloves to keep my hands warm⊙

2. My ⟨mit⟩ helps me catch baseballs⊙

3. My mittens ⟨fitt⟩ over my fingers like a sock⊙

1. have

2. mitt

3. fit

Writing a Description

Describe something you wear on your hands. Try to use as many **list words** as you can. Proofread your description. Fix any mistakes.

_____

_____

_____

_____

_____

_____

BONUS WORDS

bit
gift
pad
stand
rack

Spelling Strategy

Write a **list word** on the board, leaving a blank for its vowel. Ask students to identify the missing vowel or vowel sound. Volunteers can write the vowel and then say the words using the correct vowel sound.

BONUS WORDS Have students write a sentence for each bonus word, using the word <u>hand</u> in each sentence. Have them trade papers with a partner and read each other's sentences aloud, telling how they are the same or different.

Spelling and Writing   *Page 16*

The **Proofreading** exercise will help students prepare to proofread their descriptions. To publish their writing, students may want to write their descriptions on cut-out mitten shapes to make a class shape book. As students complete the writing activity, encourage them to brainstorm ideas, write a first draft, revise, and proofread their work.

Writer's Corner Words that have multiple meanings and that are used in common idioms are the source of much amusement in the Amelia Bedelia stories by Peggy Parish. The class may enjoy reading or hearing one of these stories. Discuss the different meanings of selected words in a story. Then have students use the words to write sentences.

Final Test

1. The **sad** story made us cry.
2. Does your dog **have** shaggy hair?
3. I need a rubber **band** for my project.
4. The library has a **list** of new books.
5. Ask **him** where he lives.
6. My **skin** really itches!
7. Please don't step on that **tack**!
8. Will your books **fit** in this box?
9. Alice **will** not eat candy.
10. Will wanted a baseball **mitt** for his birthday.

Objective
To spell words with short *u* and short *o*

Correlated Phonics Lessons
MCP Phonics, Level B,
Lessons 13–14, 16–17

Spelling Words in Action   *Page 17*

In this selection, students discover that some words are spelled the same both forward and backward. You may wish to read the passage aloud with them. After reading, invite students to brainstorm other palindromes, such as *dad*, *tot*, and *did*. Then encourage them to think of other words that make a new word when spelled backward, such as *but*, *not*, and *dam*.

Encourage students to look back at the words in dark print. Ask volunteers to say each word and name its vowel sound.

Warm-Up Test
1. Please do not chew **gum** in school.
2. We cook stew in a big **pot**.
3. There is a lot of **dust** on the table.
4. I saw a **frog** in the pond.
5. We **must** brush our teeth every day.
6. I lost a green **sock**.
7. That big dog was once a little **pup**.
8. The nurse gave me a flu **shot**.
9. My kitten is **soft** and cuddly.
10. Please help me **tug** this door open.

Spelling Practice   *Pages 18–19*

Introduce the spelling rule and have students read the **list words** aloud. Encourage students to look back at their **Warm-Up Tests** and apply the spelling rule to any misspelled words.

As students work through the **Spelling Practice** exercises, remind them to look back at their **list words** or in their dictionaries if they need help. For the **Word Puzzle**, you might want to remind students how to complete a crossword puzzle.

for ESL students See Charades/Pantomime, page 15

Spelling Words in Action

Can you think of a word that is spelled the same backward and forward?

Inside Out

In English, words are spelled from left to right. You **must** always spell them that way.

Some words are spelled the same backward or forward. Spell **pup** backward. It still spells p-u-p. Pop is still pop. Mom is always mom. Can you think of some others?

Try some spelling magic. With backward spelling, some words become other words. The word **tug** becomes gut. A **pot** becomes a top. With backward magic, a bus can go underwater because it turns into a sub.

When you spell **frog** backward, you get gorf. Gorf is not a real word. It sounds funny, though. Try to make up a funny meaning for your new nonsense word.

Look back at the words in dark print. Say each word. How many different vowel sounds do you hear?

17

Spelling Practice

TIP
Each **list word** has the short u sound or the short o sound. You hear the short u sound in <u>must</u> and <u>pup</u>. You hear the short o sound in <u>soft</u> and <u>pot</u>.

LIST WORDS
1. gum
2. pot
3. dust
4. frog
5. must
6. sock
7. pup
8. shot
9. soft
10. tug

Identifying Short Vowel Sounds

Write each **list word** under the heading that shows its short-vowel sound.

u as in <u>up</u>

1. gum   2. dust
3. must   4. pup
5. tug

o as in <u>hot</u>

6. pot   7. frog
8. sock   9. shot
10. soft

Missing Words

Look at the pictures. Write a **list word** to finish each sentence.

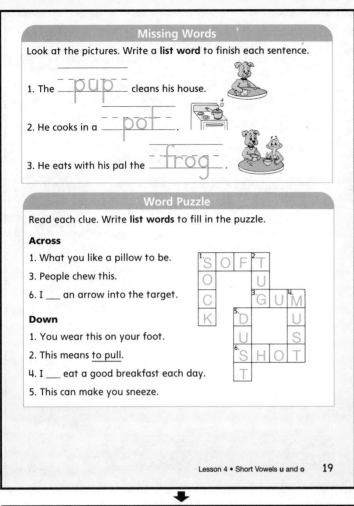

1. The ___pup___ cleans his house.

2. He cooks in a ___pot___ .

3. He eats with his pal the ___frog___ .

Word Puzzle

Read each clue. Write **list words** to fill in the puzzle.

Across

1. What you like a pillow to be.
3. People chew this.
6. I ___ an arrow into the target.

Down

1. You wear this on your foot.
2. This means to pull.
4. I ___ eat a good breakfast each day.
5. This can make you sneeze.

Crossword answers: SOFT, SOCK, GUM, DUST, SHOT, TUG, MUST

Lesson 4 • Short Vowels **u** and **o**   19

Spelling and Writing

Proofreading

Proofreading Marks

⬭ spelling mistake
≡ capital letter

Each sentence has two mistakes. Use the proofreading marks to fix each mistake. Write the misspelled **list words** correctly on the lines.

1. Carla has a pupp named snowball.

2. snowball's favorite toy is an old sok.

3. carla and her pup play tuge of war with it.

1. ___pup___

2. ___sock___

3. ___tug___

Writing a Story

Some people can swim backwards. Sometimes cars and trucks drive backwards. Write a story about something you think would be fun to do backwards. Proofread your story. Fix any mistakes.

_____
_____
_____
_____
_____
_____
_____

BONUS WORDS

stuck
stop
fog
just
lock

20   Lesson 4 • Short Vowels **u** and **o**

Spelling Strategy

Invite students to use their arms to make the shape of the vowel sound they hear in each **list word**, *o* or *u*. As you say each **list word**, have students form the letter they hear: for *o*, they can raise their arms over their heads to form a circle; for *u*, they can open their arms to form a horseshoe shape. Encourage students to repeat each word as they form the letter that stands for each sound.

BONUS WORDS

Have students write a sentence for each bonus word with a blank where the bonus word belongs. Then have them trade papers with a partner to figure out the correct bonus word for each sentence.

Spelling and Writing   *Page 20*

The **Proofreading** exercise will help students prepare to proofread their stories. As students complete the writing activity, encourage them to brainstorm ideas, write a first draft, revise, and proofread their work. To publish their writing, students may want to read their stories aloud to the class.

Writer's Corner Invite students to use palindromes to write their own riddles. Students may also enjoy spoonerisms, anagrams, and other word-play activities described in *A Children's Almanac of Words at Play* by Willard R. Espy, or in a similar book.

Final Test

1. To ring the bell, you must **tug** on the rope.
2. The little tadpole grew into a big **frog**.
3. Did you ever get **gum** stuck on your nose?
4. Children **must** come to school on time.
5. Anna **shot** the ball through the hoop.
6. Is there really a **pot** of gold at the end of a rainbow?
7. The mother seal takes care of her **pup**.
8. Your dog chewed a hole in my **sock**!
9. Isn't this pillow **soft**?
10. I will **dust** the book shelf with a soft cloth.

Short Vowel e

Objective
To spell words with short *e*

Correlated Phonics Lessons
MCP Phonics, Level B,
Lessons 18–19

Spelling Words in Action   *Page 21*

Read the opening question and ask if students can guess what this poem is about. After reading the poem, invite students to discuss ways we take care of our teeth.

Encourage students to look back at the words in dark print. Ask volunteers to say each word and name the vowel sound.

Warm-Up Test

1. Baby teeth are your first **set** of teeth.
2. My **head** hurts.
3. Please **help** me carry this.
4. The other team is not here **yet**.
5. I toast **bread** for a snack.
6. A **belt** will hold up your pants.
7. When we camp we sleep in a **tent**.
8. Mom **said** we could go to the fair.
9. Make your **bed** before you leave for school.
10. The boys will **sell** lemonade at their stand.

Spelling Practice   *Pages 22–23*

Introduce the spelling rule and have students read the **list words** aloud. Encourage students to look back at their **Warm-Up Tests** and apply the spelling rule to any misspelled words.

As students work through the **Spelling Practice** exercises, remind them to look back at their list words or in their dictionaries if they need help. For the **Riddle Puzzle** exercise, work through the directions and the first item with students, having students use their fingers to trace where the answer will appear in the puzzle. Be sure students understand how to use the shaded boxes to complete the riddle.

 See Letter Cards, page 15

Spelling Words in Action

What are white and can bite?

Shiny White, Shiny Bright

There's a **set** of things inside your **head**.
They're strong. They're hard. They bite!
They're shiny, small, and when you smile,
they make a lovely sight.

At school and home, they **help** you speak.
They help you chew your **bread**.
They chatter when the day is cold.
They're white, not blue or red.

Brush them before you go to **bed**,
and floss them, don't forget!
Brushing after every meal is even
better **yet**.

Just remember what I **said**,
and you'll keep your teeth inside your head.

Look back at the words in dark print. Say each word. What vowel sound do you hear in each word?

Spelling Practice

TIP

Each **list word** spells the short e sound in one of these ways:
e, as in s<u>e</u>t and h<u>e</u>lp
ea, as in h<u>ea</u>d
ai, as in s<u>ai</u>d

LIST WORDS

1. set
2. head
3. help
4. yet
5. bread
6. belt
7. tent
8. said
9. bed
10. sell

Writing the Short e Sound

Write the missing letter or letters that make the **e** sound in the words. Trace the letters to spell **list words**.

1. tent
2. belt
3. yet
4. help
5. sell
6. head
7. said
8. bed
9. set
10. bread

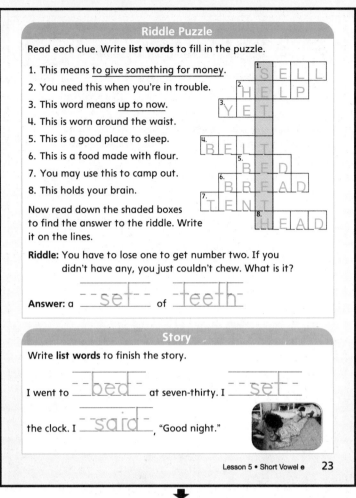

Riddle Puzzle

Read each clue. Write **list words** to fill in the puzzle.

1. This means <u>to give something for money</u>.
2. You need this when you're in trouble.
3. This word means <u>up to now</u>.
4. This is worn around the waist.
5. This is a good place to sleep.
6. This is a food made with flour.
7. You may use this to camp out.
8. This holds your brain.

Now read down the shaded boxes to find the answer to the riddle. Write it on the lines.

Riddle: You have to lose one to get number two. If you didn't have any, you just couldn't chew. What is it?

Answer: a ___set___ of ___teeth___

Story

Write **list words** to finish the story.

I went to ___bed___ at seven-thirty. I ___set___ the clock. I ___said___, "Good night."

Lesson 5 • Short Vowel e   23

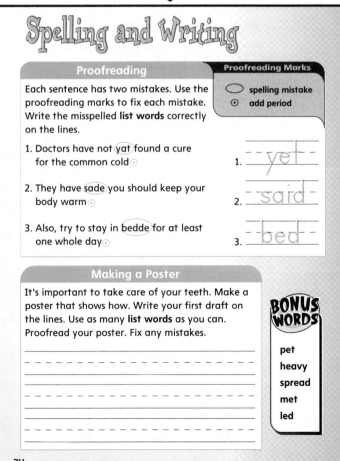

Spelling and Writing

Proofreading

Each sentence has two mistakes. Use the proofreading marks to fix each mistake. Write the misspelled **list words** correctly on the lines.

Proofreading Marks

⬭ spelling mistake
⊙ add period

1. Doctors have not (yat) found a cure for the common cold⊙

2. They have (sade) you should keep your body warm⊙

3. Also, try to stay in (bedde) for at least one whole day⊙

1. ___yet___

2. ___said___

3. ___bed___

Making a Poster

It's important to take care of your teeth. Make a poster that shows how. Write your first draft on the lines. Use as many **list words** as you can. Proofread your poster. Fix any mistakes.

_____
_____
_____
_____
_____

BONUS WORDS

pet
heavy
spread
met
led

24   Lesson 5 • Short Vowel e

Spelling Strategy

Write the different ways to spell *e* on the board, *e*, *ea*, and *ai*. Say each **list word** and have a volunteer write the word on the board under the correct heading. After each word has been written, have volunteers read the words for each different spelling aloud, identifying the letter(s) in each word that stand for the *e* sound.

BONUS WORDS Ask students to write a sentence for each bonus word, then trade papers with a partner. Have students circle the bonus words in their partners' sentences.

Spelling and Writing   Page 24

The **Proofreading** exercise will help students prepare to proofread the posters they are writing. As students complete the writing activity, encourage them to brainstorm ideas, write a first draft, revise, and proofread their work. To publish their writing, students may want to display their posters around the school or offer them to local pediatricians for office display.

Writer's Corner Bring in cereal boxes and point out the nutritional information and ingredients list. Talk about how this information can help us choose healthy foods. Students could then write a note to their families, recommending certain cereals and telling why.

Final Test
1. Ted has a fancy buckle on his **belt**.
2. I like my **bread** with butter on it.
3. We cannot leave **yet**!
4. A hat will keep your **head** warm.
5. Will your sister **help** make the poster?
6. Ivy **said**, "It is time to go."
7. Mom bought a new **set** of dishes.
8. Our **tent** is small and cozy inside.
9. We gave Dad breakfast in **bed**.
10. I will **sell** my old bicycle at a yard sale.

Lesson 6 — Review Lessons 1–5

Objective
To review spelling words with consonants and short-vowel sounds *a, i, u, o,* and *e*

Check Your Spelling Notebook
Pages 25–28

Based on your observations, note which words are giving students the most difficulty and offer assistance for spelling them correctly. Watch for the frequently misspelled word *said*.

To give students extra help and practice in taking standardized tests, you may want to have them take the **Warm-Up Test** for this lesson on pages 30–31. After scoring the tests, return them to students so that they can record their misspelled words in their spelling notebooks.

Invite students to practice their troublesome words by finger-writing each one on the desk while a partner spells the word aloud. After practicing their troublesome words, students can work through the exercises for lessons 1–5 and the cumulative review, **Show What You Know**. Before they begin each exercise, you may want to go over the spelling rule.

 Take It Home

Invite students to listen for and use the **list words** in lessons 1–5 at home during mealtime conversations. For a complete list of the words, encourage students to take their *Spelling Workout* books home. Students can also use the **Take It Home Master 1** on pages 32–33 to help them do the activity. In class, they can discuss the special words they used.

28

In Lessons 1 through 5, you learned to spell words with consonants and short vowel sounds.

Check Your Spelling Notebook
Look at the words in your spelling notebook. Which words for Lessons 1 through 5 did you have the most trouble with? Write them here.

_____

_____

_____

Lesson 1
 TIP Any letter that is not a vowel is a consonant. Listen for the consonant sounds in these words: **fox, wind.**

List Words
moon
all
new
saw

Write a **list word** that rhymes with each word.

1. soon _____moon_____

2. jaw _____saw_____

3. chew _____new_____

4. ball _____all_____

25

Lesson 2
 TIP Consonants are the building blocks for all words. Listen for the consonant sounds in these words: **took, also.**

List Words
ask
old
his
get

Write a **list word** that means the opposite of each word.

1. hers _____his_____   2. give _____get_____

3. new _____old_____   4. answer _____ask_____

Lesson 3
TIP You can hear the short a sound in **band** and **sad**. Listen for the short i sound in **fit** and **skin**.

List Words
have
tack
mitt
will

Write a **list word** to finish each sentence.

1. We _____will_____ go now.

2. Let's _____have_____ a party.

3. You can _____tack_____ up the sign.

4. This is my baseball _____mitt_____.

26   Lesson 6 • Review

Lesson 4

TIP Some words have the short **u** sound or the short **o** sound. Listen for the short **u** sound in **gum** and **must**. Listen for the short **o** sound in **pot** and **sock**.

List Words
frog
soft
pup
tug

Write a **list word** that means the same or almost the same as each word.

1. pull _tug_   2. toad _frog_

3. dog _pup_   4. gentle _soft_

Lesson 5

TIP The short **e** sound is spelled in different ways: **e**, as in **help**; **ea**, as in **bread**; and **ai**, as in **said**.

List Words
head
set
said
tent

Write a **list word** to match each clue.

1. You do this to the dinner table. _set_

2. You sleep here on a camping trip. _tent_

3. This word means the same as spoke. _said_

4. This is at the top of your body. _head_

Lesson 6 • Review   27

Show What You Know

Lessons 1–5 Review

One word is misspelled in each set of **list words**. Fill in the circle next to the **list word** that is spelled incorrectly.

1. ○ fit   ● foks   ○ hill   ○ tack
2. ● gom   ○ pup   ○ put   ○ new
3. ○ bed   ● sett   ○ saw   ○ will
4. ○ head   ○ let   ○ sad   ● healp
5. ○ list   ● winde   ○ tent   ○ all
6. ○ sock   ○ old   ○ skin   ● kut
7. ○ get   ○ tell   ○ new   ● brede
8. ● touk   ○ dust   ○ ask   ○ also
9. ○ fox   ○ sell   ● lisst   ○ moon
10. ○ set   ○ mitt   ● hiz   ○ him
11. ○ will   ● fel   ○ band   ○ frog
12. ● hav   ○ had   ○ sat   ○ yet
13. ○ must   ○ bed   ○ shot   ● bellt
14. ○ took   ○ pot   ● saft   ○ all
15. ○ cut   ● auld   ○ tug   ○ sad
16. ● hil   ○ help   ○ mitt   ○ wind
17. ○ sell   ○ fell   ● frogg   ○ his
18. ○ have   ○ sat   ● schot   ○ sock
19. ○ said   ○ soft   ○ gum   ● muon
20. ● tugg   ○ belt   ○ bread   ○ put

28   Lesson 6 • Review

Final Test

1. Jim wore **new** shoes on the first day of school.
2. May we **get** some books at the library?
3. They **will** eat lunch in the cafeteria.
4. Mia had to **tug** on the handle to open the door.
5. It's fun to sleep in a **tent** when we go camping.
6. Pedro **saw** that movie more than five times!
7. My **old** sneakers are very comfortable.
8. Maria helped me **tack** the map to the wall.
9. The kitten made a **soft** purring sound.
10. Who owns that **set** of matching luggage?
11. **All** of us came to the party.
12. Chan lost **his** best pair of gloves.
13. The catcher wears a special **mitt**.
14. We chose the spotted **pup** with the long ears.
15. Mom **said** that I can go to the park after school.
16. The **moon** was shining brightly on the lake.
17. Lori raised her hand to **ask** a question.
18. We all **have** time to shop after we eat dinner.
19. A bright green **frog** hopped into the pond.
20. This hat is much too big for my **head**!

Check Your Spelling Notebook

Before writing each word, students can name the letters that spell each short-vowel sound and the consonants that begin or end each word.

Lesson Review Test (Side A)

Lesson 6

Read each set of words. Fill in the circle next to the word that is spelled correctly.

1. ⓐ wil   ⓑ wile
   ⓒ wiil   ⓓ will

2. ⓐ ask   ⓑ aske
   ⓒ assk   ⓓ asck

3. ⓐ mune   ⓑ muen
   ⓒ mone   ⓓ moon

4. ⓐ softe   ⓑ suft
   ⓒ soft   ⓓ sofft

5. ⓐ all   ⓑ awle
   ⓒ aul   ⓓ alle

6. ⓐ hise   ⓑ hizz
   ⓒ hiz   ⓓ his

7. ⓐ miet   ⓑ mitt
   ⓒ mitte   ⓓ mit

8. ⓐ sead   ⓑ said
   ⓒ sed   ⓓ sedd

9. ⓐ noo   ⓑ nue
   ⓒ new   ⓓ newe

Lesson Review Test (Side B)

Read each set of words. Fill in the circle next to the word that is spelled correctly.

10. ⓐ oled   ⓑ old
     ⓒ owld   ⓓ oald

11. ⓐ tak   ⓑ taek
     ⓒ taick   ⓓ tack

12. ⓐ sau   ⓑ saw
     ⓒ sawe   ⓓ saww

13. ⓐ tente   ⓑ teent
     ⓒ tent   ⓓ tentt

14. ⓐ hav   ⓑ havv
     ⓒ have   ⓓ havve

15. ⓐ frog   ⓑ frogg
     ⓒ frogge   ⓓ fruge

16. ⓐ gette   ⓑ geet
     ⓒ get   ⓓ gett

17. ⓐ hedd   ⓑ hed
     ⓒ hedt   ⓓ head

18. ⓐ tug   ⓑ tuge
     ⓒ tugg   ⓓ tugge

Take It Home 1

Your child has learned to spell many new words in Lessons 1–5 and would like to share them with you and your family. Here are some great ways to turn your child's spelling review into family fun.

Sound Bites!

Here's a "tasteful" idea! Help your child listen for and use spelling words during mealtime conversations. It's a sure-fire recipe for spelling success! Start things off by using a word that interests you. (For example, "I remember the first time astronauts landed on the **moon**.") What words hold special meanings or memories for your child? Encourage your child to use and jot down those words.

Lesson 1
1. all
2. cut
3. fox
4. hill
5. moon
6. new
7. put
8. saw
9. tell
10. wind

Lesson 2
1. also
2. ask
3. fell
4. get
5. had
6. his
7. let
8. old
9. sat
10. took

Lesson 3
1. band
2. fit
3. have
4. him
5. list
6. mitt
7. sad
8. skin
9. tack
10. will

Lesson 4
1. dust
2. frog
3. gum
4. must
5. pot
6. pup
7. shot
8. sock
9. soft
10. tug

Lesson 5
1. bed
2. belt
3. bread
4. head
5. help
6. said
7. sell
8. set
9. yet
10. tent

What a Card!

Cut out the word cards on this page and make more of your own using the spelling words. Then place the cards in two stacks.
Take turns drawing one card from each stack and using the two words in a silly sentence.

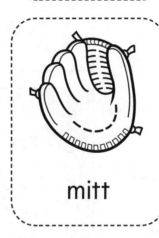

frog

head

tent

moon

mitt

bread

"Did you ever see a **frog** standing on its **head**?"

"Did you ever catch the **moon** in your baseball **mitt**?"

Objective
To spell words with long *a* spelled *a_e* and *ai*

Phonics | Correlated Phonics Lesson
MCP Phonics, Level B, Lesson 23

Spelling Words in Action   *Page 29*

In this selection, students read to learn about some surprising new cars that have been invented. You may wish to read the passage aloud with them. After reading, invite students to tell you what car they found most amazing.

Encourage students to look back at the words in dark print. Ask volunteers to say each word and identify the long-vowel sound they hear.

Warm-Up Test

1. Carl will **save** his money to buy his Mom some flowers.
2. There are big fish in the **lake**.
3. Wear a smile on your **face**.
4. Mark and Matt are reading the **same** book.
5. Please close the **gate**.
6. It is fun to **rake** leaves.
7. Use **tape** to fix that rip.
8. Look at the pretty **sail** on that boat.
9. I will **paint** the car red.
10. Is your cat **afraid** of dogs?

Spelling Practice   *Pages 30–31*

Introduce the spelling rules and have students read the **list words** aloud. Encourage students to look back at their **Warm-Up Tests** and apply the spelling rules to any misspelled words.

As students work through the **Spelling Practice** exercises, remind them to look back at their **list words** or in their dictionaries if they need help.

for ESL students See Charades / Pantomime, page 15

34

Spelling Words in Action

What kind of car would you like to drive someday?

Future Cars

Driving will never be the **same** again! Amazing new cars are changing the **face** of driving. The Skycar won't get stuck in traffic jams. It will **sail** right over them. The Skycar can lift off straight into the air. It can land the same way.

Some people are **afraid** to fly. They might like a car that swims. It goes from highway to **lake** with no problem. That could **save** drivers a lot of time.

Some drivers could save money, too. The Solar Phantom has special panels. The panels allow the car to run on sunlight instead of gas.

These are some of the cars of the future. Who knows? Maybe you will design an amazing car yourself someday.

Look back at the words in dark print. Say each word. What vowel sound do you hear?

29

Spelling Practice

TIP

The long **a** sound is the vowel sound you hear in save and sail. Each **list word** has the long **a** sound spelled in one of these ways: a_e or ai.

Writing the Long a Sound

Write each **list word** under the heading that shows its long **a** spelling pattern.

LIST WORDS

1. save
2. lake
3. face
4. same
5. gate
6. rake
7. tape
8. sail
9. paint
10. afraid

ai

1. sail   2. paint

3. afraid

a_e

4. save   5. lake

6. face   7. same

8. gate   9. rake

10. tape

Mixed Up Words

The underlined **list word** in each sentence does not make sense.
Write the **list word** that does make sense on the line.

1. It is fun to swim in the <u>paint</u>.   lake

2. I help my mother <u>tape</u> leaves in the fall.   rake

3. Open the <u>sail</u> to enter the garden.   gate

4. I <u>face</u> the planet by recycling.   save

Word Puzzle

Read each clue.
Write **list words** to fill in the puzzle.

Across

3. scared
5. It has eyes, a nose, and a mouth.
6. This makes things stick together.
8. This catches the wind on a boat.
9. a door in a fence

Down

1. take leaves off the grass
2. a kind of big pond
4. alike
7. This is one way to color a picture.
8. put money in a bank

Crossword answers:
- 3 Across / 1,2 Down area: R, L at top
- 3. A F R A I D
- 5. F A C E
- 6. T A P E
- 8. S A I L
- 9. G A T E
(Down words include RAKE, LAKE, SAME, PAINT, SAVE)

Spelling and Writing

Proofreading

Each sentence has two mistakes. Use the proofreading marks to fix each mistake. Write the misspelled **list words** correctly on the lines.

Proofreading Marks

⬭ spelling mistake
≡ capital letter
⊙ add period

1. The boat with the red ⬭sale was ≡sam's.   1. sail

2. ≡it flew across the ⬭ak⊙   2. lake

3. Sam wasn't ⬭afrade and he won the race⊙   3. afraid

Writing a News Story

A good news story always tells <u>who</u> or <u>what</u> the story is about and <u>where</u> and <u>when</u> it happened. Write a news story about someone who did a good deed. Then proofread your news story and fix any mistakes.

_____
_____
_____
_____
_____

BONUS WORDS

plane
bait
brave
tame
trail

Spelling Strategy

To reinforce spelling the long *a* sound, students can choose crayons or markers of two colors—one color they associate with *cake,* and the other with *pail.* With the corresponding colors, they can draw the outlines of a cake and a pail on a sheet of paper and label each drawing. Students can write other **list words** spelled *a_e* on the cake drawing and those spelled *ai* on the pail drawing.

BONUS WORDS Have students write a story title using each bonus word. Then have them join a partner to compare their titles.

Spelling and Writing   Page 32

The **Proofreading** exercise will help students prepare to proofread their news stories. As students complete the writing activity, encourage them to brainstorm ideas, write a first draft, revise, and proofread their work. To publish their writing, students may want to

- add their stories to a class newsletter
- read their stories aloud as if they were reporters for the "Nightly News."

Writer's Corner Clip a few short articles and pictures that feature children from your local newspapers. Read each article aloud, asking students to listen for the four W's: *who, what, where,* and *when.* Challenge students to write a headline for each story that includes one important fact.

Final Test

1. Let Sal **paint** with the big brush.
2. Let's **rake** the leaves into a big pile!
3. I need some **tape** for my project.
4. We must unlock the **gate** to get in.
5. If I **save** my money, can I buy that book?
6. The ducks have a nest near the **lake**.
7. Did you wash your hands and **face**?
8. No, I am not **afraid** of the dark.
9. Look! Our sneakers are the **same** color!
10. The **sail** on my new boat is red.

Lesson 8 — Long Vowel i

Objective
To spell words with long *i*

 Correlated Phonics Lesson
MCP Phonics, Level B, Lesson 24

Spelling Words in Action — *Page 33*

In this selection, students find out that an important part of winning a race is determination, right to the very end. You may wish to read the passage aloud with them. After reading, invite students to discuss how they think this same lesson might apply to other things they do.

Encourage students to look back at the words in dark print. Ask volunteers to say each word and name the long-vowel sound they hear.

Warm-Up Test
1. The river is too **wide** to cross.
2. I live a **mile** away from the school.
3. The students stood in **line** to buy pizza.
4. We can **hide** under that chair.
5. Mom made a **fire** in the grill.
6. We have such **nice** friends!
7. It is a **fine** day to go fishing.
8. Did Carl change his **mind** about going?
9. I must **find** the book I lost.
10. I left my bike **behind** the school.

Spelling Practice — *Pages 34–35*

Introduce the spelling rule and have students read the **list words** aloud. Encourage students to look back at their **Warm-Up Tests** and apply the spelling rule to any misspelled words.

As students work through the **Spelling Practice** exercises, remind them to look back at their **list words** or in their dictionaries if they need help.

 for ESL students See Tape Recording, page 15

36

Long Vowel i — Lesson 8

Spelling Words in Action

What is your favorite kind of race?

Friends Come First

Mike stood on **line** for the bike race. The race was one **mile** long, and the prizes were great. It would be **nice** to win one.

Mike felt a tap on his arm. His best friend, Sarah, was **behind** him. She wore a **wide** smile on her face. "I knew I would **find** you here," she said. "I am racing, too."

It was a **fine** day for a race. Would Mike's red bike be as fast as a **fire** engine? The race began. Mike pedaled as hard as he could.

"You can't **hide** from me!" Sarah called. Soon, her bike was next to Mike's. Mike pedaled even faster.

At last, Mike zoomed past the finish line a few inches ahead of Sarah. Mike won the race!

"Congratulations!" Sarah told him. "I don't **mind** losing so much because my best friend won."

Say each word in dark print in the paragraphs. What vowel sound do you hear in each word?

33

Spelling Practice

 TIP
Each list word has the long i sound. Sometimes the sound is spelled **i_e**, as in **mile**. Sometimes the long i is spelled **i _ _**, as in **find**.

LIST WORDS
1. wide
2. mile
3. line
4. hide
5. fire
6. nice
7. fine
8. mind
9. find
10. behind

Spelling the Long i Sound
Write each **list word** under the heading that shows its long i spelling pattern.

i_e
1. wide
2. mile
3. line
4. hide
5. fire
6. nice
7. fine

i _ _
8. mind
9. find
10. behind

34   Lesson 8 • Long Vowel i

Word Clues

Write the **list word** that matches each clue.

1. This means kind.   nice
2. You use this to think.   mind
3. It is hot. Be careful!   fire
4. Can you run this far?   mile
5. This tells how you feel.   fine
6. This means in back of.   behind

Missing Words

Write a **list word** to finish each sentence.

1. The ___line___ for the movie is very long.
2. I hope we can ___find___ good seats.
3. This is a very ___wide___ movie screen.
4. If the movie is scary, I will ___hide___ under my chair.

Spelling and Writing

Proofreading

Each sentence has two mistakes. Use the proofreading marks to fix each mistake. Write the misspelled **list words** correctly on the lines.

Proofreading Marks

◯ spelling mistake
⊙ add period

1. I keep these rules in min when I ride a bike⊙   1. mind
2. I stay on whyd roads⊙   2. wide
3. I use a mirror to see behine me⊙   3. behind

Writing a Paragraph

Remember the day you learned how to do something for the first time? Write a paragraph telling about that day. Proofread your paragraph. Fix any mistakes.

BONUS WORDS

wire
pipe
pint
bite
kind

Spelling Strategy

Ask the class to listen carefully as you call out each **list word**. Invite students to
• name the vowel sound they hear
• tell you whether the word is spelled *i_e* or *i_*.
Call on a volunteer to write the word on the board.

BONUS WORDS Have students write sentences using scrambled bonus words. Then have them trade papers with a partner to unscramble each word and write it correctly.

Spelling and Writing   *Page 36*

The **Proofreading** exercise will help students prepare to proofread their paragraphs. As students complete the writing activity, encourage them to brainstorm ideas, write a first draft, revise, and proofread their work. To publish their writing, students may want to
• illustrate and display their paragraphs
• exchange and discuss their paragraphs with a partner.

Writer's Corner Students may enjoy making a series of posters that illustrate bike safety rules. One group of students could write to the local police department and another group to the library, asking for pamphlets or handouts about rules or other safe-riding practices.

Final Test
1. There is a big tree **behind** my house.
2. This box is deep and **wide**.
3. My cat likes to **hide** under my bed.
4. Who can **find** my new pen?
5. The fire truck helped put out the **fire**.
6. We paid a **fine** on the library book.
7. Please write a **nice** thank-you note to Grandma.
8. The **line** for the circus was very long.
9. The post office is a **mile** from the library.
10. Keep your **mind** on your homework!

Long Vowel u

Objective
To spell words with the long *u* sound

 Correlated Phonics Lesson
MCP Phonics, Level B, Lesson 26

Spelling Words in Action   *Page 37*

In this selection, students read to find out how to make nachos, a simple snack of corn chips and melted cheese. After reading, ask students whether they have ever tasted nachos, and if not, ask if they would like to try them.

Encourage students to look back at the words in dark print. Ask volunteers to say each word and name the long-vowel sound they hear.

Warm-Up Test
1. Follow the **rule** for safety.
2. I always **use** soap to wash my hands.
3. He hummed a happy **tune**.
4. A **mule** looks a little like a horse.
5. Our homework is **due** tomorrow.
6. Is that a **true** story?
7. The tree **grew** very tall.
8. We planted a **few** flowers in the garden.
9. I love **you**.
10. That hamster is so **cute**.

Spelling Practice   *Pages 38–39*

Introduce the spelling rule and have students read the **list words** aloud. Encourage students to look back at their **Warm-Up Tests** and apply the spelling rule to any misspelled words.

As students work through the **Spelling Practice** exercises, remind them to look back at their **list words** or in their dictionaries if they need help. For the **Mixed Up Words** exercise, be sure students understand that the underlined word does not belong in the sentence and that they need to replace it with the correct **list word**.

 See Letter Cards, page 15

38

Spelling Words in Action

What are nachos?

A Fun Snack

It's **true**! Nachos are fun to make and fun to eat. Here's a recipe to make nachos for **you** and a **few** of your amigos. (Amigos is Spanish for friends.)

First, you will need a grown-up to help you. You will also need a package of corn chips, a large baking dish, and some grated cheese. **Use** Monterey Jack cheese or cheddar.

Heat the oven to 350 degrees. Spread the corn chips around in the bottom of the baking dish. Sprinkle the cheese over the chips. Bake in the oven for about 10 minutes until the cheese is melted. Be sure to use an oven mitt when you take your nachos out of the oven. That's an important **rule**! Let the nachos cool for a bit and dig in. Mmmmm.

Say each word in dark print in the paragraphs. What vowel sound do you hear?

37

Spelling Practice

TIP
Each list word has a long u sound. The long u can be spelled ew, as in few; u_e, as in rule; ue, as in true; and ou, as in you.

Writing the Long u Sounds

Write each **list word** under the heading that shows its long **u** sound spelling.

u_e, as in June

1. rule   2. use
3. tune   4. mule
5. cute

ew, as in new

6. grew   7. few

ue, as in blue

8. due   9. true

ou, as in soup

10. you

LIST WORDS
1. rule
2. use
3. tune
4. mule
5. due
6. true
7. grew
8. few
9. you
10. cute

Mixed Up Words

The underlined **list word** in each sentence does not make sense. Write the **list word** that does make sense.

1. We sang a happy <u>rule</u> in our holiday concert.

2. My spelling homework is <u>true</u> tomorrow.

3. I want to <u>tune</u> the phone.

4. "Be kind to others," is a good <u>mule</u>.

5. The story was cute and also <u>grew</u>.

tune

due

use

rule

true

Story

Write **list words** to complete the story.

My pet ___mule___ is smaller than a horse. When he was

a baby, his fuzzy ears were so ___cute___. When he

___grew___ bigger, his ears looked different. I've only ridden

my mule a ___few___ times. ___You___ can ride him, too.

Spelling and Writing

Proofreading

Each sentence has two mistakes. Use the proofreading marks to fix them. Write the misspelled **list words** correctly on the lines.

Proofreading Marks
- ⬭ spelling mistake
- ≡ capital letter
- ⌃ add something

1. Do you want the myool to sing to you?

2. she will sing her favorite toon.

3. her voice changed as she grue up.

1. mule

2. tune

3. grew

Writing a Recipe

A finger food is a snack you eat with your fingers, such as nachos. What other finger food do you like? Tell what it is and how to make it.

BONUS WORDS
knew
threw
clue
tube
huge

Spelling Strategy

Write several cloze sentences on the board for the **list words**. Next to each blank, include each word's long *u* spelling as a clue. For example, *That song has a catchy (u_e)*. Invite students to read the sentence, decide which **list word** goes in the blank, and write the word.

BONUS WORDS
Have students write their own definitions for each bonus word, but not the word itself. Then have them trade papers with a partner to figure out the correct list word for each definition.

Spelling and Writing   *Page 40*

The **Proofreading** exercise will help them prepare to proofread their descriptions. As students complete the writing activity, encourage them to brainstorm ideas, write a first draft, revise, and proofread their work. To publish their writing, students may want to put together a class recipe book called "Super Snacks!"

Writer's Corner *The Kid's Cookbook* by Patricia Barrett-Dragan and Rosemary Dalton offers child-tested recipes collected by two teachers. Use this or other cookbooks to show students that recipes have both a list of ingredients and a set of step-by-step directions. Ask students to write a description of a meal they would like to make for their family.

Final Test
1. I am **due** home at four o'clock.
2. A **few** of my friends collect stamps.
3. The farmer **grew** corn and carrots.
4. A **mule** has larger ears than a horse.
5. A good friendship **rule** is to be a good listener.
6. My kitten has a **cute** nose.
7. It is **true** that bats sleep during the day.
8. Does Dad remember the **tune** of that song?
9. Always **use** a backpack to carry your books.
10. I have a great birthday present for **you**!

Objective
To spell words with long *o*

 Phonics Correlated Phonics Lesson
MCP Phonics, Level B, Lesson 29

Spelling Words in Action   *Page 41*

In this selection, students read to find out about the origins of the yo-yo and learn that yo-yo is a Philippine word. After reading, help students locate the Philippine Islands on a globe or world map. Ask them why yo-yo is a good name for this toy.

Encourage students to look back at the words in dark print. Ask volunteers to say each word and name the long-vowel sound they hear.

Warm-Up Test
1. I like **those** apples best.
2. I put the plant on a **low** shelf.
3. We saw a **goat** at the farm.
4. This is my very **own** room.
5. It's nice to have a warm **coat** when it is cold.
6. Martina will **go** to school today.
7. I **hope** you like your new home.
8. Yo-yos are **sold** in most toy stores.
9. Can we climb **over** that fence?
10. My grandparents were born a long time **ago**.

Spelling Practice   *Pages 42–43*

Introduce the spelling rule and have students read the **list words** aloud. Encourage students to look back at their **Warm-Up Tests** and apply the spelling rule to any misspelled words.

As students work through the **Spelling Practice** exercises, remind them to look back at their **list words** or in their dictionaries if they need help. In the verse in the **Alphabetical Order** exercise, you might have students find long *o* sound words that are not list words: *old, bold,* and *motorboat*. Discuss what a bold coat might look like, explaining that bold colors or patterns are bright and eye-catching.

for ESL students   See Variant Spellings, page 14

Spelling Words in Action

Who invented the yo-yo?

One of the Oldest Toys in the World

No one knows who invented the yo-yo. Children in ancient Greece played with yo-yos 2,500 years **ago**. In the 1800s, grown-ups in France had yo-yos of their **own**. Today, yo-yos are **sold** all **over** the world.

If you **go** to a museum, you may see some old pictures of yo-yos. **Those** old yo-yos were made of wood or clay. Some were made of metal.

In the Philippines, the word yo-yo means to bounce back. Yo-yos were popular there for hundreds of years. Then Pedro Flores moved to California from the Philippines. He opened a yo-yo factory in 1928. It started a yo-yo craze in this country. If you have a yo-yo, you have Pedro Flores to thank.

Look back at the words in dark print. Say each word. Do you hear the long <u>o</u> sound in each word?

41

Spelling Practice

TIP
Each **list word** has the long **o** sound, spelled in one of the following five ways: o_e, as in those; ow, as in low; oa, as in coat; o, as in go; or old, as in sold.

LIST WORDS
1. those
2. low
3. goat
4. own
5. coat
6. go
7. hope
8. sold
9. over
10. ago

Writing the Long o Sound

Write the missing letter or letters for the long **o** sound in each word. Trace the letters to spell **list words**.

1. own   2. over
3. ago   4. low
5. go   6. sold
7. those   8. hope
9. coat   10. goat

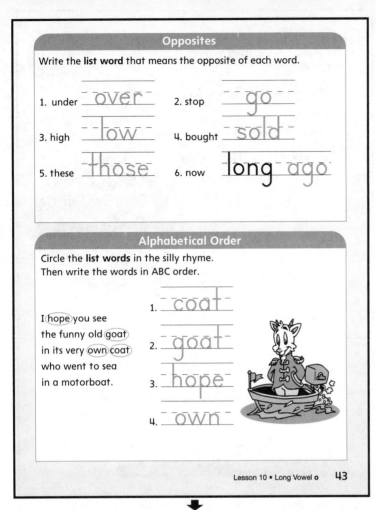

Opposites

Write the **list word** that means the opposite of each word.

1. under __over__ 2. stop __go__

3. high __low__ 4. bought __sold__

5. these __those__ 6. now __long ago__

Alphabetical Order

Circle the **list words** in the silly rhyme.
Then write the words in ABC order.

I (hope) you see
the funny old (goat)
in its very (own) (coat)
who went to sea
in a motorboat.

1. __coat__

2. __goat__

3. __hope__

4. __own__

Spelling and Writing

Proofreading

Each sentence has two mistakes. Use
the proofreading marks to fix each
mistake. Write the misspelled **list
words** correctly on the lines.

Proofreading Marks

⬭ spelling mistake
^ add something

1. How many millions of teddy bears do you
   think have been (solde)?

2. Do you know that even grown-ups (owne)
   teddy bears?

3. Why do you think (thoes) bears are
   so popular?

1. __sold__

2. __own__

3. __those__

Writing a Description

Write about your favorite toy. Tell when you got
it, how it works, and what it does. Use as many
list words as you can. Proofread your description.
Fix any mistakes.

_____

_____

_____

_____

_____

BONUS WORDS

fold

so

nose

boat

blow

Spelling Strategy

Write the five ways to spell the long *o* sound
(*o_e, ow, oa, o, old*) on the board as separate
column headings. Then invite students to suggest
list words and other words that go with each
pattern. Write each word on the board in the
appropriate column and circle the letter or letters
that stand for the long *o* sound.

BONUS WORDS

Have students write the bonus words
across the top of a page and then write a
rhyming list word below each bonus word.
Pair students into teams to write a poem
using the rhyming words.

Spelling and Writing   Page 44

The **Proofreading** exercise will help students
prepare to proofread their descriptions. Before they
begin the exercise, remind students that the
proofreading mark ^ is used to add something. It
could be a question mark or an exclamation mark.
As students complete the writing activity,
encourage them to brainstorm ideas, write a first
draft, revise, and proofread their work. To publish
their writing, students may want to

• use their descriptions to create an ad for
  their toy
• put together a class "Favorite Toys Catalog."

Writer's Corner The class might enjoy researching
yo-yo tricks and trivia online or in the library. Have
them write a paragraph describing their favorite
yo-yo trick or trivia.

Final Test

1. Dinosaurs lived a long time **ago**.
2. Dad put a new **coat** of paint on my bike.
3. Is it time to **go** home now?
4. This milk came from our pet **goat**.
5. We **hope** to win the game.
6. The music is so **low** I can hardly hear it.
7. I put on a sweater **over** my shirt.
8. **Those** shoes belong to Maria.
9. She likes to do things in her **own** way.
10. Joey **sold** lemonade at the fair.

Long Vowel e

Objective
To spell words with long *e* spelled *ee* and *ea*

Correlated Phonics Lesson
MCP Phonics, Level B, Lesson 31

Spelling Words in Action   *Page 45*

In this selection, students read to find out what makes growing up so hard for a baby sea turtle that is left to hatch and survive on its own. After reading, invite students to explain in their own words why grown sea turtles are so big and so strong.

Encourage students to look back at the words in dark print. Ask volunteers to say each word and name the vowel sound spelled by *ee* or *ea*.

Warm-Up Test
1. I **feed** my fish every day.
2. Many turtles live in the **sea**.
3. I want you to **meet** a new student.
4. This necklace is made of **real** gold.
5. Can we **keep** this kitten?
6. Friday is my favorite day of the **week**!
7. The water is too **deep** at that end.
8. It is **easy** to run faster than a turtle.
9. Who wants to go to the **beach** with us?
10. Make sure your hands are **clean** before you eat.

Spelling Practice   *Pages 46–47*

Introduce the spelling rule and have students read the **list words** aloud. Encourage students to look back at their **Warm-Up Tests** and apply the spelling rule to any misspelled words.

As students work through the **Spelling Practice** exercises, remind them to look back at their **list words** or in their dictionaries if they need help. Afterward, you might want to point out that four of the **list words** are homophones and identify them using both spellings of long *e*: *sea-see, meet-meat, real-reel,* and *week-weak.*

for ESL students   See Picture Clues, page 15

42

Long Vowel e   Lesson 11

Spelling Words in Action

What is green, breathes air, and lives in water?

Making It on Their Own

Green **sea** turtles are reptiles. They live in the ocean, but they are born on land.

A mother sea turtle crawls onto a **beach** when she is ready to lay her eggs. She lays her eggs and goes back into the water.

When the baby turtles hatch, they are on their own. First they must crawl into the sea. It is not **easy** for them to get there. Sea turtles move very slowly on land. This puts them in **real** danger. They may **meet** a hungry seagull or crab along the way. These animals will **feed** on baby sea turtles. Still, the baby turtles **keep** on crawling.

When the baby turtles reach the sea, they swim for one or two days to get to **deep** water. In deep water, the baby turtles are safe.

Say each word in dark print in the paragraphs. What vowel sound do you hear?

Spelling Practice

TIP
The long e sound is the vowel sound you hear in <u>feed</u> and se<u>a</u>. Each list word has the long e sound spelled in one of these ways: **ee** or **ea**.

LIST WORDS
1. feed
2. sea
3. meet
4. real
5. keep
6. week
7. deep
8. easy
9. beach
10. clean

Writing the Long e Sound

Write the missing letters for the long **e** sound in each word. Trace the letters to spell **list words**.

1. deep
2. easy
3. clean
4. sea
5. meet
6. beach
7. keep
8. real
9. week
10. feed

Opposites

Write the **list word** that means the opposite of each word.

1. dirty **clean**
2. lose **keep**
3. fake **real**
4. shallow **deep**
5. hard **easy**
6. starve **feed**

Rhyming Clues

Read each clue. Then write the **list word** that rhymes.

1. It is seven days.
   It rhymes with <u>peek</u>. **week**

2. This is sand by the ocean.
   It rhymes with <u>teach</u>. **beach**

3. This is salty water.
   It rhymes with <u>tea</u>. **sea**

4. This is when you see someone.
   It rhymes with <u>feet</u>. **meet**

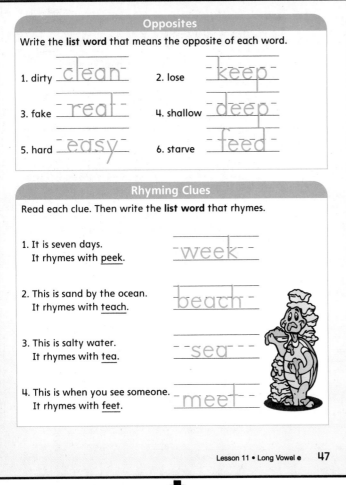

Spelling and Writing

Proofreading

Each sentence has two mistakes. Use the proofreading marks to fix each mistake. Write the misspelled **list words** correctly on the lines.

Proofreading Marks

- ◯ spelling mistake
- ⊙ add period

1. Snapping turtles don't live in the see⊙   1. **sea**

2. You might mete one in a river or lake⊙   2. **meet**

3. If you see one, kepe away from its strong jaws⊙   3. **keep**

Writing a Journal Entry

Write a journal entry telling what you would like to do at a beach or lake. Proofread your work. Fix any mistakes.

_____

- - - - - - - - - - - - - - - - - -

_____

- - - - - - - - - - - - - - - - - -

_____

BONUS WORDS

sheep
sleep
heat
heel
teach

Spelling Strategy

Students can use writing with color to help them distinguish between the two spellings for the long *e* sound. With crayons or markers in shades of green and peach, show them how to draw two boxes on their paper, labeling each box at the top with the name of the color. As you read the **list words**, they can write the words spelled with *ee* in the green box and those spelled with *ea* in the peach box.

BONUS WORDS Ask students to write a sentence for each bonus word, but to leave a blank where the bonus word belongs. Then have them trade papers with a partner and see if they can fill in the correct bonus words.

Spelling and Writing   *Page 48*

The **Proofreading** exercise will help students prepare to proofread their paragraphs. As students complete the writing activity, encourage them to brainstorm ideas, write a first draft, revise, and proofread their work. To publish their writing, students may want to create a bulletin-board display of a beach scene and display their journal entries.

Writer's Corner You might want to bring in information about endangered species and what is being done to help them. Discuss what children can do to help. Then invite students to write a description of the endangered animal they would most like to save.

Final Test

1. He sailed a boat across the **sea**.
2. That hole is very **deep**.
3. My **real** name is Jason, but my friends call me Jake.
4. It is **easy** to play jump rope.
5. Please **feed** my cat when I am away.
6. We can **meet** in front of the school.
7. We will visit my grandmother for one **week**.
8. It is fun to play on the **beach**.
9. I always **keep** my room neat.
10. Pets need **clean** cages to stay healthy.

Objective

To review spelling words with long-vowel sounds *a, i, u (yoo* or *oo), o,* and *e*

Check Your Spelling Notebook
Pages 49–52

Based on your observations, note which words are giving students the most difficulty and offer assistance for spelling them correctly. Here are some frequently misspelled words to watch for: *easy, nice, week,* and *you.*

To give students extra help and practice in taking standardized tests, you may want to have them take the **Warm-Up Test** for this lesson on pages 46–47. After scoring the tests, return them to students so that they can record their misspelled words in their spelling notebooks.

Invite students to practice writing their troublesome words with a partner. Have them take turns saying each word, naming the long-vowel sound in the word, and then writing it. After practicing their words, students can work through the exercises for lessons 7–11 and the cumulative review, **Show What You Know.** Before they begin each exercise, you may want to go over the spelling rule.

 Take It Home

Invite students to listen carefully for the **list words** in lessons 7–11 at home while they are reading, watching TV, or listening to the radio or their favorite CDs or tapes. For a complete list of the words, encourage students to take their *Spelling Workout* books home. Students can also use the **Take It Home Master 2** on pages 48–49 to help them do the activity. They can share the words they collected with the class.

In Lessons 7–11, you learned how to spell words with long vowel sounds.

Check Your Spelling Notebook

Look at the words in your spelling notebook. Which words for Lessons 7 through 11 did you have the most trouble with? Write them here.

_____
_____
_____
_____

Lesson 7

TIP The long a sound can be spelled a_e, as in <u>lake</u>, and ai, as in <u>afraid</u>.

List Words
face
save
paint
sail

Write the **list word** that belongs in each group.

1. brush, picture, _____ paint

2. eyes, nose, _____ face

3. money, bank, _____ save

4. boat, water, _____ sail

49

Lesson 8

TIP Sometimes the long i sound is spelled i_e, as in <u>hide</u>. Other times it is spelled i_ _, as in <u>find</u>.

List Words
mind
line
nice
mile

Write a **list word** that rhymes with each word.

1. smile _____ mile   2. twice _____ nice

3. kind _____ mind   4. mine _____ line

Lesson 9

TIP The long u sound can be spelled ue, as in <u>due</u>; u_e, as in <u>use</u>; and ew, as in <u>grew</u>.

List Words
few
true
cute
tune

Write a **list word** to match each clue.

1. pretty _____ cute

2. not many _____ few

3. song _____ tune

4. not false _____ true

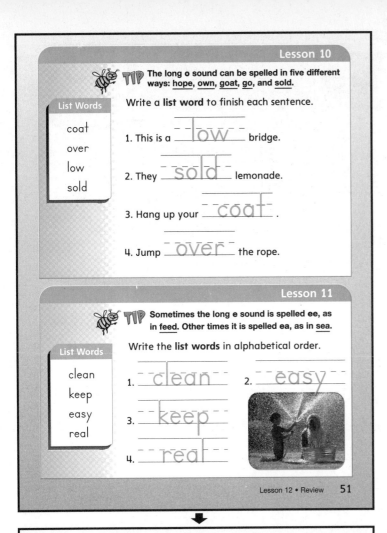

Lesson 10

🐝 **TIP** The long o sound can be spelled in five different ways: <u>hope</u>, <u>own</u>, <u>goat</u>, <u>go</u>, and <u>sold</u>.

List Words

coat
over
low
sold

Write a **list word** to finish each sentence.

1. This is a __low__ bridge.

2. They __sold__ lemonade.

3. Hang up your __coat__.

4. Jump __over__ the rope.

Lesson 11

🐝 **TIP** Sometimes the long e sound is spelled ee, as in <u>feed</u>. Other times it is spelled ea, as in <u>sea</u>.

List Words

clean
keep
easy
real

Write the **list words** in alphabetical order.

1. __clean__   2. __easy__

3. __keep__

4. __real__

Lesson 12 • Review   **51**

Show What You Know

Lessons 7–11 Review

One word is misspelled in each set of **list words**. Fill in the circle next to the **list word** that is spelled incorrectly.

1. ● owne	○ sea	○ tune	○ go
2. ○ paint	○ wide	● raik	○ deep
3. ○ mind	● lak	○ rule	○ mile
4. ○ sail	○ over	● yu	○ feed
5. ○ due	○ tape	○ cute	● lin
6. ● eazy	○ hide	○ true	○ face
7. ○ hope	○ grew	● afrayd	○ few
8. ○ mule	○ meet	● cleen	○ fire
9. ● behin	○ ago	○ coat	○ low
10. ○ goat	● reall	○ use	○ week
11. ● keap	○ nice	○ gate	○ those
12. ○ fine	○ sold	● sav	○ same
13. ○ beach	● finde	○ due	○ wide
14. ○ sea	○ hide	● mil	○ line
15. ○ own	○ ago	○ afraid	● taip
16. ○ rake	○ keep	● soled	○ use
17. ○ clean	● fayce	○ coat	○ fire
18. ● deap	○ over	○ easy	○ find
19. ○ you	○ paint	○ mule	● trew
20. ● loe	○ save	○ few	○ mind

Final Test

1. Jacob sold quite a **few** tickets to the play.
2. I had to scrub hard to get my hands **clean**.
3. This **coat** has a zipper and buttons, too.
4. I just can't make up my **mind** about this!
5. The clown made a funny **face** at the audience.
6. What a **cute** little puppy that is!
7. This problem is **easy** if you think about it.
8. The truck would not fit under the **low** bridge.
9. I am lucky to have so many **nice** friends.
10. Let's **paint** the doghouse bright green.
11. Gina read a **true** story about the first astronauts.
12. Chico wants to **keep** the frog as a pet.
13. We had fun jumping **over** the puddles.
14. Draw a **line** under the correct answer.
15. Does Angie like to **save** picture postcards?
16. That **tune** is one of my favorite songs.
17. The fruit looked **real**, but it was made of wax.
18. We **sold** all our old toys at a yard sale.
19. Jon's house is exactly one **mile** from his school.
20. Nina likes to **sail** on the lake in the summer.

Check Your Spelling Notebook

Before writing each word, students can say it, name the long-vowel sound, and point out the spelling pattern used for the long-vowel sound.

Name _____

Read each set of words. Fill in the circle next to the word that is spelled wrong.

1. (a) rule   (b) paint
   (c) miel   (d) hide

2. (a) afraid   (b) cewt
   (c) own   (d) due

3. (a) cleen   (b) same
   (c) line   (d) sea

4. (a) ago   (b) fase
   (c) use   (d) cute

5. (a) beach   (b) true
   (c) paint   (d) keap

6. (a) nice   (b) fire
   (c) soald   (d) lake

7. (a) fue   (b) mule
   (c) grew   (d) go

8. (a) minde   (b) rake
   (c) wide   (d) line

9. (a) feed   (b) saile
   (c) line   (d) paint

Name _____

Lesson Review Test (Side B)

Read each set of words. Fill in the circle next to the word that is spelled wrong.

10. ⓐ you   ⓑ tape
     ⓒ behind   ⓓ cuet

11. ⓐ fine   ⓑ those
     ⓒ nise   ⓓ goat

12. ⓐ week   ⓑ ovur
     ⓒ mind   ⓓ few

13. ⓐ paint   ⓑ line
     ⓒ meet   ⓓ troo

14. ⓐ find   ⓑ fire
     ⓒ saiv   ⓓ feed

15. ⓐ face   ⓑ gate
     ⓒ sold   ⓓ eazy

16. ⓐ you   ⓑ loe
     ⓒ mile   ⓓ line

17. ⓐ toon   ⓑ hope
     ⓒ clean   ⓓ paint

18. ⓐ reale   ⓑ rake
     ⓒ deep   ⓓ line

Take It Home 2

Your child has learned to spell many new words and would like to share them with you and your family. Here are some ideas for helping your child review some of the words in Lessons 7–11.

Now Hear This!

You and your child will be "all ears" once you are on the alert for spelling words at home. You can collect "heard words" as you read aloud, watch TV, or listen to the radio or your favorite tapes. You can even record a spelling-word message of your own, using a tape recorder or an answering machine!

Lesson 7
1. afraid
2. face
3. gate
4. lake
5. paint
6. rake
7. sail
8. same
9. save
10. tape

Lesson 8
1. behind
2. find
3. fine
4. fire
5. hide
6. line
7. mile
8. mind
9. nice
10. wide

Lesson 9
1. cute
2. due
3. few
4. grew
5. mule
6. rule
7. true
8. tune
9. use
10. you

Lesson 10
1. ago
2. coat
3. go
4. goat
5. hope
6. low
7. over
8. own
9. sold
10. those

Lesson 11
1. beach
2. clean
3. deep
4. easy
5. feed
6. keep
7. meet
8. real
9. sea
10. week

Word Search Star

Circle all the spelling words in each of the five squares. Write the
remaining letters on the lines below. They spell out a special message
that you can read to your child! Read the letters in the order in which the
stars are numbered.

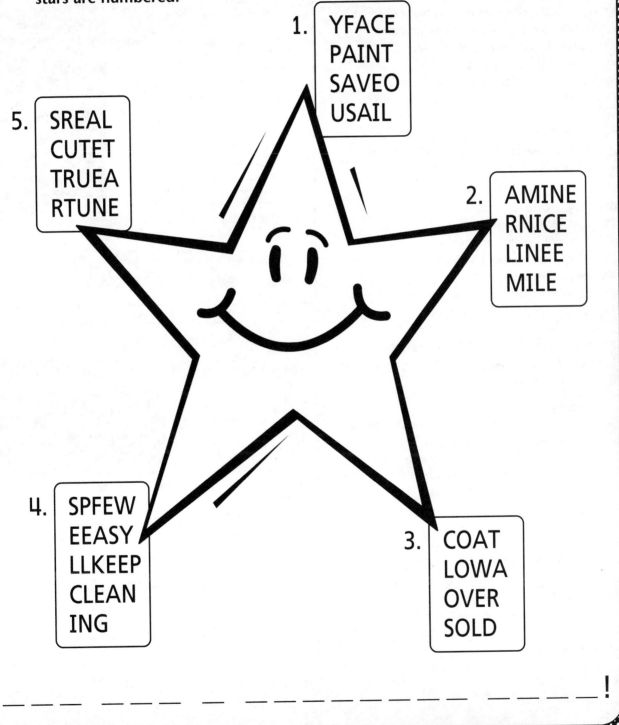

1. YFACE
PAINT
SAVEO
USAIL

5. SREAL
CUTET
TRUEA
RTUNE

2. AMINE
RNICE
LINEE
MILE

4. SPFEW
EEASY
LLKEEP
CLEAN
ING

3. COAT
LOWA
OVER
SOLD

_____ !

Blends with l and r

Objective
To spell words with *l* or *r* blends

Phonics **Correlated Phonics Lesson**
MCP Phonics, Level B, Lesson 48

Spelling Words in Action   *Page 53*

In this selection, students read to find out what is special about a giant redwood tree named General Sherman. Afterward, ask students to estimate the height of a particular tree near their school (for example, "*as high as a two-story house*"). Ask how many times taller than that tree General Sherman is.

Encourage students to look back at the words in dark print. Ask volunteers to say each word and name the consonant sounds they hear.

Warm-Up Test
1. Please stay off the **grass**.
2. The **trunk** of that tree is hollow.
3. What big tires this **truck** has!
4. The plane **flew** very fast.
5. Find a **flat** place to set up the tent.
6. Are Jane and Yon Jin in your **class**?
7. There is a slice of pizza on my **plate**.
8. My dog is three feet long **from** head to tail.
9. I lost one **glove** at school.
10. Bill is my best **friend**.

Spelling Practice   *Pages 54–55*

Introduce the spelling rule and have students read the **list words** aloud, helping them identify the blend at the beginning of each word. Then encourage students to look back at their **Warm-Up Tests** and apply the spelling rule to any misspelled words.

As students work through the **Spelling Practice** exercises, remind them to look back at their **list words** or in their dictionaries if they need help. For the **Scrambled Letters** exercise, you may want to model how another **list word** that is not being used, such as *plate*, fits into a shape drawn on the blackboard.

for ESL students See Picture Clues, page 15

Spelling Words in Action

How tall is General Sherman?

Wooden Soldier

The day of the **class** trip was finally here. The students followed their teacher across the **grass**. A bird flew overhead. They all looked up. Then they saw it. The tree was huge. Its **trunk** was as wide as a **truck** is long.

The students were visiting Sequoia National Park in California. They were looking at the tallest tree in the world. It is a sequoia named General Sherman. It is 272 feet tall. The students looked up **from** the **flat** land around the tree. It was like looking at a 20-story building.

General Sherman is still growing in Sequoia National Park. Maybe you will visit it someday.

Look back at the words in dark print. What do you notice about their spelling? Say each word. What consonant sounds do you hear?

53

Spelling Practice

TIP
In a consonant **blend**, two or more consonants come together in a word. The sound of each consonant can be heard. You can hear the l blend in class and the r blend in grass.

Identifying l and r Blends
Write each **list word** under the heading that shows its blend.

LIST WORDS
1. grass
2. trunk
3. truck
4. flew
5. flat
6. class
7. plate
8. from
9. glove
10. friend

l blend
1. flew   2. flat
3. class   4. plate
5. glove

r blend
6. grass   7. trunk
8. truck   9. from
10. friend

Word Groups

Write the **list word** that belongs with each group of words.

1. hat, coat, <u>glove</u>
2. pal, buddy, <u>friend</u>
3. spoon, glass, <u>plate</u>
4. school, teacher, <u>class</u>
5. car, bus, <u>truck</u>
6. box, chest, <u>trunk</u>

Scrambled Letters

Unscramble the letters to spell **list words**. The word shapes will help you.

1. morf f r o m
2. sargs g r a s s
3. falt f l a t
4. welf f l e w
5. renifd f r i e n d
6. kurct t r u c k

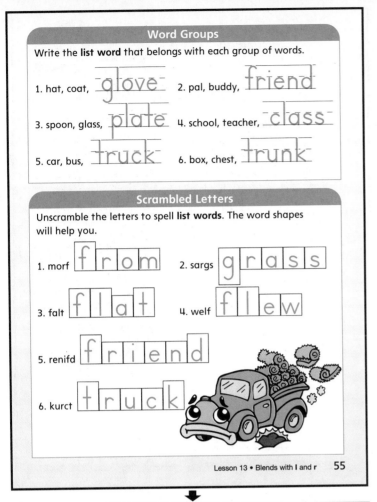

Spelling and Writing

Proofreading

Each sentence has two mistakes. Use the proofreading marks to fix each mistake. Write the misspelled **list words** correctly on the lines.

Proofreading Marks
⬭ spelling mistake
≡ capital letter

1. Jackie bought a (flate) piece of land in oregon.

2. it has lots of green (grase)

3. My (frend) jackie likes it there.

1. <u>flat</u>
2. <u>grass</u>
3. <u>friend</u>

Writing a Poem

Trees give us shade, fruit, and branches to climb. Write a poem about a tree. Proofread your poem and fix any mistakes.

_____
_____
_____
_____
_____

BONUS WORDS

growl
fresh
plan
blanket
crown

Spelling Strategy

Show students how to fold a sheet of paper in half lengthwise to divide it into two columns. Have them write the letter *l* at the top of one column and the letter *r* at the top of the other. As you read each **list word** aloud, invite students to write it in the *l* or the *r* column, depending on which letter they hear in the beginning consonant blend.

BONUS WORDS Ask students to write a sentence for each bonus word, but instead of writing out the whole word, have them write only the beginning consonant blend. Next, have them trade papers with a partner to fill in the correct word in each sentence.

Spelling and Writing　　*Page 56*

The **Proofreading** exercise will help students prepare to proofread their poems. As students complete the writing activity, encourage them to brainstorm ideas, write a first draft, revise, and proofread their poems. To publish their writing, students may want to

- cut out leaf shapes and paste their poems on them
- take part in a poetry reading group.

Writer's Corner Students might enjoy looking at pictures from the gardening section of a newspaper. Read the captions to students and then invite them to write their own captions for the pictures, or to find other pictures that they can write captions for.

Final Test

1. The sea gulls **flew** over the water.
2. Today the teacher let the **class** out early.
3. I will visit my **friend** in Ohio next week.
4. I got a letter **from** France in the mail.
5. I stepped on my hat and now it is **flat**.
6. Brenda found my **glove** in her backyard.
7. I set the table with a fork by each **plate**.
8. The **grass** tickles my bare feet!
9. My mom painted my toy **truck** red.
10. This tree **trunk** is so big you can drive a car through it.

Objective
To spell words with initial or final <u>s</u> blends

 Correlated Phonics Lesson
MCP Phonics, Level B, Lesson 46

Spelling Words in Action   *Page 57*

In this selection, students find out how to behave if they happen to see a snake. After reading, invite them to share a personal experience they may have had with a snake or another reptile, such as a turtle or a lizard.

Encourage students to look back at the words in dark print. Ask volunteers to say each word and name the consonant blend with *s* that they hear.

Warm-Up Test
1. A **snake** hissed in the grass.
2. I love the way roses **smell**.
3. My little brother is **still** asleep.
4. A wisp of **smoke** rose from the chimney.
5. Do you think it is easy to **spell** words?
6. Emily likes to **swim** in the pool.
7. Please butter my **slice** of bread.
8. **Most** people like funny movies.
9. Lee will **strike** out if his bat misses the ball.
10. Can you find a **story** about a dragon?

Spelling Practice   *Pages 58–59*

Introduce the spelling rule and have students read the **list words** aloud. Encourage students to look back at their **Warm-Up Tests** and apply the spelling rule to any misspelled words.

As students work through the **Spelling Practice** exercises, remind them to look back at their **list words** or in their dictionaries if they need help. For the **Scrambled Letters**, invite students to discuss the two meanings of scales to explain the riddle.

 See Categorizing, page 15

Spelling Words in Action

What should you do if you see a snake?

Hissss!

Have you ever seen a **snake**? There are over 2,000 kinds of snakes. Water snakes **swim** in oceans, lakes, and rivers. Land snakes stay on the ground. Many people are afraid of snakes, but **most** snakes are harmless.

If you see a snake, stand very **still**. A snake will only **strike** at you if you come too close.

Snakes are different from other animals. They use their tongues to help them **smell**. Their tongues can also feel fast movements. Most snakes are helpful. They eat bugs and other pests. When you see a snake, just walk slowly away.

Say each word in dark print in the paragraphs. What consonant blend with <u>s</u> do you hear in each word?

Spelling Practice

TIP
The letter **s** can work with two or more letters to make a blend, as in **still** and **strike**. A blend can begin a word or end a word. Listen for the **s** blend in each **list word**.

LIST WORDS
1. snake
2. smell
3. still
4. smoke
5. spell
6. swim
7. slice
8. most
9. strike
10. story

Identifying s Blends
Write each **list word** under the heading that shows its **s** blend.

st
1. still   2. most
3. story

str   **sp**
4. strike   5. spell

sn   **sl**
6. snake   7. slice

sm
8. smell   9. smoke

sw
10. swim

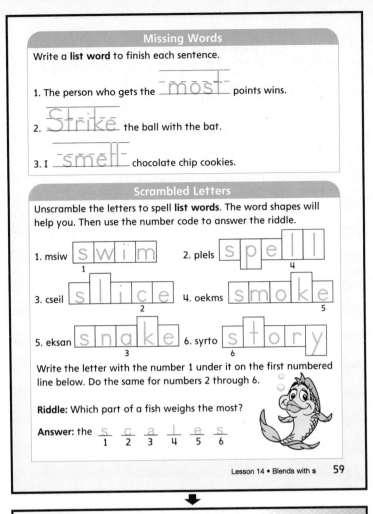

Missing Words

Write a **list word** to finish each sentence.

1. The person who gets the __most__ points wins.

2. __Strike__ the ball with the bat.

3. I __smell__ chocolate chip cookies.

Scrambled Letters

Unscramble the letters to spell **list words**. The word shapes will help you. Then use the number code to answer the riddle.

1. msiw __s w i m__
   1

2. plels __s p e l l__
   4

3. cseil __s l i c e__
   2

4. oekms __s m o k e__
   5

5. eksan __s n a k e__
   3

6. syrto __s t o r y__
   6

Write the letter with the number 1 under it on the first numbered line below. Do the same for numbers 2 through 6.

Riddle: Which part of a fish weighs the most?

Answer: the __s c a l e s__
   1 2 3 4 5 6

Spelling and Writing

Proofreading

Each sentence has two mistakes. Use the proofreading marks to fix each mistake. Write the misspelled **list words** correctly on the lines.

Proofreading Marks

- ◯ spelling mistake
- ⊙ add period
- ℓ take out something

1. A snaek and a turtle are alike because they are both reptiles.?

2. Like mose reptiles, they both lay eggs⊙

3. When scared, a turtle will snap, but a snake will stryke with its tongue⊙

1. __snake__

2. __most__

3. __strike__

Making a Sign

Snakes are helpful animals. They eat bugs and other pests. Make a sign that asks people to be kind to snakes. Write your first draft on the lines. Then copy it onto another sheet of paper and add a picture.

_____

_____

_____

_____

BONUS WORDS

stream
splash
stamp
beast
sleepy

Spelling Strategy

Draw seven boxcars on the board, end to end, and write a different consonant blend above each one: *st, str, sl, sn, sm, sp,* and *sw.* Then call on volunteers to help you "load the s-blend train" by writing a **list word** or words in each boxcar containing the matching *s* blend.

BONUS WORDS Ask students to draw a picture for each bonus word, then trade papers with a partner to write the correct list word for each picture.

Spelling and Writing   *Page 60*

The **Proofreading** exercise will help students prepare to proofread their snake signs. As students complete the writing activity, encourage them to brainstorm ideas, write a first draft, revise, and proofread their work. To publish their writing, students may want to

- post their signs around the school
- create a class "Be Kind to Snakes" booklet.

Writer's Corner Students might enjoy listening to a story about an imaginary snake, such as *Crictor* by Tomi Ungerer. Afterward, students can draw a picture of an imaginary snake of their own and write a paragraph to tell about it.

Final Test

1. My favorite **story** is *The Ugly Duckling.*
2. My name is not hard for me to **spell**.
3. I saw a small green **snake** in the garden.
4. Do you know how to **swim**?
5. Yes, you may eat a **slice** of cheese.
6. Can you **smell** the bread that is baking?
7. I like **most** people that I meet.
8. I promise I will never **smoke**.
9. Sit **still** and stop wiggling!
10. Did you hear the clock **strike** at noon?

Objective
To spell words in which y plus a vowel spells either the long *a* sound or the *oi* sound

 Phonics Correlated Phonics Lessons
MCP Phonics, Level B,
Lessons 84, 97

Spelling Words in Action   *Page 61*

In this selection, students find out about boys and girls who are digging for dinosaurs in the Junior Paleontologist program. After reading, invite students to discuss what they might look for if they went on an archeological dig, i.e., old coins, pieces of pottery, bones, or other artifacts.

Encourage students to look back at the words in dark print. Ask volunteers to say each word and identify the vowel sound they hear.

Warm-Up Test
1. My friend Manuel **plays** the piano.
2. Please don't **say** no to me.
3. Some day you and I **may** go to the moon.
4. Who left dirty dishes on the **tray**?
5. The sky is full of **gray** clouds.
6. Are you going to visit your aunt **today**?
7. Australia is very far **away**.
8. **They** will arrive at three o'clock.
9. There are two **boys** named Tom in my class.
10. It is a **joy** to hear you sing!

Spelling Practice   *Pages 62–63*

Introduce the spelling rule and have students read the **list words** aloud. Encourage students to look back at their **Warm-Up Tests** and apply the spelling rule to any misspelled words.

As students work through the **Spelling Practice** exercises, remind them to look back at their **list words** or in their dictionaries if they need help. For the **Spelling Practice**, remind students not to write any **list word** more than once. You may also want to review the way to fill in the **Word Puzzle** answers.

 **See Spelling Aloud, page 14**

54

---

y with a Vowel

Lesson 15

Spelling Words in Action

How can you tell the difference between a bone and a rock?

Dinosaur Dig

A paleontologist is someone who studies fossils. **Today**, Project Exploration helps **boys** and girls become Junior Paleontologists. **They** call themselves JPs for short. It **may** sound like fun to look for dinosaur bones. It can be a lot of hard work, too.

First the JPs train for two weeks. Then **they** travel far **away** from their homes.

The JPs go to the badlands of Montana. There they crawl on the ground. They use picks and paint brushes to search for tiny, **gray** fossils. They use their hands, eyes, brains, and even their tongues! Scientists **say** that one way to tell a bone from a rock is to lick it. If it sticks to your tongue, it is probably a bone.

Imagine the **joy** of finding a dinosaur fossil! Maybe someday you will not have to imagine it. You will really do it.

Look back at the words in dark print. The letter **y** with **a**, **e**, or **o** can spell vowel sounds. Say each word. What vowel sounds do you hear?

61

Spelling Practice

TIP
The letter **y** can team up with **a**, **e**, or **o** to spell vowel sounds. The long **a** sound can be spelled **ay**, as in s**ay**, or **ey**, as in th**ey**. The **oi** sound can also be spelled **oy**, as in j**oy**.

Spelling Vowel Sounds with y

Write each **list word** under the heading that shows the vowel sound **y** spells.

oy spells oi

1. boys   2. joy

ay spells long a

3. plays   4. say
5. may   6. tray
7. gray   8. today
9. away

ey spells long a

10. they

LIST WORDS
1. plays
2. say
3. may
4. tray
5. gray
6. today
7. away
8. they
9. boys
10. joy

62   Lesson 15 • **y** with a Vowel

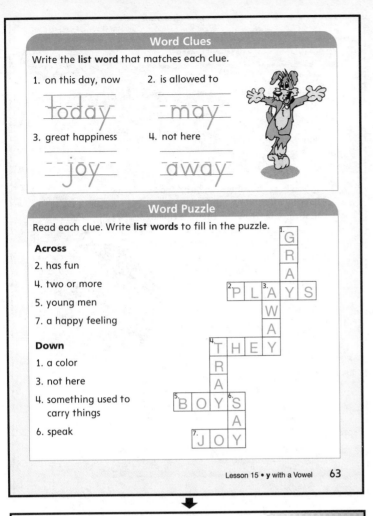

Word Clues

Write the **list word** that matches each clue.

1. on this day, now

today

2. is allowed to

may

3. great happiness

joy

4. not here

away

Word Puzzle

Read each clue. Write **list words** to fill in the puzzle.

Across

2. has fun
4. two or more
5. young men
7. a happy feeling

Down

1. a color
3. not here
4. something used to carry things
6. speak

Crossword:
- 1 Down: GRAY
- 2 Across: PLAYS
- 4 Down: TRAY
- 4 Across: THEY
- 5 Across: BOYS
- 6 Down: SAY
- 7 Across: JOY
- WAY (2 down area)

Lesson 15 • **y** with a Vowel   63

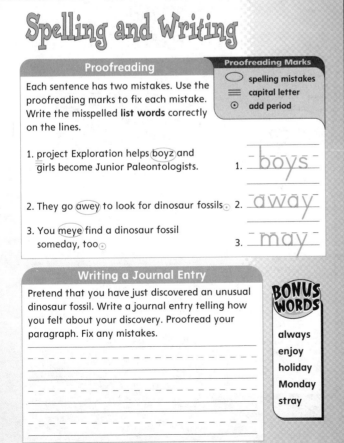

Spelling and Writing

Proofreading

Each sentence has two mistakes. Use the proofreading marks to fix each mistake. Write the misspelled **list words** correctly on the lines.

Proofreading Marks

⬭ spelling mistakes
≡ capital letter
⊙ add period

1. project Exploration helps boyz and girls become Junior Paleontologists.

2. They go awey to look for dinosaur fossils.

3. You meye find a dinosaur fossil someday, too.

1. boys

2. away

3. may

Writing a Journal Entry

Pretend that you have just discovered an unusual dinosaur fossil. Write a journal entry telling how you felt about your discovery. Proofread your paragraph. Fix any mistakes.

BONUS WORDS

always
enjoy
holiday
Monday
stray

64   Lesson 15 • **y** with a Vowel

Spelling Strategy

Write *oy*, *ey*, and *ay* on separate sheets of paper and have three volunteers stand in different corners of the classroom, each holding a sheet of paper. Then call out each **list word** and invite the class to

- point toward the sign whose letters spell the vowel sound in the word
- finger-write the word in the air.

BONUS WORDS Ask students to draw a picture for each bonus word. Then have them trade papers with a partner and write the bonus word that goes with each picture.

Spelling and Writing   *Page 64*

The **Proofreading** exercise will help students prepare to proofread their journal entries. As students complete the writing activity, encourage them to brainstorm ideas, write a first draft, revise, and proofread their work. To publish their writing, students may want to read their journal entries aloud in a group.

Writer's Corner The class might enjoy listening to you read *Dinosaur Ghosts: The Mystery of Coelophysis* by J. Lynett Gillette. Afterward, invite students to write questions that they would like to ask dinosaurs if they could.

Final Test

1. Please move the chair **away** from the wall.
2. Who owns the **gray** coat in the closet?
3. Please let the dogs out if **they** bark.
4. The **boys** in the front row are twins.
5. My sister often **plays** checkers with me.
6. Use this **tray** to carry the teacups.
7. Carla went straight home from school **today**.
8. I feel great **joy** when I see a rainbow.
9. Will the teacher **say** each spelling word twice?
10. You **may** sit down now.

y as a Vowel

Objective
To spell words in which *y* as a vowel spells the long *e* sound or the long *i* sound

Phonics Correlated Phonics Lessons
MCP Phonics, Level B, Lessons 49-50

Spelling Words in Action   *Page 65*

In this selection, students discover how a certain kind of fish "flies." After reading, invite students to read aloud the part of the selection they liked the best.

Encourage students to look back at the words in dark print. Ask volunteers to say each word and name the vowel sound that *y* stands for.

Warm-Up Test
1. This **bunny** is so cute!
2. I saw **many** kinds of animals at the zoo.
3. Can we **fry** the fish I caught for lunch?
4. I am the **only** girl in my art class.
5. I found a **lucky** coin this morning.
6. Is that your book on the floor **by** the table?
7. My dog is so **tiny**, it fits in my pocket.
8. Did anyone lose a **penny**?
9. I think I know **why** Matt is absent.
10. We could not leave until Dad found the car **key**.

Spelling Practice   *Pages 66–67*

Introduce the spelling rule and have students read the **list words** aloud. Encourage students to look back at their **Warm-Up Tests** and apply the spelling rule to any misspelled words.

As students work through the **Spelling Practice** exercises, remind them to look back at their **list words** or in their dictionaries if they need help. For the **Dictionary** exercise, explain that the number of syllables in a word is the same as the number of vowel sounds. Have students tap the number of syllables as you say *monkey, try, pony, cry, fly,* and *funny.*

for ESL students **See Tape Recording, page 15**

Spelling Words in Action

How does a flying fish fly?

A Fish Out of Water

You have probably seen birds and bugs fly **many** times. Did you know that some fish can fly? They are called flying fish.

Flying fish do not fly the same way as a bird or a bug. It **only** looks as if they do. Flying fish have fins shaped like wings. The fish swim very fast just below the surface of the water. Then they wiggle their tails. **By** wiggling their tails very fast, they are able to jump high out of the water. They sail through the air with their fins held out like wings. That is **why** it looks as if they are flying.

The trip lasts only a few seconds, but these **tiny** fish are fast. They can fly up to 30 miles an hour. Some can fly 1,000 feet in just one jump!

Say each word in dark print in the paragraphs. What vowel sound does the *y* stand for in each word?

65

Spelling Practice

TIP
The letter *y* can team up with *a*, *e*, or *o* to spell vowel sounds. It can also spell vowel sounds all by itself, such as the long *e* sound in *many* and the long *i* sound in *fry*.

LIST WORDS
1. bunny
2. many
3. fry
4. only
5. lucky
6. by
7. tiny
8. penny
9. why
10. key

Identifying y as a Vowel
Write each **list word** under the heading that shows its long vowel sound.

Long e sound

1. bunny   2. many

3. only   4. lucky

5. tiny   6. penny

7. key

Long i sound

8. fry   9. by

10. why

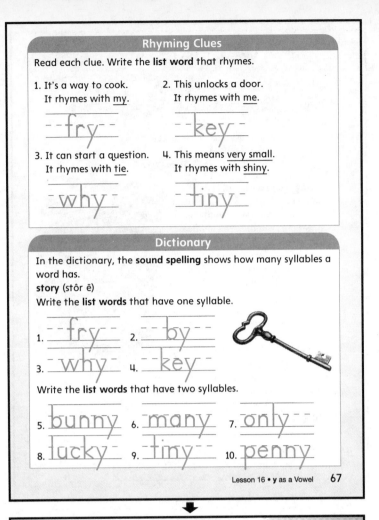

Rhyming Clues

Read each clue. Write the **list word** that rhymes.

1. It's a way to cook.
   It rhymes with <u>my</u>.

   fry

2. This unlocks a door.
   It rhymes with <u>me</u>.

   key

3. It can start a question.
   It rhymes with <u>tie</u>.

   why

4. This means <u>very small</u>.
   It rhymes with <u>shiny</u>.

   tiny

Dictionary

In the dictionary, the **sound spelling** shows how many syllables a word has.

story (stôr ē)

Write the **list words** that have one syllable.

1. _fry_
2. _by_
3. _why_
4. _key_

Write the **list words** that have two syllables.

5. _bunny_
6. _many_
7. _only_
8. _lucky_
9. _tiny_
10. _penny_

Spelling and Writing

Proofreading

Each sentence has two mistakes. Use the proofreading marks to fix each mistake. Write the misspelled **list words** correctly on the lines.

Proofreading Marks

- ⬯ spelling mistake
- ⊙ add period
- ℮ take out something

1. The flying fish is not the (onelee) strange sea animal⊙

   1. _only_

2. The sea horse looks like a (tinee) horse.?

   2. _tiny_

3. The electric eel has shocked (menny) people⊙

   3. _many_

Writing a Description

There are many different kinds of fish. Write a description of a fish you have seen or heard about. Proofread your description. Fix any mistakes.

_____
_____
_____
_____
_____

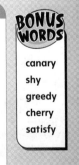

BONUS WORDS

canary
shy
greedy
cherry
satisfy

Spelling Strategy

Tell students that the letter *y* usually makes

- the long *e* sound at the end of a two-syllable word (*funny*)
- the long *i* sound at the end of a one-syllable word (*try*).

Then ask volunteers to come to the board and write **list words**, telling how many syllables they have and naming the sound that *y* makes. Point out that *key* is an exception to the spelling rules above.

BONUS WORDS Ask students to try to write a story using all of the bonus words. Then have them trade stories with a partner to read aloud to the class.

Spelling and Writing   *Page 68*

The **Proofreading** exercise will help students prepare to proofread their descriptions. As students complete the writing activity, encourage them to brainstorm ideas, write a first draft, revise, and proofread their work. To publish their writing, students may want to illustrate their descriptions and use their drawings and writings to create a bulletin-board display.

Writer's Corner You might want to bring in picture books or magazines about marine life. Encourage students to pretend that they have an aquarium and to write about a sea creature or plant they would like to keep in it.

Final Test

1. Do you believe that four-leaf clovers are **lucky**?
2. Line up **by** the door when you are ready.
3. What long ears that **bunny** has!
4. Can you tell me how to **fry** chicken?
5. **Why** do trees lose their leaves in the fall?
6. Of course I will lend you a **penny**.
7. In **many** places, children ride buses to school.
8. We have **only** a few minutes to finish writing.
9. Our cat looks big compared to the **tiny** kitten.
10. You don't need a **key** to open this door.

Objective
To spell words with final *le*

Spelling Words in Action   *Page 69*

In this passage, students learn about John Chapman, and find out what kind of seeds he planted. Afterward, invite students to discuss what kind of fruit or flower they would like to plant. If a map of John Chapman's planting route is available in a book or on-line, have students trace the trail with their fingers and count how many states it passes through.

Encourage students to look back at the words in dark print. Ask volunteers to say each word and name the sound that *le* makes at the end of the word.

Warm-Up Test
1. There are two **apple** trees in our yard.
2. Be careful! That **handle** is hot!
3. Sandy is **able** to tell time.
4. Please open the **bottle** of juice now.
5. Will you please set the **table**?
6. My **uncle** loves hot cider.
7. The baby had one **candle** on his birthday cake.
8. Is **purple** his favorite color?
9. The **turtle** swam across the pond.
10. How many **people** came to the town fair?

Spelling Practice   *Pages 70–71*

Introduce the spelling rule and have students read the **list words** aloud, tapping out the syllables as they say them. Then encourage students to look back at their **Warm-Up Tests** and apply the spelling rule to any misspelled words.

As students work through the **Spelling Practice** exercises, remind them to look back at their **list words** or in their dictionaries if they need help. For **Mixed Up Words**, remind students that the underlined word does not belong in the sentence and that they need to replace it with the correct **list word**.

 for ESL students See Picture Clues, page 15

58

Spelling Words in Action

What kind of seeds did John Chapman plant?

America's Apple Man

Have you ever heard of John Chapman? In the 1800s he walked thousands of miles through many states. As he walked, he planted **apple** seeds.

People began to call him Johnny Appleseed. He wore old clothes and an old pot for a hat. When he was ready to cook, he grabbed the **handle** of the pot, took it off his head, and put it on the fire!

He was kind to wild animals and was **able** to get very close to them. Most of all, Johnny loved his apple trees. The next time you bite into an apple or see a **bottle** of apple juice, think of Johnny Appleseed. Some of the apple trees he planted so long ago are still growing.

Look back at the words in dark print. Say each word. What sound does <u>le</u> make at the end of each word?

69

Spelling Practice

 TIP
Words with the **le** spelling at the end always have at least two syllables, as in **apple**. Listen for the sound **le** makes at the end of each **list word**.

LIST WORDS
1. apple   *apple*
2. handle   *handle*
3. able   *able*
4. bottle   *bottle*
5. table   *table*
6. uncle   *uncle*
7. candle   *candle*
8. purple   *purple*
9. turtle   *turtle*
10. people *people*

Identifying le Endings

Write each **list word** under the heading that shows its second syllable.

ble
1. able   2. table

tle
3. bottle   4. turtle

cle
5. uncle

ple
6. apple   7. purple
8. people

dle
9. handle   10. candle

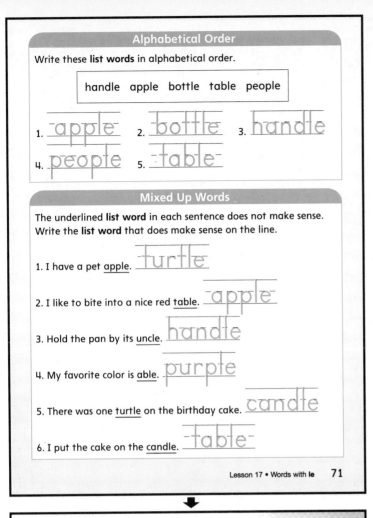

Alphabetical Order

Write these **list words** in alphabetical order.

handle   apple   bottle   table   people

1. apple   2. bottle   3. handle
4. people   5. table

Mixed Up Words

The underlined **list word** in each sentence does not make sense. Write the **list word** that does make sense on the line.

1. I have a pet apple. turtle

2. I like to bite into a nice red table. apple

3. Hold the pan by its uncle. handle

4. My favorite color is able. purple

5. There was one turtle on the birthday cake. candle

6. I put the cake on the candle. table

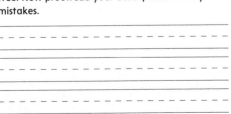
Spelling and Writing

Proofreading

Each sentence has two mistakes. Use the proofreading marks to fix each mistake. Write the misspelled **list words** on the lines.

1. an appel a day keeps the doctor away.

2. My uncal says that may be true ⊙

3. He is not a doctor, but he knows what is good for pepol ⊙

Proofreading Marks

◯ spelling mistake
═ capital letter
⊙ add period

1. apple
2. uncle
3. people

Writing a Description

What other kinds of fruits grow on trees? Write a description of your favorite fruit that grows on a tree. Now proofread your description. Fix any mistakes.

_____
_____
_____
_____
_____
_____

BONUS WORDS

nibble
eagle
gentle
tumble
sparkle

Spelling Strategy

Remind students that words with final *le* always have at least two syllables. Then write each **list word** on the board, drawing a line between the syllables (*han/dle*, *ap/ple*). Next, write *all*, *bell*, *will*, and *doll* on the board, pointing out that they are one-syllable words, and have students say them. Help students recognize the difference between the sound for *l* and the spelling pattern at the end of the one-syllable words and the sound for *l* and the spelling pattern at the end of the **list words**.

BONUS WORDS Ask students to write a story about an eagle using all of the bonus words. Then have them trade stories with a partner to read aloud and invent new endings for the stories.

Spelling and Writing   *Page 72*

The **Proofreading** exercise will help students prepare to proofread their decsriptions. As students complete the writing activity, encourage them to brainstorm ideas, write a first draft, revise, and proofread their work. To publish their writing, students may want to work in a group to make a large drawing of a fruit tree, and then tape their descriptions to its branches.

Writer's Corner You might want to bring in supermarket advertising inserts from your local newspaper and help students read the fresh produce section. Work with the class to write math word problems based on the prices of the fruit being featured.

Final Test
1. My **uncle** is a farmer.
2. He owns an **apple** orchard.
3. **People** visit his farm every fall.
4. Are they **able** to pick their own fruit?
5. My cousin Kim sells cider at a **table** by the road.
6. She pours the golden cider from a big **bottle**.
7. What is the name of those **purple** flowers?
8. The **candle** flame flickered in the wind.
9. The sign on the road said, "Slow, **turtle** crossing."
10. When I picked up the suitcase, its **handle** broke!

Lesson 18

Review Lessons 13–17

Objective

To review spelling words with consonant blends with *l*, *r*, or *s*; *y* as a vowel; words with the *le* ending

Check Your Spelling Notebook

Pages 73–76

Based on your observations, note which words are giving students the most difficulty and offer assistance for spelling them correctly. Here are some frequently misspelled words to watch for: *from*, *they*, *many*, and *people*.

Students can practice their troublesome words by writing them in a list and then trading lists with a partner to check each other's work. After practicing their words, students can work through the exercises for lessons 13–17 and the cumulative review, **Show What You Know**. Before they begin each exercise, you may want to go over the spelling rule.

To give students extra help and practice in taking standardized tests, you may want to have them take the **Warm-Up Test** for this lesson on pages 62–63. After scoring the tests, return them to students so that they can record their misspelled words in their spelling notebooks.

 Take It Home

Invite students to collect everyday phrases they hear at home that contain **list words** from lessons 13–17 (best *friend*, bedtime *story*, *slice* of pizza). For a complete list of the words, encourage them to take their *Spelling Workout* books home. Students can also use the **Take It Home Master 3** on pages 64–65 to help them do the activity. They can bring their lists to school and see whether any of their classmates heard the same phrases they did.

Lessons 13–17 · Review

Lesson 18

In Lessons 13–17 you learned how to spell words with consonant blends r, l, and s, y with a vowel and y as a vowel, and words with le at the end.

Check Your Spelling Notebook

Look at the words in your spelling notebook. Which words in Lessons 13 through 17 did you have the most trouble with? Write them here.

_____

_ _

Lesson 13

🐝 **TIP** In a blend, you can hear each of the consonants that go together. Listen for the l blend in <u>flew</u> and the r blend in <u>truck</u>.

List Words
class
from
friend
glove

Write the **list word** that rhymes.

1. love **glove**   2. glass **class**

3. send **friend**   4. drum **from**

73

Lesson 14

🐝 **TIP** The letter s can work with two or more letters to make a blend at the beginning or the end of a word. Listen for the s blends in the words <u>smell</u> and <u>most</u>.

List Words
slice
smoke
spell
swim

Write the **list word** that belongs in each group.

1. pool, water,   2. letters, words,
swim   **spell**

3. fire, chimney,   4. pizza, pie,
smoke   **slice**

Lesson 15

🐝 **TIP** The letter y with a vowel can have the long a sound, as in <u>say</u> or <u>they</u>. It can also have the oi sound, as in <u>joy</u>.

List Words
boys
they
joy
today

Write the **list word** that matches each clue.

1. This is great happiness. **joy**

2. She and he together. **they**

3. These are young men. **boys**

4. This day is now. **today**

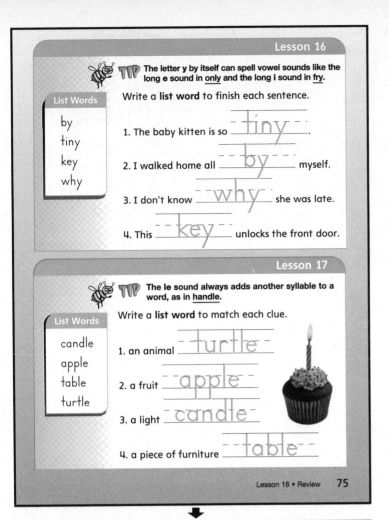

Lesson 16

TIP The letter y by itself can spell vowel sounds like the long e sound in <u>only</u> and the long i sound in <u>fry</u>.

List Words

by
tiny
key
why

Write a **list word** to finish each sentence.

1. The baby kitten is so _tiny_.

2. I walked home all _by_ myself.

3. I don't know _why_ she was late.

4. This _key_ unlocks the front door.

Lesson 17

TIP The le sound always adds another syllable to a word, as in <u>handle</u>.

List Words

candle
apple
table
turtle

Write a **list word** to match each clue.

1. an animal _turtle_

2. a fruit _apple_

3. a light _candle_

4. a piece of furniture _table_

Lesson 18 • Review   75

Show What You Know

Lessons 13–17 Review

One word is misspelled in each set of **list words**. Fill in the circle next to the **list word** that is spelled incorrectly.

1. ○ plays	● tiney	○ uncle	○ only
2. ○ flew	○ many	● sae	○ swim
3. ○ why	● playt	○ table	○ trunk
4. ● peeple	○ joy	○ snake	○ penny
5. ○ able	○ smell	○ grass	● smok
6. ○ flat	● buny	○ may	○ truck
7. ○ story	○ key	○ purple	● gluv
8. ○ bottle	○ today	○ flat	● mosht
9. ○ gray	○ by	● thay	○ from
10. ○ spell	● appel	○ friend	○ lucky
11. ● ownlee	○ fry	○ people	○ class
12. ● chruck	○ handle	○ away	○ say
13. ○ glove	○ slice	○ turtle	● joi
14. ○ candle	○ boys	● tabl	○ bunny
15. ○ they	○ tray	● smeell	○ strike
16. ○ still	○ apple	○ uncle	● gra
17. ○ most	● kee	○ by	○ flew
18. ● frend	○ swim	○ class	○ tiny
19. ○ away	○ snake	○ plate	● botle
20. ○ grass	○ smoke	● menny	○ purple

Final Test

1. Joline is my very best **friend**.
2. Did Nick learn to **swim** in his uncle's pool?
3. Our class is going on a field trip **today**.
4. John will explain **why** he was late.
5. He lit a **candle** when the power failed.
6. This red **glove** belongs to Mia.
7. **Smoke** poured out of the burning building.
8. **They** rode to school together on their bikes.
9. That bug is so **tiny** I can hardly see it!
10. Whose turn is it to set the **table** for dinner?
11. How far is it **from** Steve's house to the park?
12. I hope you will **spell** all these words correctly.
13. Are those tears of **joy** or tears of sadness?
14. Juanita lost the **key** to her front door.
15. Dad puts an **apple** in my lunch every day.
16. Mrs. Wing's **class** is making finger puppets.
17. Would you like a **slice** of freshly baked bread?
18. The family next door has three **boys**.
19. Your book reports are due **by** next Friday.
20. A giant sea **turtle** swam close to our boat.

Check Your Spelling Notebook

Before writing each word, students can name the consonants in a blend, the vowel sound *y* stands for, or the words with the *le* ending.

Lesson Review Test (Side A)

Lesson
18

Read each set of words. Fill in the circle next to the word that is spelled correctly.

1. ⓐ frum   ⓑ from
   ⓒ frome   ⓓ fromm

2. ⓐ todae   ⓑ tooday
   ⓒ tuday   ⓓ today

3. ⓐ joye   ⓑ joi
   ⓒ joy   ⓓ jooy

4. ⓐ slise   ⓑ sliec
   ⓒ slies   ⓓ slice

5. ⓐ tiney   ⓑ tiny
   ⓒ tinnie   ⓓ tinney

6. ⓐ turdle   ⓑ tertle
   ⓒ turtle   ⓓ turtel

7. ⓐ friend   ⓑ freind
   ⓒ frend   ⓓ frennd

8. ⓐ smoak   ⓑ smook
   ⓒ smoek   ⓓ smoke

9. ⓐ key   ⓑ kee
   ⓒ kea   ⓓ keye

Lesson Review Test (Side B)

Lesson 18

Read each set of words. Fill in the circle next to the word that is spelled correctly.

10. ⓐ gluv   ⓑ glov
     ⓒ glove   ⓓ gluve

11. ⓐ spell   ⓑ spele
     ⓒ speal   ⓓ spel

12. ⓐ aple   ⓑ appel
     ⓒ appul   ⓓ apple

13. ⓐ classe   ⓑ class
     ⓒ clas   ⓓ clase

14. ⓐ thay   ⓑ tey
     ⓒ thae   ⓓ they

15. ⓐ tabble   ⓑ table
     ⓒ tabel   ⓓ tabbel

16. ⓐ why   ⓑ whay
     ⓒ whie   ⓓ wy

17. ⓐ candel   ⓑ candl
     ⓒ canedle   ⓓ candle

18. ⓐ boys   ⓑ boize
     ⓒ boyz   ⓓ boyes

Take It Home 3

Your child has learned to spell many new spelling words and would enjoy sharing them with you and your family. Here are some ways to help your child review the words in Lessons 13–17 and have some family fun too!

Slice of Life

Best friend, why not, slice of pizza—these are just some of the everyday phrases that contain your child's spelling words. Help your child come up with and list even more. Encourage your child to share the list at school.

Lesson 13
1. class
2. flat
3. flew
4. friend
5. from
6. glove
7. grass
8. plate
9. truck
10. trunk

Lesson 14
1. snake
2. smell
3. still
4. smoke
5. spell
6. swim
7. slice
8. most
9. strike
10. story

Lesson 15
1. away
2. boys
3. gray
4. joy
5. may
6. plays
7. say
8. they
9. today
10. tray

Lesson 16
1. bunny
2. by
3. fry
4. key
5. lucky
6. many
7. only
8. penny
9. tiny
10. why

Lesson 17
1. apple
2. handle
3. able
4. bottle
5. table
6. uncle
7. candle
8. purple
9. turtle
10. people

Word Search

You and your child will be off and running—well, off and spelling!—with this easy-to-play board game. For markers, use anything from buttons to your child's favorite miniature cars, figurines, or other tiny toys. Then, simply flip a penny for each turn you take—heads, move one space; tails, move two spaces. As you move your markers around the board, read aloud the spelling word on each square. Off you go!

START
people | apple | class | friend
table
uncle | key | tiny | smoke
today | joy | slice
swim | END
boys | glove
why | spell | from | they | by

Objective
To spell words with consonant digraphs *sh* or *th*

 Correlated Phonics Lessons
MCP Phonics, Level B, Lessons 53–54

Spelling Words in Action   *Page 77*

In "See with Your Ears!" students find out about a type of entertainment that was popular fifty years ago. Afterward, ask students what kinds of stories they like to listen to on the radio.

Encourage students to look back at the words in dark print. Ask volunteers to say each word and to tell how many consonant sounds they hear at the beginning of *shout* and *then*.

Warm-Up Test
1. Please do not **shout** when people are sleeping.
2. The wind blew the door **shut**.
3. That loud **crash** made me jump!
4. First I ate my dinner, and **then** I ate dessert.
5. Please cut me a **thin** slice of watermelon.
6. I did my **math** homework first.
7. I **think** mystery stories are fun to read.
8. Daniel and Kelly walk to school **together**.
9. I could see **nothing** in the fog.
10. Do you know **anything** about horses?

Spelling Practice   *Pages 78–79*

Introduce the spelling rule, helping students recognize the two sounds that *th* stands for. Then have students read the **list words** aloud. Encourage them to look back at their **Warm-Up Tests** and apply the spelling rule to any misspelled words.

As students work through the **Spelling Practice** exercises, remind them to look back at their **list words** or in their dictionaries if they need help.

 See Categorizing, page 15

Spelling Words in Action

What did people do before they had TV?

See with Your Ears!

Three actors stand **together** in a studio. One man begins to **shout**, "**Shut** the door! I'm freezing!"

Crash! You can hear the sound of a door slamming, but there is no door to see. These actors are performing on the radio.

Today, many people listen to music on the radio. Fifty years ago, people listened to stories. There was no TV back **then**.

What did the listeners look at? **Nothing**! With a radio story, you don't see the pictures. You **think** them! The radio gives you the words and sounds. Your mind makes the pictures.

Did you know you can still hear radio stories? Why not tune in and listen?

> Look back at the words in dark print. Say each word. How many consonant sounds do you hear at the beginning of the words?

Spelling Practice

TIP
When two consonants make one sound it is called a **consonant digraph**. Listen for the sound th makes in think and then. Listen for the sound sh makes in shut and shout.

LIST WORDS
1. shout   *shout*
2. shut   *shut*
3. crash   *crash*
4. then   *then*
5. thin   *thin*
6. math   *math*
7. think   *think*
8. together   *together*
9. nothing   *nothing*
10. anything   *anything*

Adding Consonant Digraphs

Add a consonant digraph to each group of letters to make a word. Trace the letters to spell **list words**.

1. think
2. shout
3. math
4. together
5. anything
6. crash
7. nothing
8. then
9. shut
10. thin

Opposites

Write the **list word** that means the opposite of the word or words.

1. thick   thin   2. whisper   shout

3. open   shut   4. everything   nothing

5. alone   together   6. now   then

7. a special thing   anything

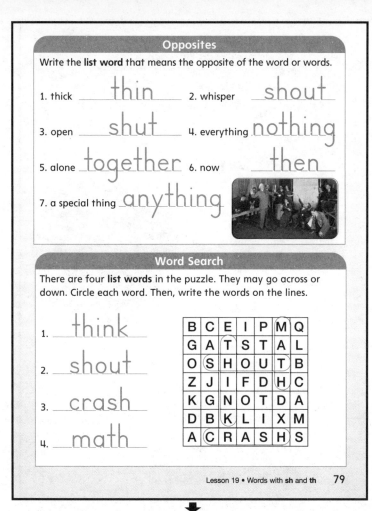

Word Search

There are four **list words** in the puzzle. They may go across or down. Circle each word. Then, write the words on the lines.

1. think
2. shout
3. crash
4. math

B	C	E	I	P	M	Q
G	A	T	S	T	A	L
O	S	H	O	U	T	B
Z	J	I	F	D	H	C
K	G	N	O	T	D	A
D	B	K	L	I	X	M
A	C	R	A	S	H	S

Spelling and Writing

Proofreading

Each sentence has two mistakes. Use the proofreading marks to fix each mistake. Write the misspelled **list words** correctly on the lines.

1. I think radio shows are are fun.

2. My brother and i listen to the radio tugethr.

3. we shet our eyes and imagine what is happening.

Proofreading Marks
- ◯ spelling mistake
- ≡ capital letter
- ℒ take out something

1. think
2. together
3. shut

Writing a Radio Play

What kind of radio story would you like to write? Write a sentence to tell what the story would be about. Write one or two sentences that actors will say in your play. Describe the sounds, too.

_____

_____

_____

BONUS WORDS
shell
gather
shape
shore
thick

Spelling Strategy

Remind students that a consonant digraph is two consonants together that make one sound, such as *sh* and *th*. Then write each **list word** on the board and call on a volunteer to circle the consonant digraph. Have the class pronounce the word in unison, stressing *sh* or *th*. Help students notice the two sounds that *th* makes.

BONUS WORDS
Ask students to try writing a story using the bonus words, but leaving a blank where the words belong. Then have them trade papers with a partner to fill in the correct words.

Spelling and Writing   *Page 80*

The **Proofreading** exercise will help students prepare to proofread their story ideas. As they complete the writing activity, encourage them to brainstorm ideas, write a first draft, revise, and proofread their work. To publish their writing, students may want to use their ideas to create and perform radio stories for another class.

Writer's Corner Students might enjoy listening to a children's radio program. Afterward, encourage them to write a paragraph telling how listening to the radio is different from watching television.

Final Test
1. The lamp fell with a loud **crash**.
2. I thought about it, and **then** I wrote the answer.
3. Do you **think** it will rain today?
4. Please **shut** the window.
5. Don't do **anything** until after you read the directions.
6. Keep your feet **together** when you dive.
7. Lisa will **shout** the score after each inning.
8. There's **nothing** left to eat!
9. I like bread that is cut into **thin** slices.
10. Will we have **math** before lunch today?

Lesson 20

Words with <u>ch</u> and <u>wh</u>

Objective
To spell words that contain consonant digraphs *ch* or *wh*

 Correlated Phonics Lessons
MCP Phonics, Level B, Lessons 53–54

Spelling Words in Action — Page 81

In "Night Jumper," students discover an unusual animal called a galago. After reading, locate Africa on the map and invite students to read aloud the part of the selection they liked best.

Encourage students to look back at the words in dark print. Ask volunteers to say each word and name the sound that *ch* or *wh* stands for.

Warm-Up Test
1. Could you tell me **what** time it is?
2. You have **such** a big dog!
3. I hope the driver knows **where** the airport is.
4. We have a **peach** tree in our back yard.
5. Too **much** rain can cause a flood.
6. **When** is the bus arriving?
7. The cowboy cracked his **whip**.
8. There is a large **arch** in St. Louis, Missouri.
9. Mrs. Kingsley is our soccer **coach**.
10. **Who** sent me this beautiful card?

Spelling Practice — Pages 82–83

Introduce the spelling rule and have students read the **list words** aloud. You may also want to point out that the letters *wh* in *who* spell the sound *h*, not *hw*. Then encourage students to look back at their **Warm-Up Tests** and apply the spelling rule to any misspelled words.

As students work through the **Spelling Practice** exercises, remind them to look back at their **list words** or in their dictionaries if they need help.

for ESL students See Student Dictation, page 14

68

Words with <u>ch</u> and <u>wh</u>

Lesson 20

Spelling Words in Action

What is a galago?

Night Jumper

Some animals have **such** funny names. One is the galago.

Galagos live in Africa **where** there are many trees. Galagos live in trees. Their long hind legs help them jump from branch to branch. Galagos can jump as far as 15 feet.

Galagos sleep during the day. They are active **when** it is night. Their large eyes help them see well in the dark.

Galagos can be as big as a squirrel or as small as a chipmunk. They have soft fur and a long tail. They have fingers and toes that help them hold on to things.

What an interesting animal a galago is. They are so **much** fun to watch. **Who** would not want to see one? The next time you visit a zoo, see if there is a galago living there.

Look back at the words in dark print. Say each word. What sound do the consonants <u>wh</u> and <u>ch</u> stand for in each word?

81

Spelling Practice

TIP
A consonant digraph is two consonants that make one sound. The letters **ch** spell one sound, as in <u>such</u>. The letters **wh** spell the sound you hear in <u>what</u>.

LIST WORDS
1. what *what*
2. such *such*
3. where *where*
4. peach *peach*
5. much *much*
6. when *when*
7. whip *whip*
8. arch *arch*
9. coach *coach*
10. who *who*

Identifying Consonant Digraphs

Write each **list word** under the heading that shows its consonant digraph.

ch

1. such   2. peach
3. much   4. arch
5. coach

wh

6. what   7. where
8. when   9. whip
10. who

82   Lesson 20 • Words with **ch** and **wh**

Word Meaning

Write the **list word** that matches each meaning.

1. A lot

much

2. A kind of fruit

peach

3. What people?

who

4. Leader of a team

coach

5. What time?

when

6. What place?

where

Rhyming Clues

Write **list words** that rhyme with the clues.

1. This word rhymes with <u>there</u>.

where

2. This word rhymes with <u>ship</u>.

whip

3. This word rhymes with <u>march</u>.

arch

4. This word rhymes with <u>mutt</u>.

what

5. These two words rhyme with each other.

such   _much_

Spelling and Writing

Proofreading

The paragraph below has six mistakes. Use the proofreading marks to fix each mistake. Write the misspelled **list words** correctly on the lines.

Have you ever seen an unusual looking animal? Whut did it look like? Was it cute? Was it funny looking? Wheen you go for a walk, look around. See how many animals you can find. Make a list that tells what they look like. Share your list with your friends. See how mech they know about the animals you saw.

Proofreading Marks
- ⬭ spelling mistake
- ⊙ add period
- ⌃ add something

1. _What_

2. _When_

3. _much_

Writing a Description

What is your favorite animal? What does it look like? Why is it your favorite? Write sentences to describe your favorite animal. Proofread your description. Fix any mistakes.

_____

_____

BONUS WORDS

child
whale
wheat
sandwich
cheese

Spelling Strategy

Show students how to fold a sheet of paper in half lengthwise to make two columns. Have them label one column *chair* and the other *white*, and point out the consonant digraph *ch* or *wh* in each word. Then call out the **list words**, guiding students to write them under the correct headings. Ask students to suggest other words with *ch* and *wh* that they could add to the columns.

BONUS WORDS

Ask students to draw a picture for each bonus word, and then trade papers with partner to write the correct word for each picture.

Spelling and Writing   *Page 84*

The **Proofreading** exercise will help students prepare to proofread their descriptions. As they complete the writing activity, encourage them to brainstorm ideas, write a first draft, revise, and proofread their work. To publish their writing, students may want to

- use their descriptions to make a book of favorite animals
- make a poster of animal favorites to display in the hall.

Writer's Corner You may want to show the class a map of your city or state and point out areas that have nature preserves or other places where animals may be observed in their natural habitats. Invite students to write a few sentences about a place they have visited or would like to visit.

Final Test

1. The recipe tells us to **whip** the cream.
2. Will you please slice a **peach** for the fruit salad?
3. We had **such** a wonderful time at the circus!
4. **Who** borrowed my tape?
5. Workers painted the **arch** of the bridge.
6. **What** book will you read for your report?
7. Our **coach** said that we played our best game.
8. **When** I was your age, I learned to swim.
9. Thank you very **much** for helping me.
10. **Where** did I leave my suitcase?

Objective
To spell words with c and ck

 Correlated Phonics Lessons
MCP Phonics, Level B, Lessons 39, 54

Spelling Words in Action   *Page 85*

In this selection, students read about a kind of sock that has nothing to do with feet. After reading, invite students to describe wind socks they may have seen and to tell what kind of wind sock they would like to make.

Encourage students to look back at the words in dark print. Ask a volunteer to say each word and tell which one begins with *c*, but has the *s* sound. Ask another volunteer to name the words that have the *k* sound.

Warm-Up Test

1. Who won the **race**?
2. A **stick** is made of wood.
3. My favorite **color** is green.
4. In soccer you must **kick** the ball into the goal.
5. You must be **quick** to win a race.
6. Can you carry this pack on your **back**?
7. The caterpillar **became** a butterfly.
8. This scarf keeps my **neck** warm.
9. One **cent** is easy to carry.
10. How many people live in this **city**?

Spelling Practice   *Pages 86–87*

Introduce the spelling rule and have students read the **list words** aloud. Encourage students to look back at their **Warm-Up Tests** and apply the spelling rule to any misspelled words.

As students work through the **Spelling Practice** exercises, remind them to look back at their **list words** or in their dictionaries if they need help.

 See Rhymes and Songs, page 14

Spelling Words in Action

What kind of sock does not go on your foot?

How to Make a Wind Sock

A wind sock is a tube of fabric that hangs on a pole or **stick**. When the wind blows, the tube fills with air. By looking at the wind sock you can tell which way the wind is blowing.

A wind sock is **quick** and easy to make. It might cost more than one **cent**, but it will not cost very much. Use a piece of cloth about two feet wide and three feet long. Use markers or paint to **color** a design on the **back**. Next, sew the long edges of the cloth together to make a tube. Then, bend thin metal or a wire coat hanger into the shape of a circle. Sew one end of the tube onto the hoop. Attach some string and tie your wind sock to a stick. Now, wait for the wind to blow!

Look back at the words in dark print. Say each word. Which word begins with c, but has the s sound? In which words can you hear the k sound?

85

 TIP

The letter **c** can make the k sound, as in color, or the s sound, as in race. When the letters **c** and **k** come together, they make the k sound, as in kick.

Spelling Practice

Showing the Sound c Makes,

Write each **list word** under the heading that shows the sound **c** spells.

LIST WORDS

1. race   *race*
2. stick   *stick*
3. color   *color*
4. kick   *kick*
5. quick   *quick*
6. back   *back*
7. became   *became*
8. neck   *neck*
9. cent   *cent*
10. city   *city*

c spells s

1. race   2. cent

3. city

ck spells k

4. stick   5. kick

6. quick   7. back

8. neck

c spells k

9. color   10. became

Word Groups

Write the **list word** that belongs with each group.

1. head, shoulders,

   neck

2. hit, strike,

   kick

3. dime, nickel,

   cent

4. town, village,

   city

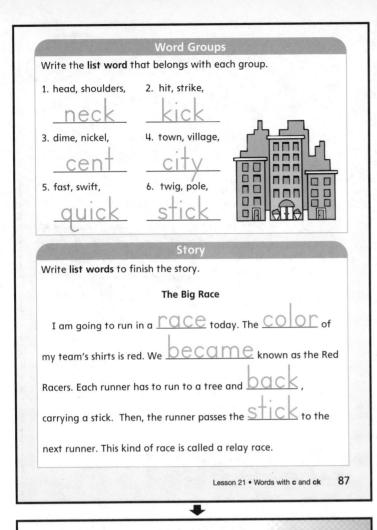

5. fast, swift,

   quick

6. twig, pole,

   stick

Story

Write **list words** to finish the story.

The Big Race

I am going to run in a _race_ today. The _color_ of my team's shirts is red. We _became_ known as the Red Racers. Each runner has to run to a tree and _back_, carrying a stick. Then, the runner passes the _stick_ to the next runner. This kind of race is called a relay race.

Lesson 21 • Words with **c** and **ck**   87

Spelling and Writing

Proofreading

Each sentence has two mistakes. Use the proofreading marks to fix each mistake. Write the misspelled **list words** correctly on the lines.

1. Our team won the the rase today!

2. We were quik on the track.

3. Next week, we'll ride to the cite to race a new team.

Proofreading Marks

⬭ spelling mistake
⊙ add period
⤴ take something out

1. _race_

2. _quick_

3. _city_

Writing Directions

Have you ever made a wind sock, a pinwheel, or a paper airplane? Write sentences that tell how to make something.

_____

_____

_____

BONUS WORDS

camera

coconut

space

pack

circle

Spelling Strategy

Write each **list word** on the board and ask the class whether the letter *c* appears alone in the word or with *k*. If *c* appears alone, ask whether it stands for the *s* sound or the *k* sound. If *c* appears with *k*, ask what sound the two letters spell. Explain that the *k* sound at the end of a short-vowel word is usually spelled with *ck*. Write these words on the board to illustrate the point: *bike, bake, back, peek, peck, luck, like, rock, joke*.

BONUS WORDS Have students write a sentence for each bonus word, but just write the first letter and leave the rest of the word blank. Then have them trade papers with a partner to fill in the correct bonus words.

Spelling and Writing   *Page 88*

The **Proofreading** exercise will help students prepare to proofread their paragraphs. As they complete the writing activity, encourage them to brainstorm ideas, write a first draft, revise, and proofread their work. To publish their writing, students may want to ask an adult family member to help them make the item they wrote about.

Writer's Corner Students might enjoy listening to a song about something fun to play with, such as *The Marvelous Toy* by Tom Paxton or *Rubber Duckie* by Jeffrey Moss. Help the class write an additional verse to add to the song.

Final Test

1. If you are **quick**, you can still catch the bus.
2. This shirt has my name written on the **back**.
3. **Kick** the ball to your teammate so he can score.
4. What is your favorite **color**?
5. In winter, the rabbit's fur **became** white.
6. Our **city** has an exciting science museum.
7. Don't wave that **stick** around!
8. I need a thirty-four **cent** stamp.
9. Is Nick running in this **race**?
10. The coach wears a whistle around her **neck**.

Objective
To spell words with the *ar* or *or* sounds

 Phonics **Correlated Phonics Lessons**
MCP Phonics, Level B, Lessons 58–59

Spelling Words in Action   *Page 89*

In "A Far Away Place," students read about an interesting way to learn about another country. Invite students to discuss special letters they have received or sent, or their own experiences with pen pals, if any.

Encourage students to look back at the words in dark print. Ask volunteers to say each word and identify the sound spelled by *ar* or *or*.

Warm-Up Test
1. Amanda likes to work on the **farm**.
2. This farm grows **corn** and carrots.
3. The work is **hard** but fun, too.
4. Matthew went to the **park** every day to practice.
5. My cousin had a good **part** in the play.
6. Did you ever ride on a **horse**?
7. Would you like **more** salad?
8. Is it **far** to Leon's house?
9. I watched the parade from a second **floor** window.
10. We visited the farm on a **warm** day in June.

Spelling Practice   *Pages 90–91*

Introduce the spelling rule and have the class read the **list words** aloud. Call attention to *floor* and *warm*, which spell the *or* sound differently than the other list words with *or* (*floor, warm*). Encourage students to look back at their **Warm-Up Tests** and apply the spelling rule to any misspelled words.

As students work through the **Spelling Practice** exercises, remind them to look back at their **list words** or in their dictionaries if they need help.

 See Rhymes and Songs, page 14

72

Spelling Words in Action

What is a fun way to learn about another country?

A Far Away Place

One girl lives on a **farm** in Iowa. Another girl lives in a big city **far** away in Japan. How can they be friends? They are pen pals.

Pen pals are friends who write letters to each other. Many groups help school children find pen pals in other countries.

The girl in Iowa might tell her pen pal about the **corn** her family grows on their farm. She might tell about the farm animals, a **horse** or a cow. She might write about what it's like at her school.

Her pen pal can tell her what things are like in Japan. They can each learn **more** about each others' country. It's not **hard** at all. It's fun!

Say each word in dark print in the paragraphs. What sounds do *ar* and *or* spell?

89

Spelling Practice

TIP
When a vowel is followed by **r**, the vowel sound is changed by the **r**. Listen for the **or** sound in *corn* and the **ar** sound in *farm*.

LIST WORDS
1. farm *farm*
2. corn *corn*
3. hard *hard*
4. park *park*
5. part *part*
6. horse *horse*
7. more *more*
8. far *far*
9. floor *floor*
10. warm *warm*

Adding or and ar
Add **ar** or **or** to make **list words**. Trace the letters to spell **list words**.

1. more   2. park
3. warm   4. corn
5. hard   6. floor
7. part   8. farm
9. far   10. horse

90   Lesson 22 • Vowels with r

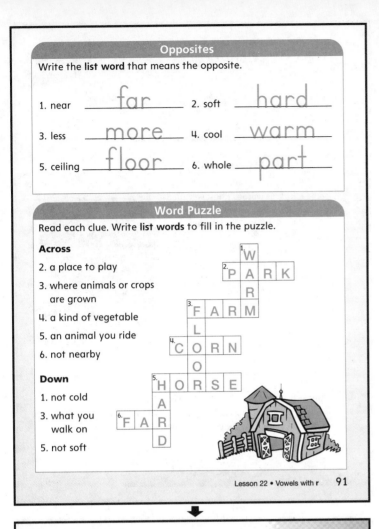

Opposites

Write the **list word** that means the opposite.

1. near _far_
2. soft _hard_
3. less _more_
4. cool _warm_
5. ceiling _floor_
6. whole _part_

Word Puzzle

Read each clue. Write **list words** to fill in the puzzle.

Across

2. a place to play
3. where animals or crops are grown
4. a kind of vegetable
5. an animal you ride
6. not nearby

Down

1. not cold
3. what you walk on
5. not soft

```
        ¹W
   ²P  A  R  K
        R
    ³F  A  R  M
        L
    ⁴C  O  R  N
        O
   ⁵H  O  R  S  E
        A
 ⁶F  A  R  D
        D
```

Spelling and Writing

Proofreading

Each sentence has two mistakes. Use the proofreading marks to fix each mistake. Write the misspelled **list words** correctly on the lines.

Proofreading Marks

⬭ spelling mistake
≡ capital letter
⌃ add something

1. Jerry visited his aunt's ⬭faerm⬭ in idaho.

   1. _farm_

2. Aunt jessie worked ⬭haard⬭ all day.

   2. _hard_

3. What ⬭parte⬭ of the farm do you like best⌃

   3. _part_

Writing a Letter

Imagine you have a pen pal in another country. Write a letter to your pen pal.

_____

_____

_____

_____

_____

BONUS WORDS

start
born
cart
forest
alarm

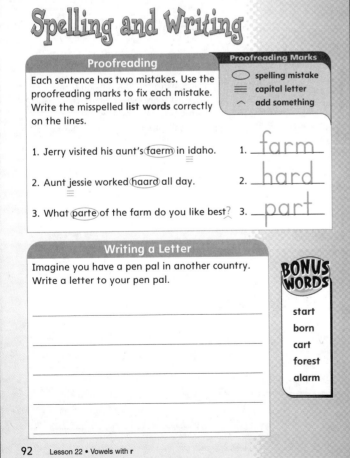

Spelling Strategy

Invite students to get together with a partner and take turns writing the **list words**. The partner who writes the word

- pronounces it, emphasizing the *ar* or *or* vowel sound
- circles the letters that stand for *ar* or *or*.

BONUS WORDS Have students use the bonus words to write a poem about life on a farm, then trade papers with a partner to read aloud.

Spelling and Writing   *Page 92*

The **Proofreading** exercise will help students prepare to proofread their letters. As students complete the writing activity, encourage them to brainstorm ideas, write a first draft, revise, and proofread their work. To publish their writing, students may want to read their letters aloud as you locate the imaginary pen pal's country on a globe or a map of the world.

Writer's Corner You may want to bring in some envelopes that contained mail sent to you. Discuss the standard form for addressing an envelope, emphasizing the need for both the delivery address and the return address, as well as ZIP codes. Students can practice this standard form by addressing an envelope (or a folded sheet of paper) to someone at their home address.

Final Test

1. This **corn** on the cob is delicious!
2. The tomatoes were grown on a nearby **farm**.
3. Lucas swept the **floor**.
4. Did you find that story **hard** to understand?
5. The **horse** nibbled on the carrot.
6. I would like **more** pie, please.
7. May we go to the **park** after dinner?
8. Tara tried out for a **part** in the school play.
9. I don't like to swim too **far** from the shore.
10. It felt **warm** when the sun came out.

Contractions

Contractions
Lesson 23

Objective
To spell contractions

Phonics Correlated Phonics Lessons
MCP Phonics, Level B, Lessons 65–68

Spelling Words in Action **Page 93**

In this selection, students are introduced to a spelling shortcut called a contraction. If necessary, help students with the pronunciation of the word *apostrophe*. Then invite the class to take the challenge in the last paragraph and name all the contractions in the passage.

Encourage students to look back at the words in dark print. Ask volunteers to say each word and identify the pair of words that form the contraction.

Warm-Up Test
1. I know **you'll** enjoy reading this book.
2. **They're** my best friends.
3. **It's** a great day for a picnic!
4. Yes, **we've** had a wonderful time.
5. Why **isn't** Zack in school today?
6. **Let's** go for a hike.
7. Why **aren't** we going to the museum tomorrow?
8. **I'm** planning to be a scientist someday.
9. My dog **can't** do many tricks.
10. **We're** happy to see you, Meg.

Spelling Practice **Pages 94–95**

Introduce the spelling rule and have students read the **list words** aloud. You may want to point out that the contraction *I'm* always begins with a capital letter because it begins with the pronoun *I*. Then encourage students to look back at their **Warm-Up Tests** and apply the spelling rule to any misspelled words.

As students work through the **Spelling Practice** exercises, remind them to look back at their **list words** or in their dictionaries if they need help.

for ESL students See Words in Context, page 14

Spelling Words in Action

Do you know what a spelling shortcut is?

Spelling Shortcuts

In this lesson, **you'll** be spelling some shortcut words. **They're** called contractions. You already say many contractions every day. **It's** an easy way to talk.

Contractions join two words into one. You might say, "**We're** going to the park." We're is a contraction. It is a short way of writing "we are."

This mark (') takes the place of the letter or letters you took away. This little mark has a big name. It's called an apostrophe. Use it to combine two words into one shorter word. **Isn't** that easy?

Let's see if you can find all the contractions in this story. It isn't hard to do. **They're** easy to see, **aren't** they? Just look for that little mark. **I'm** sure you can do it. You just **can't** miss!

Look back at the words in dark print. Say each word. What two words make up the contraction? What letter or letters does the apostrophe replace?

93

Spelling Practice

TIP A **contraction** is two words combined into one. One or more letters are dropped. A mark called an **apostrophe** (') replaces the missing letters.

LIST WORDS
1. you'll *you'll*
2. they're *they're*
3. it's *it's*
4. we've *we've*
5. isn't *isn't*
6. let's *let's*
7. aren't *aren't*
8. I'm *I'm*
9. can't *can't*
10. we're *we're*

Adding Apostrophes

The apostrophe (') is missing from each **list word** below. Write the correct **list word** on the line. Put the apostrophe in the right place.

1. youll
you'll

2. lets
let's

3. cant
can't

4. Im
I'm

5. were
we're

6. its
it's

7. theyre
they're

8. isnt
isn't

9. arent
aren't

10. were
we're

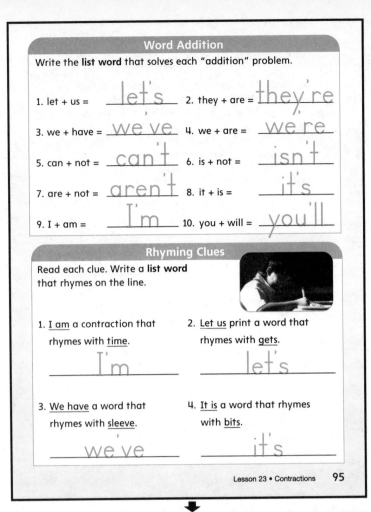

Word Addition

Write the **list word** that solves each "addition" problem.

1. let + us = **let's**
2. they + are = **they're**
3. we + have = **we've**
4. we + are = **we're**
5. can + not = **can't**
6. is + not = **isn't**
7. are + not = **aren't**
8. it + is = **it's**
9. I + am = **I'm**
10. you + will = **you'll**

Rhyming Clues

Read each clue. Write a **list word** that rhymes on the line.

1. <u>I am</u> a contraction that rhymes with <u>time</u>.

I'm

2. <u>Let us</u> print a word that rhymes with <u>gets</u>.

let's

3. <u>We have</u> a word that rhymes with <u>sleeve</u>.

we've

4. <u>It is</u> a word that rhymes with <u>bits</u>.

it's

Spelling and Writing

Proofreading

Each sentence has two mistakes. Use the proofreading marks to fix each mistake. Write the **list words** correctly on the lines.

Proofreading Marks	
⌄	add apostrophe
≡	capital letter
⊙	add period

1. On the Fourth of July, youll see many families in the parks⊙

1. **you'll**

2. usually, they're eating or playing games.

2. **they're**

3. Its a day for singing the "Star spangled Banner."

3. **It's**

Writing a Description

A contraction is a kind of shortcut. Shortcuts save time. Write a description of a shortcut you know at home or at school.

_____

_____

_____

_____

BONUS WORDS

doesn't

I'd

weren't

you've

mustn't

Spelling Strategy

To help students understand contractions, write *we have* and *are not* on the board and explain that there are "shortcut" words used to say these phrases. Then write *we've* next to *we have* and *aren't* next to *are not*, and identify the new words as contractions. Ask students to tell you

- what words have been combined to make each contraction
- which letter or letters the apostrophe takes the place of.

Repeat this procedure with other **list words**.

BONUS WORDS

Have students write a sentence for each bonus word, but write the two full words that form each contraction instead of the correct word. Then have them trade papers with a partner to replace the two word combinations with the correct contraction bonus word.

Spelling and Writing   **Page 96**

The **Proofreading** exercise will help students prepare to proofread their descriptions. As they complete the writing activity, encourage them to brainstorm ideas, write a first draft, revise, and proofread their work. To publish their writing, students may want to

- create a class newsletter called "Time Savers"
- exchange descriptions with a partner.

Writer's Corner You might want to display comic strips that contain contractions in the dialogue. Ask students what else the characters in the comic strips might say. Help them use contractions in the new dialogue.

Final Test

1. Jamal and Alice **aren't** here today.
2. I **can't** find my baseball cap anywhere.
3. **I'm** going to tell you a story.
4. Why **isn't** my book in my book bag?
5. If **it's** a nice day, we will play outside.
6. **Let's** all go to the beach!
7. Did Marco and Ginny say **they're** coming, too?
8. **We're** taking a picnic lunch to the beach.
9. **We've** spent many happy hours at the park.
10. Do you think **you'll** have a good time?

Lesson 24

Review Lessons 19–23

Objective
To review spelling words with *sh, th, ch,* or *wh*; with *c* or *ck*; with the *ar* or *or* sound; and with contractions

Check Your Spelling Notebook
Pages 97–100

Based on your observations, note which words are giving students the most difficulty and offer assistance for spelling them correctly. Here are some frequently misspelled words to watch for: *together, then, when, where, much, color, they're, it's, let's, can't,* and *we're.*

To give students extra help and practice in taking standardized tests, you may want to have them take the **Warm-Up Test** for this lesson on pages 78–79. After scoring the tests, return them to students so that they can record their misspelled words in their spelling notebooks.

Invite students to practice their troublesome words by having a partner check the words as they spell them aloud. After practicing their words, students can work through the exercises for lessons 19–23 and the cumulative review, **Show What You Know.** Before they begin each exercise, you may want to go over the spelling rule. For the Lesson 20 review on page 98, you may want to point out that students may need to capitalize some of the **list words** used.

 Take It Home

Invite students to listen for and use the **list words** in lessons 19–23 at home. Suggest that they ask family members to use the words in conversation and to point out **list words** that they hear or see. For a complete list of the words, have students take their *Spelling Workout* books home. Students can also use **Take It Home Master 4** on pages 80–81 to help them do the activity. Encourage them to share the words they collected with the class and to discuss which words were the most difficult to use or find.

For the Lesson 20 review on page 98, you may want to point out that students may need to capitalize some of the **list words** used.

76

Lessons 19–23 · Review

In Lessons 19–23 you learned how to spell words with consonant digraphs and words with vowels and the letter **r**. You also learned the sounds that **c** and **ck** can make and how to write contractions.

Check Your Spelling Notebook

Look at the words in your spelling notebook. Which words for Lessons 19 through 23 did you have the most trouble with? Write them here.

_____

_____

Lesson 19

TIP Some consonant pairs spell one sound. They are called **consonant digraphs.** Listen for the **sh** sound, as in <u>crash</u>, and the **th** sound, as in <u>then</u>.

List Words
nothing
shout
shut
thin

Write the **list word** that means the same or almost the same each word.

1. skinny _thin_ 2. yell _shout_

3. zero _nothing_ 4. close _shut_

97

Lesson 20

TIP The letter pairs **ch** and **wh** are consonant digraphs. Listen for the **ch** sound, as in <u>coach</u>, and the **wh** sound, as in <u>whip</u>.

List Words
much
peach
when
where

Write a **list word** to finish each sentence.

1. _When_ will the movie begin?

2. _Where_ do you live?

3. How _much_ does it cost?

4. May I eat the _peach_?

Lesson 21

TIP You can hear the **k** sound with the letter **c** in <u>became</u>. The letter **c** can also make the **s** sound, as in <u>cent</u>. When the letters **c** and **k** come together, you hear the **k** sound, as in <u>neck</u>.

List Words
cent
race
color
stick

Write each **list word** next to its dictionary sound-spelling.

1. (kul' ər) _color_ 2. (rās) _race_

3. (stik) _stick_ 4. (sent) _cent_

98 Lesson 24 • Review

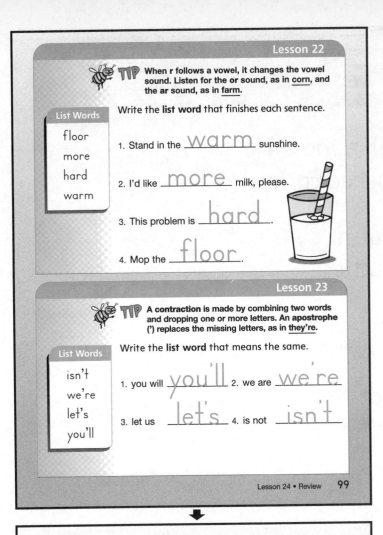

Lesson 22

TIP When r follows a vowel, it changes the vowel sound. Listen for the or sound, as in <u>corn</u>, and the ar sound, as in <u>farm</u>.

List Words

floor
more
hard
warm

Write the **list word** that finishes each sentence.

1. Stand in the _warm_ sunshine.

2. I'd like _more_ milk, please.

3. This problem is _hard_.

4. Mop the _floor_.

Lesson 23

TIP A contraction is made by combining two words and dropping one or more letters. An apostrophe (') replaces the missing letters, as in they're.

List Words

isn't
we're
let's
you'll

Write the **list word** that means the same.

1. you will _you'll_   2. we are _we're_

3. let us _let's_   4. is not _isn't_

Lesson 24 • Review   99

Show What You Know

Lessons 19–23 Review

One word is misspelled in each set of **list words**. Fill in the circle next to the **list word** that is spelled incorrectly.

1. ○ think	● citie	○ such	○ floor
2. ● cann't	○ far	○ kick	○ what
3. ○ became	○ much	○ corn	● togeter
4. ○ cent	○ let's	● parc	○ where
5. ○ thin	● arche	○ hard	○ color
6. ● moore	○ who	○ back	○ it's
7. ● krash	○ farm	○ when	○ race
8. ○ coach	○ part	○ neck	● you'l
9. ○ shut	● whipp	○ quick	○ warm
10. ○ I'm	○ then	○ it's	● stik
11. ○ anything	○ horse	● isnn't	○ math
12. ○ they're	● nothin	○ shout	○ who
13. ○ thin	○ back	○ peach	● flore
14. ● rase	○ hard	○ what	○ aren't
15. ● peech	○ cent	○ then	○ we've
16. ○ it's	○ much	○ kick	● schut
17. ○ such	○ color	● farr	○ math
18. ○ when	● quik	○ we're	○ corn
19. ○ neck	○ think	○ part	● we'er
20. ● arenn't	○ warm	○ coach	○ think

100   Lesson 24 • Review

Final Test

1. I think **you'll** have a great time at the beach.
2. A penny equals one **cent**.
3. Why does a new bike cost so **much** money?
4. Rachel found **nothing** wrong with the kite string.
5. Is there any **more** popcorn in the bowl?
6. Dad said **we're** moving to a new town.
7. The sky was a purplish-red **color** at sunset.
8. This **peach** is from the tree in our yard.
9. Please don't **shout** or you will wake the baby.
10. Practice **hard** and you'll be a better player.
11. **Let's** pretend that this bench is a rocket ship.
12. Joshua couldn't wait to try the sack **race**.
13. **When** will your sister go to college?
14. Maria forgot to **shut** the door to the tool shed.
15. The **floor** was very shiny after it was waxed.
16. Lindsey **isn't** going because she has a bad cold.
17. The dog ran to fetch the **stick** that Karen threw.
18. Adam can't remember **where** he left his notebook.
19. The wire was so **thin** we could hardly see it.
20. If it gets too **warm**, may we open the windows?

Check Your Spelling Notebook

Before writing each word, students can say the word and name the consonant digraph, the vowel sound they hear, the two words that make up a contraction, or they can circle the *c* or *ck*.

Lesson Review Test (Side A)

Lesson 24

Read each set of words. Fill in the circle next to the word that is spelled correctly.

1. ⓐ mutch   ⓑ mutsh
   ⓒ much   ⓓ muche

2. ⓐ shet   ⓑ shut
   ⓒ shutt   ⓓ shawt

3. ⓐ is'nt   ⓑ is'ot
   ⓒ isnt   ⓓ isn't

4. ⓐ color   ⓑ coler
   ⓒ collor   ⓓ coller

5. ⓐ flor   ⓑ floore
   ⓒ flore   ⓓ floor

6. ⓐ nuthing   ⓑ nothing
   ⓒ nothin   ⓓ notting

7. ⓐ peech   ⓑ peatch
   ⓒ peach   ⓓ peash

8. ⓐ harde   ⓑ hard
   ⓒ harred   ⓓ hared

9. ⓐ shote   ⓑ showt
   ⓒ shout   ⓓ shuot

Name _____

Read each set of words. Fill in the circle next to the word that is spelled correctly.

10. (a) maur   (b) more
     (c) mor   (d) maure

11. (a) stik   (b) stick
     (c) sticke   (d) stic

12. (a) le'ts   (b) lets'
     (c) let's   (d) letus

13. (a) wene   (b) whenn
     (c) when   (d) wenn

14. (a) thin   (b) tchin
     (c) thinn   (d) thinne

15. (a) ras   (b) rac
     (c) rase   (d) race

16. (a) whare   (b) where
     (c) weare   (d) wheer

17. (a) you'll   (b) youw'll
     (c) you'l   (d) youll

18. (a) cint   (b) cinte
     (c) cente   (d) cent

Take It Home

4

Your child will enjoy trying out new spelling words in Lessons 19–23 with you and your family. Be sure to check out these activities to make spelling review F-U-N!

Tell and Spell

Here's an idea that's sure to cause some talk! Encourage your child to ask you and your other family members to use spelling words in conversations. You can also keep your eyes and ears open for spelling words that come up in the news, on the phone, or in a favorite family magazine. As you and your child come across spelling words, you can "tell (and spell) all"!

Lesson 19
1. anything
2. crash
3. math
4. nothing
5. shout
6. shut
7. then
8. thin
9. think
10. together

Lesson 20
1. arch
2. coach
3. much
4. peach
5. such
6. what
7. when
8. where
9. whip
10. who

Lesson 21
1. back
2. became
3. cent
4. city
5. color
6. kick
7. neck
8. quick
9. race
10. stick

Lesson 22
1. corn
2. far
3. farm
4. floor
5. hard
6. horse
7. more
8. park
9. part
10. warm

Lesson 23
1. aren't
2. can't
3. I'm
4. isn't
5. it's
6. let's
7. they're
8. we're
9. we've
10. you'll

Word Treasures

You and your child can collect a treasure of words by labeling all of the things in this picture that represent spelling words. Remember, you can't just name the words—you have to spell them too!

Lesson 25 — Vowels with r

Objective
To spell words containing vowels followed by *r*

 Correlated Phonics Lessons
MCP Phonics, Level B, Lessons 59–60

Spelling Words in Action   **Page 101**

In this section, students read about people who grow giant vegetables. After reading, help students locate Pennsylvania and North Carolina on a map. Invite them to share information they might know about these states.

Encourage students to look back at the words in dark print. Ask volunteers to say each word and name the vowel sound they hear.

Warm-Up Test

1. We all wish for **world** peace.
2. There's a new **girl** in our class.
3. My new **skirt** is red and black.
4. What is **her** name?
5. When is the **first** day of vacation?
6. That giant pumpkin is **worth** a lot of money.
7. Write each **word** very carefully.
8. Thank you for helping me, **sir**.
9. When will that tadpole **turn** into a frog?
10. All my friends **were** at my party.

Spelling Practice   **Pages 102–103**

Introduce the spelling rule and have students read the **list words** aloud. Encourage students to look back at their **Warm-Up Tests** and apply the spelling rule to any misspelled words.

As students work through the **Spelling Practice** exercises, remind them to look back at their **list words** or in their dictionaries if they need help.

 See Charades/Pantomime, page 15

82

Vowels with r — Lesson 25

Spelling Words in Action

How much does a giant pumpkin weigh?

The **Bigger** the Better

Some people like to grow giant fruits and vegetables. They want to break **world** records.

A woman in Pennsylvania grew a pumpkin that weighed 1,131 pounds! **Her** pumpkin was really big.

In North Carolina, a man named Harry Hurley broke the biggest bean record for the **first** time in 1996. The bean was 4 feet long! One year later, he had another **turn** to break the world record. This time his giant bean was 4 feet 3 1/2 inches long.

In 2000, a company in England grew the largest tomato plant in the world. It grew to be 65 feet tall! That was **worth** a world record, too. People **were** able to pick 1,000 tomatoes off the giant plant.

> Look back at the words in dark print. Say each word. What vowel sounds do you hear?

101

Spelling Practice

TIP
When r follows the vowels **e, i, o,** or **u,** it can make the **ur** sound you hear in **her** and **sir.** That sound is spelled **er, ir, or,** or **ur.**

LIST WORDS

1. world *world*
2. girl *girl*
3. skirt *skirt*
4. her *her*
5. first *first*
6. worth *worth*
7. word *word*
8. sir *sir*
9. turn *turn*
10. were *were*

Adding Vowels with r

Add **er, ir, or,** or **ur** to each word to make a **list word.** Trace the letters to spell **list words.**

1. her   2. girl
3. were   4. world
5. turn   6. worth
7. sir   8. skirt
9. word   10. first

102   Lesson 25 • Vowels with r

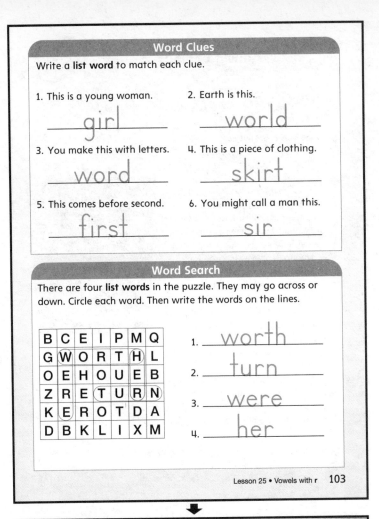

Word Clues

Write a **list word** to match each clue.

1. This is a young woman.
   girl

2. Earth is this.
   world

3. You make this with letters.
   word

4. This is a piece of clothing.
   skirt

5. This comes before second.
   first

6. You might call a man this.
   sir

Word Search

There are four **list words** in the puzzle. They may go across or down. Circle each word. Then write the words on the lines.

B	C	E	I	P	M	Q
G	W	O	R	T	H	L
O	E	H	O	U	E	B
Z	R	E	T	U	R	N
K	E	R	O	T	D	A
D	B	K	L	I	X	M

1. worth
2. turn
3. were
4. her

Spelling and Writing

Proofreading

Each sentence has two mistakes. Use the proofreading marks to fix each mistake. Write the misspelled **list words** correctly on the lines.

Proofreading Marks

◯ spelling mistake
⊙ add period
︿ add something

1. The largest carrot in the worle weighed over 18 pounds.

2. It was the furst carrot ever to grow that big.

3. What do you think a carrot that size is werth?

1. world
2. first
3. worth

Writing an Ad

Write an ad for the world's biggest pizza. How big will it be? How many slices will it have? Proofread your ad and fix any mistakes.

_____

_____

_____

BONUS WORDS

beaver
curtain
dirt
shirt
worm

Spelling Strategy

Ask students to close their eyes and listen carefully as you call out each **list word**. Encourage them to picture the word, focusing on the letters (*er*, *ir*, *or*, or *ur*) that stand for the *ur* sound. After students open their eyes, ask the class to name the letters that spell the vowel sound. Then call on a volunteer to write the word on the board and circle *er*, *ir*, *or*, or *ur*.

BONUS WORDS

Have the class draw a picture for each bonus word, then trade pictures with a partner. Partners should write a sentence for each picture using the correct bonus word.

Spelling and Writing   Page 104

The **Proofreading** exercise will help students prepare to proofread their ads. As they complete the writing activity, encourage them to brainstorm ideas, write a first draft, revise, and proofread their work. To publish their writing, students may want to post their ads in the lunchroom or other place and invite all students to vote which pizza sounds best.

Writer's Corner Students might enjoy listening as you read some of the entries in a book of records, such as the *Guiness Book of World Records*. Afterward, invite students to create a book of humorous class records. Categories might include "shortest pencil" or "messiest corner."

Final Test

1. A baby's **first** food is usually milk.
2. What is the name of that **girl**?
3. Grandma drove **her** car to the beach.
4. Follow me, **sir**, and I will show you your seat.
5. What a pretty **skirt** you are wearing!
6. Will this caterpillar **turn** into a butterfly?
7. All the students **were** reading quietly.
8. Does this **word** have the *ur* sound in it?
9. All over the **world**, people love to sing.
10. His old baseball card is **worth** a lot of money.

Objective
To spell words with the suffixes *ing*, *ed*, and *s* or *es*

 Correlated Phonics Lessons
MCP Phonics, Level B, Lessons 69–71

Spelling Words in Action *Page 105*

In this selection, students learn about lookouts and what it was like to work in a tower on top of a mountain. Ask students how they would feel if they were a lookout.

Encourage students to look back at the words in dark print. Ask volunteers to say each word and name its ending.

Warm-Up Test
1. Ray **worked** in a tall tower.
2. The airline is **sending** our tickets in the mail.
3. Who **wants** to watch the game?
4. Dad filled our **glasses** with cider.
5. Michelle **sees** a deer in the woods.
6. The fire is **burning** out of control!
7. The baby **reached** out and grabbed my hand.
8. We packed our dishes in cardboard **boxes**.
9. The farmer **wishes** it would rain soon.
10. Where is the **opening** in the fence?

Spelling Practice *Pages 106–107*

Introduce the spelling rule and have students read the **list words** aloud, helping them identify the base word and the ending for each word. Then encourage students to look back at their **Warm-Up Tests** and apply the spelling rule to any misspelled words.

As students work through the **Spelling Practice** exercises, remind them to look back at their **list words** or in their dictionaries if they need help. For the **Scrambled Letters** exercise, you may want to point out how this activity differs from previous versions where word shape boxes were used.

 See Comparing / Contrasting, page 15

84

Spelling Words in Action

What does a lookout do?

Sky High

The U.S. Forest Service began **sending** people to live in lookout towers in the 1930s. These tall towers are usually built on top of mountains, so a lookout **sees** a long, long way.

Hundreds or even thousands of steps had to be climbed before a lookout **reached** the top of the tower. The small room at the top of the tower was where a lookout lived and **worked**.

Lookouts watched for signs of **burning** forest fires. They used field **glasses**, or binoculars, to help them. Then they'd call for help.

Nowadays there are not many jobs for lookouts. There are still many lookout towers, though. Some are rented to campers. If you think you would like to sleep hundreds of feet above the ground, a lookout tower might be for you.

Say each word in dark print in the paragraphs. How many different endings do you hear?

105

Spelling Practice

 TIP

All of the **list words** have been built from base words and the endings **s** or **es**, **ed**, or **ing**. Add **es** to words that end in **x**, **s**, **sh**, or **ch**, such as <u>wishes</u> or <u>boxes</u>. Just add **s** to words ending in other letters, such as <u>wants</u> or <u>sees</u>.

LIST WORDS
1. worked *worked*
2. sending *sending*
3. wants *wants*
4. glasses *glasses*
5. sees *sees*
6. burning *burning*
7. reached *reached*
8. boxes *boxes*
9. wishes *wishes*
10. opening *opening*

Adding Endings

Add **s**, **es**, **ed**, or **ing** to each word to make a **list word**. Trace the letters to spell **list words**.

1. sees
2. reached
3. wants
4. wishes
5. worked
6. boxes
7. glasses
8. burning
9. sending
10. opening

106 Lesson 26 • Adding Endings

Word Meaning

Write the **list word** that matches each meaning.

1. uses the eyes _sees_

2. wishes to have _wants_

3. you drink from these _glasses_

4. a place to go through _opening_

5. on fire _burning_

6. mailing _sending_

Scrambled Letters

Unscramble the letters to make **list words**. Then use the number code to answer the riddle.

1. esndgin

S	E	N	D	I	N	G
	1		4			

2. antws

W	A	N	T	S
		3		

3. shiwes

W	I	S	H	E	S
6		2			

4. obxse

B	O	X	E	S
			5	

Find the letter with the number 1 under it. Write that letter on the line below that has the number 1 under it. Do the same for the numbers 2 through 6.

Riddle: What is dark but made by light?

Answer: S H A D O W
       1 2 3 4 5 6

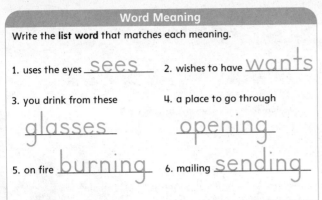

Spelling and Writing

Proofreading

Each sentence has two mistakes. Use the proofreading marks to fix each mistake. Write the misspelled **list words** correctly on the lines.

Proofreading Marks
- ⬭ spelling mistake
- ≡ capital letter
- ⊙ add period

1. the firefighters workt hard to put out the fire.

   1. _worked_

2. The fire reachd the river.

   2. _reached_

3. The firefighters were happy the fire had stopped burnning.

   3. _burning_

Writing a Thank You Letter

For many years, Smokey the Bear has been helping to prevent forest fires. Write a letter to Smokey thanking him for doing such a great job.

BONUS WORDS

pushed

marching

rushes

sweeps

crashes

Spelling Strategy

Have students write each **list word** as you call it out and
- draw a box around the base word
- underline the ending.

Ask volunteers to write the words, with boxes and underscores, on the board. For words that end in *s* and *es*, ask the volunteers to explain the spelling rule for adding these endings.

BONUS WORDS Ask students to write a sentence for each bonus word using the word *firefighter* in each sentence. Then have them trade papers with a partner to compare their sentences.

Spelling and Writing   **Page 108**

The **Proofreading** exercise will help students prepare to proofread their letters. As students complete the writing activity, encourage them to brainstorm ideas, write a first draft, revise, and proofread their work. To publish their writing, students may want to exchange letters with a partner. Afterward, invite the class to discuss what people can do to help prevent forest fires.

Writer's Corner You might want to invite a forest service worker or an experienced camper to speak to the class about the responsibilities people have when they use forests for recreational purposes. Encourage students to write questions for the speaker before the visit.

Final Test

1. The forest fire has been **burning** for days.
2. I'll be **sending** you a postcard.
3. All the **boxes** tumbled to the floor.
4. My **glasses** help me see better.
5. Do you need help **opening** that jar?
6. Who **wants** another piece of pizza?
7. Sean **reached** for the dictionary on the top shelf.
8. An owl **sees** better at night than during the day.
9. How great it would be to have three **wishes**!
10. Matt **worked** to earn money for a new bike.

Adding Endings

Adding Endings

Lesson 27

Objective
To spell words with the suffixes *ing*, *ed*, *er*, or *est*

 Correlated Phonics Lessons
MCP Phonics, Level B,
Lessons 70, 72, 78

Spelling Words in Action   *Page 109*

In this selection, students find out about the physical benefits of jumping rope. After reading, ask students if they like to jump rope and what their favorite exercise is.

Encourage students to look back at the words in dark print. Ask volunteers to say each word and name the double consonants.

Warm-Up Test
1. **Jogging** is great exercise.
2. He is **running** to the finish line.
3. The barber just finished **trimming** his hair.
4. She loves **skipping** rope with her friends.
5. We **shopped** for a new bed.
6. After we lost the game, Mary was **sadder** than I was.
7. Tom is the **gladdest** of all the boys.
8. The bunny **hopped** across the grass.
9. **Winning** is much more fun than losing.
10. We **mixed** the pancake batter with a big spoon.

Spelling Practice   *Pages 110–111*

Introduce the spelling rule and have students read the **list words** aloud. Also point out the exception to the spelling rule (*mixed*). Then encourage students to look back at their **Warm-Up Tests** and apply the spelling rule to any misspelled words.

As students work through the **Spelling Practice** exercises, remind them to look back at their **list words** or in their dictionaries if they need help.

 See Spelling Aloud, page 14

Spelling Words in Action

What are some different ways to jump rope?

Jump!
Jump!

It's as good for you as **jogging** or swimming. It's as fast as **running**. It can make your heart and lungs stronger. You can do it indoors or out, and it's a lot of fun. What is it? It's jumping rope.

There are many ways to jump rope. You can jump in place. You can try **skipping** forward or backward as you jump. Double Dutch is when two people spin the rope and two people jump at the same time.

There are many jump rope clubs around the country. Club members go to contests all over the country. They are **gladdest** when their team is **winning**. Even when they're not winning, though, they all love jumping rope.

> Look back at the words in dark print. Say each word. What consonants are doubled to make each ending?

Spelling Practice

 TIP
The final consonant in most short-vowel words is doubled when an ending is added. This rule works for most of the list words:
jog + ing = jogging

LIST WORDS
1. jogging *jogging*
2. running *running*
3. trimming *trimming*
4. skipping *skipping*
5. shopped *shopped*
6. sadder *sadder*
7. gladdest *gladdest*
8. hopped *hopped*
9. winning *winning*
10. mixed *mixed*

Adding Endings
Add **ed**, **ing**, **er**, or **est** to each base word to make a **list word**. Double the final consonant of all words except one. Trace the letters to spell **list words**.

1. shopped
2. trimming
3. skipping
4. mixed
5. winning
6. sadder
7. hopped
8. running
9. gladdest
10. jogging

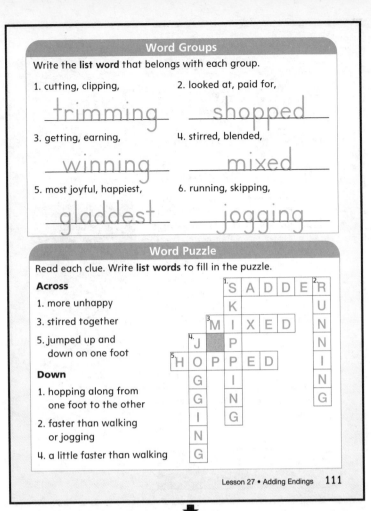

Word Groups

Write the **list word** that belongs with each group.

1. cutting, clipping,

   trimming

2. looked at, paid for,

   shopped

3. getting, earning,

   winning

4. stirred, blended,

   mixed

5. most joyful, happiest,

   gladdest

6. running, skipping,

   jogging

Word Puzzle

Read each clue. Write **list words** to fill in the puzzle.

Across

1. more unhappy
3. stirred together
5. jumped up and down on one foot

Down

1. hopping along from one foot to the other
2. faster than walking or jogging
4. a little faster than walking

Crossword answers:
- 1 Across: SADDER
- 3 Across: MIXED
- 5 Across: HOPPED
- 1 Down: SKIPPING
- 2 Down: RUNNING
- 4 Down: JOGGING

Spelling and Writing

Proofreading

Each sentence has two mistakes. Use the proofreading marks to fix each mistake. Write the misspelled **list words** correctly on the lines.

1. Some people like joging, because it's good exercise.
2. Other people like ronning because they go faster.
3. Wining a race isnt important, but staying healthy is.

1. jogging
2. running
3. winning

Proofreading Marks

- ⬭ spelling mistake
- ⊙ add period
- ⌄ add apostrophe

Writing a Rhyme

"One, two, buckle my shoe. Three, four, shut the door." Jump rope rhymes are fun. Write your own jump rope rhyme. Proofread your rhyme and fix any mistakes.

_____

_____

_____

BONUS WORDS

thinnest
napped
madder
begged
hugging

Spelling Strategy

Divide the class into four groups and assign each group a different ending from the lesson: *ing*, *ed*, *er*, or *est*. Then invite the groups to

- write the **list word** or words that contain their assigned ending
- circle the ending
- list other words that have the same ending
- share their list with another group.

BONUS WORDS

Ask students to write a sentence for each bonus word, but to leave the bonus word blank. Then have them trade papers with a partner to fill in the correct bonus word in each sentence.

Spelling and Writing   *Page 112*

The **Proofreading** exercise will help students prepare to proofread their rhymes. As they complete the writing activity, encourage students to brainstorm ideas, write a first draft, revise, and proofread their work. To publish their writing, students may want to

- play jump rope, using their rhymes
- chant their rhymes one after another in class.

Writer's Corner The class can read some of the tips on healthy eating and exercise on the President's Council on Physical Fitness and Sports Web sites, www.fitness.gov and www.surgeongeneral.gov. Students can use this information to create a class fitness poster describing their favorite healthy snacks and exercises.

Final Test

1. They are glad, but I am **gladdest** of all.
2. Janelle **hopped** on one foot.
3. Sometimes I go **jogging** with my father.
4. Who **mixed** all the paints together?
5. Pat is **running** for class president.
6. I felt **sadder** than my sister when our kitten ran away.
7. Dad and I **shopped** for a present for Mom.
8. I like **skipping** stones along the lake.
9. Lamar is **trimming** the dead branches off the tree.
10. The **winning** entry in the contest gets a blue ribbon.

Lesson 28

Adding Endings

Objective
To spell words with the suffixes *ing*, *ed*, *s*, or *es*, *er*, and *est*

 Phonics

Correlated Phonics Lessons
MCP Phonics, Level B,
Lessons 69–73, 78

Spelling Words in Action   *Page 113*

In this selection, students discover the importance and versatility of potatoes. Ask students to tell you what they learned about potatoes that they never knew before.

Encourage students to look back at the words in dark print. Ask volunteers to say each word and identify the spelling change in the base word when the ending is added.

Warm-Up Test

1. We are **having** chicken and rice for dinner.
2. When are they **serving** lunch?
3. Everyone **loves** french fries.
4. Who **baked** the brownies?
5. Tara **trades** recipes with her friend Ali.
6. Do you like **fried** chicken?
7. Healthy food helps our **bodies** grow strong.
8. Some people are **luckier** than others.
9. Anne always tells the **funniest** jokes!
10. Ryan **carries** the groceries to the car.

Spelling Practice   *Pages 114–115*

Introduce the spelling rule and have students read the **list words** aloud. Encourage students to look back at their **Warm-Up Tests** and apply the spelling rule to any misspelled words.

As students work through the **Spelling Practice** exercises, remind them to look back at their **list words** or in their dictionaries if they need help.

 for ESL students   See Change or No Change, page 15

88

Spelling Words in Action

What is your favorite way to eat potatoes?

Are You a Potato-Head?

If you like to eat potatoes, you are not alone. The average American **loves** them. Every day, fast-food places are **serving** millions of pounds of french fries, **fried** potatoes. Maybe you will be **having** potatoes with your dinner tonight. They may be fried, **baked**, or mashed.

Potatoes are not only good to eat. They are good for you. They contain lots of Vitamin C. Our **bodies** need Vitamin C to help us grow strong and healthy.

Potatoes are not just for eating, though. One of the **funniest** ways potatoes are used is in Shelley, Idaho. This town holds an annual festival with a mashed potato tug-of-war. Instead of mud, the loser gets pulled through a giant pile of mashed potatoes!

Look at each word in dark print. What do you notice about the spelling of the base word when the ending is added?

113

 **TIP**

When a word ends in silent e, drop the e to add endings that begin with a vowel, such as es, ed, or ing.
  have + ing = having
  bake + ed = baked
When a word ends in y after a consonant, change y to i to add the endings ed, es, er, and est.
  lucky + er = luckier

Spelling Practice

Adding Endings

The headings tell which ending made the **list word**. Write each **list word** under the right heading.

LIST WORDS

1. having   *having*
2. serving   *serving*
3. loves   *loves*
4. baked   *baked*
5. trades   *trades*
6. fried   *fried*
7. bodies   *bodies*
8. luckier   *luckier*
9. funniest   *funniest*
10. carries   *carries*

added s
1. loves   2. trades

dropped final e
3. having   4. serving
5. baked

changed y to i
6. fried   7. bodies
8. luckier   9. funniest
10. carries

Word Clues

Write **list words** to match each clue.

1. People exercise to keep these fit.

   bodies

2. The waitress is doing this to our lunch.

   serving

3. This describes someone who tells the best jokes.

   funniest

4. Matt does this with his baseball cards.

   trades

5. The cook did this to make a cake.

   baked

6. When more good things happen to you, you are this.

   luckier

7. The mailman does this with letters he brings.

   carries

8. When you are eating, you are doing this to a meal.

   having

Rhyming

Write a **list word** that rhymes with the underlined word.

1. It is a way to cook. It rhymes with tried.

   fried

2. This is a way of feeling. It rhymes with doves.

   loves

Lesson 28 • Adding Endings   115

Spelling and Writing

Proofreading

Each sentence has two mistakes. Use the proofreading marks to fix each mistake. Write the misspelled **list words** correctly on the lines.

Proofreading Marks
- ⬭ spelling mistake
- ⌃ add something
- ⊙ add period

1. Are you haveing three balanced meals a day?

2. You should eat one serveing of fruit or vegetables with every meal

3. Remember, healthy bodys need healthy food

1. having

2. serving

3. bodies

Writing a Recipe

What is your favorite food? Write sentences that tell about your favorite food and how to make it.

BONUS WORDS

healthier
sleepiest
tired
palest
blueberries

116   Lesson 28 • Adding Endings

Spelling Strategy

To help students apply the spelling rules, write *serve/serving* on the board. Call on a volunteer to come to the front of the class and

- circle the ending in *serving*
- explain how the base word *serve* was changed to *serving*.

Follow this procedure for the rest of the **list words**. Have students note that when *s* is added, the base does not change, as in *trades* and *loves*.

BONUS WORDS Ask students to write a definition for each bonus word, but not the word itself. Then have them trade papers with a partner to fill in the correct word for each definition.

Spelling and Writing   Page 116

The **Proofreading** exercise will help students prepare to proofread their recipes. As students complete the writing activity, encourage them to brainstorm ideas, write a first draft, revise, and proofread their work. To publish their writing, students may want to create a class favorite cookbook with their recipes.

Writer's Corner Students might be interested in looking through seed catalogs to learn about different kinds of potatoes or other root vegetables. Encourage them to write a short poem or a verse about a vegetable they like.

Final Test

1. Sharon is **luckier** than anyone I know.
2. How can we take better care of our **bodies**?
3. A **fried** egg makes a good breakfast.
4. Chan **carries** his books in his backpack.
5. Nicole **trades** baseball cards with Scott.
6. That was the **funniest** movie I ever saw!
7. Jamie **loves** eating at Angela's house.
8. Are they **having** Chinese food tonight?
9. Mrs. Lopez is **serving** grilled cheese sandwiches.
10. Who **baked** this carrot cake?

Objective
To spell words containing vowel pairs

 Correlated Phonics Lessons
MCP Phonics, Level B, Lessons 84–86

Spelling Words in Action   *Page 117*

In this section, students learn about different kinds of frogs. Invite them to talk about any frogs they may have seen, either in the wild or at a nature preserve or zoo.

Encourage students to look back at the words in dark print. Ask volunteers to say each word and name the vowel sound they hear.

Warm-Up Test

1. Please don't **beat** the drum so loudly.
2. How many **roads** cross this highway?
3. Red lights **mean** "stop."
4. Chickens **lay** brown or white eggs.
5. The **main** street in our town is wide and shady.
6. My sister sleeps in the **lower** bunk bed.
7. I love apple **pie**.
8. He can **tie** his shoes all by himself.
9. I have holes in the **toes** of my blue socks.
10. **Read** what the sign says.

Spelling Practice   *Pages 118–119*

Introduce the spelling rule and have students read the **list words** aloud. Encourage students to look back at their **Warm-Up Tests** and apply the spelling rule to any misspelled words.

As students work through the **Spelling Practice** exercises, remind them to look back at their **list words** or in their dictionaries if they need help. For **Scrambled Letters**, explain how students can compare the scrambled words with **list words** and use the consonants as well as the word length to help them figure out the correct **list word**.

for ESL students   See Charades/Pantomime, page 15

90

Spelling Words in Action

Where do frogs live?

Creature Feature

They have bulging eyes and long back legs. They live on land and in water. They catch bugs with their tongues. They **lay** eggs. What are they? They're frogs!

Frogs vary in color and size. The **main** colors are green or brown. Cricket frogs are only 1/2 inch long. Bullfrogs can grow to be 8 inches long. The biggest is the Goliath frog in Africa. It can be one foot long.

Tree frogs live on the **lower** branches of trees near ponds and streams. Suction pads on their **toes** help them climb trees.

Read about frogs in your area. Then the next time you're near a pond or stream, see how many you can spot. Look by the water, but don't forget to look in the trees, too.

Look back at the words in dark print. Say each word. What vowel sound do you hear in each one?

117

Spelling Practice

TIP
Two vowels that come together in a word can spell a long-vowel sound. In a word with a **vowel pair**, you can hear the sound of the vowel that comes first, as in <u>toes</u> and <u>tie</u>.

LIST WORDS

1. beat   *beat*
2. roads   *roads*
3. mean   *mean*
4. lay   *lay*
5. main   *main*
6. lower   *lower*
7. pie   *pie*
8. tie   *tie*
9. toes   *toes*
10. read   *read*

Grouping Vowel Pairs

Write each **list word** under the heading that shows its vowel sound.

long **a** sound

1. lay   2. main

long **e** sound

3. beat   4. mean
5. read

long **i** sound

6. pie   7. tie

long **o** sound

8. roads   9. lower
10. toes

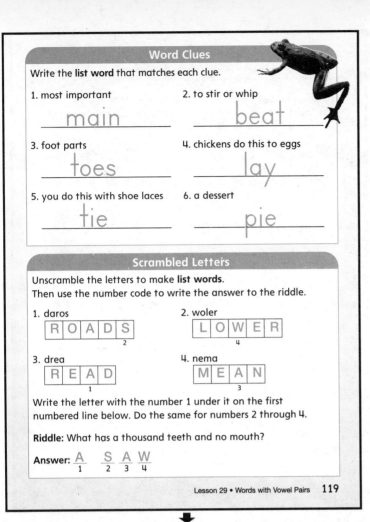

Word Clues

Write the **list word** that matches each clue.

1. most important

    main

2. to stir or whip

    beat

3. foot parts

    toes

4. chickens do this to eggs

    lay

5. you do this with shoe laces

    tie

6. a dessert

    pie

Scrambled Letters

Unscramble the letters to make **list words**.
Then use the number code to write the answer to the riddle.

1. daros

R	O	A	D	S
	2			

2. woler

L	O	W	E	R
		4		

3. drea

R	E	A	D
1			

4. nema

M	E	A	N
		3	

Write the letter with the number 1 under it on the first numbered line below. Do the same for numbers 2 through 4.

Riddle: What has a thousand teeth and no mouth?

Answer: $\underset{1}{A}\ \ \underset{2}{S}\ \underset{3}{A}\ \underset{4}{W}$

Spelling and Writing

Proofreading

Each sentence has two mistakes. Use the proofreading marks to fix each mistake. Write the misspelled **list words** correctly on the lines.

Proofreading Marks

- ⬭ spelling mistake
- ⊙ add period
- ≡ capital letter

1. Frogs have webbed tose for swimming⊙

2. frogs ley their eggs in the water.

3. A frog's mane diet is insects and worms⊙

1. toes

2. lay

3. main

Writing a Description

Write a description of a frog you've seen or would like to see. Proofread your description and fix any mistakes.

_____

_____

_____

BONUS WORDS

team

faint

toast

bowl

lie

Spelling Strategy

You may want to teach students this mnemonic device: *When two vowels go walking, the first one does the talking.* Explain that this sentence will help them remember that the first vowel in a pair is usually the one heard in the vowel pair sound. Then have students work with a partner to write each **list word**, say it aloud, circle the vowel pair, and point to the "talking" vowel. Explain that even though *w* is not a vowel, it is considered part of the vowel pair (*ow*) in the word *lower*.

BONUS WORDS Ask students to write a sentence for each bonus word, but leave the bonus word blank. Then have them trade papers with a partner to fill in the correct word in each sentence.

Spelling and Writing   Page 120

The **Proofreading** exercise will help students prepare to proofread their descriptions. As students complete the writing activity, encourage them to brainstorm ideas, write a first draft, revise, and proofread their work. To publish their writing, students may want to get together with a partner and use their descriptions to role-play telling a friend about the frogs.

Writer's Corner The class can learn more about frogs by visiting various frog-related Web sites. Have them research and write about one new frog fact they learned in this way.

Final Test

1. Alligators and chickens both **lay** eggs.
2. There are many cars on the **roads** today.
3. Dinner is usually our **main** meal of the day.
4. Could we have pumpkin **pie** for dessert?
5. I **beat** the pancake batter until it was smooth.
6. Let me **read** the directions to you.
7. I may speak softly but I **mean** what I say.
8. I put the biggest plates on the **lower** shelves.
9. I taught my brother how to **tie** his shoes.
10. Do you like to dig your **toes** into warm sand?

Lesson 30 — Review Lessons 25–29

Objective
To review spelling words with vowels followed by *r*; with suffixes: *ing, ed, s, es, er,* and *est*; with vowel pairs

Check Your Spelling Notebook
Pages 121–124

Based on your observations, note which words are giving students the most difficulty and offer assistance for spelling them correctly. Here are some frequently misspelled words to watch for: *having, first, were, running,* and *read.*

To give students extra help and practice in taking standardized tests, you may want to have them take the **Warm-Up Test** for this lesson on pages 94–95. After scoring the tests, return them to students so that they can record their misspelled words in their spelling notebooks.

Students can practice their troublesome words with a partner. One partner spells the word aloud as the other finger-writes it in the air. After practicing their words, students can work through the exercises for lessons 25–29 and the cumulative review, **Show What You Know**. Before they begin each exercise, you may want to go over the spelling rule.

 Take It Home

Invite students to look for the **list words** in lessons 25-29 at home. For a complete list of the words, encourage them to take their *Spelling Workout* books home. Students can also use **Take It Home Master 5** on pages 96–97 to help them do the activity. In class, students can discuss their experiences searching for words.

In Lessons 25–30, you learned how to spell words with the endings ing, ed, s or es, er, and est. You also learned the sound of vowels followed by r and the sound of vowel pairs.

Check Your Spelling Notebook
Look at the words in your spelling notebook. Which words for Lessons 25 through 29 did you have the most trouble with? Write them here.

_____

_____

Lesson 25
 TIP When **r** follows the vowels **e, i, o,** or **u,** it can make the **ur** sound, as in girl and word.

List Words
first
turn
her
world

Write a **list word** that belongs in each group.

1. them, him, ____her____
2. Earth, planet, ____world____
3. third, second, ____first____
4. twirl, twist, ____turn____

121

Lesson 26
TIP The endings ing, ed, and s or es are added to base words to make new words, as in glasses. Add es to words that end in x, s, sh, or ch, as in boxes.

List Words
opening
wants
wishes
worked

Write a **list word** that has the same base word as each word.

1. wishing ____wishes____
2. wanted ____wants____
3. working ____worked____
4. opened ____opening____

Lesson 27
TIP The final consonant in most short-vowel words is doubled when an ending is added: jog + ing = jogging.

List Words
gladdest
running
mixed
sadder

Write a **list word** that means the same or almost the same as each word.

1. racing ____running____
2. unhappier ____sadder____
3. happiest ____gladdest____
4. blended ____mixed____

122   Lesson 30 • Review

92

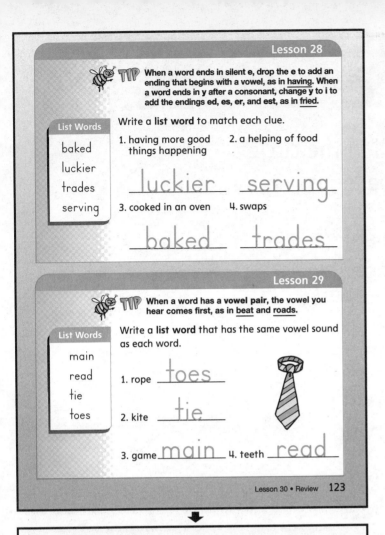

Lesson 28

TIP When a word ends in silent e, drop the e to add an ending that begins with a vowel, as in having. When a word ends in y after a consonant, change y to i to add the endings ed, es, er, and est, as in fried.

List Words

baked
luckier
trades
serving

Write a **list word** to match each clue.

1. having more good things happening

2. a helping of food

luckier   _serving_

3. cooked in an oven

4. swaps

baked   _trades_

Lesson 29

TIP When a word has a **vowel pair**, the vowel you hear comes first, as in beat and roads.

List Words

main
read
tie
toes

Write a **list word** that has the same vowel sound as each word.

1. rope _toes_

2. kite _tie_

3. game _main_   4. teeth _read_

Lesson 30 • Review   **123**

Show What You Know

Lessons 25–29 Review

One word is misspelled in each set of **list words**. Fill in the circle next to the **list word** that is spelled incorrectly.

1. ○ wants	● gurl	○ mixed	○ fried
2. ○ loves	○ sadder	○ boxes	● roods
3. ● wishs	○ sir	○ baked	○ pie
4. ○ lay	○ her	● triming	○ sees
5. ○ word	● bodys	○ beat	○ worked
6. ○ tie	○ first	● wining	○ burning
7. ○ reached	○ having	○ turn	● meen
8. ● skurt	○ jogging	○ mean	○ were
9. ○ trades	● gladest	○ sending	○ toes
10. ○ read	○ running	● openning	○ world
11. ○ lower	○ glasses	○ worth	● funnyest
12. ○ beat	● skiping	○ luckier	○ worked
13. ● carrys	○ hopped	○ turn	○ read
14. ○ serving	○ boxes	● shoped	○ first
15. ○ baked	○ mixed	○ main	● wurld
16. ○ her	● toze	○ wants	○ burning
17. ● haveing	○ word	○ lower	○ sending
18. ○ sees	○ her	○ beat	● fryed
19. ○ pie	○ sending	● glases	○ lay
20. ● luves	○ were	○ reached	○ running

124   Lesson 30 • Review

Final Test

1. The **main** street in the village is a dirt road.
2. **Turn** off the light when you leave the room.
3. Wouldn't it be great if your **wishes** came true?
4. Look at all the people **running** after the bus!
5. I felt **luckier** after I found the bright gold coin.
6. Juan likes to **read** for an hour before going to bed.
7. Dana looked everywhere for **her** missing shoe.
8. Our teacher **wants** us to enjoy learning things.
9. Julio **mixed** blue and red paint to make purple.
10. Jesse always **trades** places in line with Erica.
11. Jenny taught Tyler how to **tie** his shoelaces.
12. The **first** one to reach the oak tree wins the race.
13. Who started **opening** this package?
14. Of all the happy children, she is the **gladdest**.
15. Do you like butter on your **baked** potato?
16. These old shoes hurt my **toes**.
17. They roamed the **world** looking for the treasure.
18. Tina **worked** on her homework for an hour.
19. When Adrian moved away, I **was** sadder than ever.
20. They are **serving** their father breakfast in bed.

Check Your Spelling Notebook

Before writing each word, students can say the word and name the letters in the vowel pair or the base word and the suffix.

Name _____

Lesson Review Test (Side A)

Read each set of words. Fill in the circle
next to the word that is spelled correctly.

1. ⓐ openning   ⓑ opening
   ⓒ opning   ⓓ oppening

2. ⓐ her   ⓑ hur
   ⓒ hure   ⓓ herr

3. ⓐ serveing   ⓑ surving
   ⓒ surveing   ⓓ serving

4. ⓐ traids   ⓑ traydes
   ⓒ traides   ⓓ trades

5. ⓐ rede   ⓑ reade
   ⓒ raed   ⓓ read

6. ⓐ running   ⓑ runing
   ⓒ runneng   ⓓ runeing

7. ⓐ mixxed   ⓑ mixd
   ⓒ mixed   ⓓ mixxd

8. ⓐ wurld   ⓑ werld
   ⓒ world   ⓓ worled

9. ⓐ toze   ⓑ tose
   ⓒ toes   ⓓ toas

Lesson Review Test (Side B)

Read each set of words. Fill in the circle next to the word that is spelled correctly.

10. ⓐ sader   ⓑ sadder
     ⓒ saddr   ⓓ sadr

11. ⓐ tirn   ⓑ turne
     ⓒ tirne   ⓓ turn

12. ⓐ luckier   ⓑ luckyer
     ⓒ luckir   ⓓ luckyr

13. ⓐ ty   ⓑ tie
     ⓒ tiy   ⓓ tiey

14. ⓐ baiked   ⓑ baekd
     ⓒ bakd   ⓓ baked

15. ⓐ wontz   ⓑ wantz
     ⓒ wants   ⓓ wonts

16. ⓐ gladest   ⓑ gladst
     ⓒ gladdest   ⓓ gladdust

17. ⓐ furst   ⓑ firste
     ⓒ ferst   ⓓ first

18. ⓐ workt   ⓑ worked
     ⓒ worket   ⓓ workd

Take It Home 5

Your child has learned to spell many new words and would enjoy sharing them with you and your family. Here's how to help your child review some of the words in Lessons 25–29 and have a good time, too!

Track Those Words!

Get on the trail of hidden household words and become a spelling detective when you and your child search for spelling words at home. You never know where the words might be lurking— in the kitchen (baked, serving), in the playroom (first, turn), on an invitation (wants, wishes)—even on a tube of toothpaste (opening)! Happy hunting!

Lesson 25

1. first
2. girl
3. her
4. sir
5. skirt
6. turn
7. were
8. word
9. world
10. worth

Lesson 26

1. boxes
2. burning
3. glasses
4. opening
5. reached
6. sees
7. sending
8. wants
9. wishes
10. worked

Lesson 27

1. gladdest
2. hopped
3. jogging
4. mixed
5. running
6. sadder
7. shopped
8. skipping
9. trimming
10. winning

Lesson 28

1. baked
2. bodies
3. carries
4. fried
5. funniest
6. having
7. loves
8. luckier
9. serving
10. trades

Lesson 29

1. beat
2. lay
3. lower
4. main
5. mean
6. pie
7. read
8. roads
9. tie
10. toes

Crossword Puzzle

Here's a crossword puzzle for you and your child to solve. Encourage your child to print the correct spelling word as you read aloud each clue.

turn	her	trades	serving	wishes
gladdest	opening	toes	luckier	tie

Across

1. to move in a circle
3. giving food
4. happiest
8. a hole
9. his or _____

Down

1. head and shoulders, knees and _____
2. gives one for another
5. having more good things happen
6. Can you _____ your shoes?
7. things you want

Objective
To spell words that contain the o͞o or o͝o sound

 Correlated Phonics Lesson
MCP Phonics, Level B, Lesson 89

Spelling Words in Action   *Page 125*
In this selection, students read about starfish. Invite students to discuss whether they would enjoy scuba-diving to see starfish and what they would wear or what special equipment they would bring if they did so.

Encourage students to look back at the words in dark print. Ask volunteers to say each word, name the vowel sound they hear, and tell how it is spelled.

Warm-Up Test
1. Ouch! I hurt my **foot**!
2. Your kitten needs **food** and water every day.
3. Will the train arrive **soon**?
4. You are all **good** students.
5. The **hood** on my jacket keeps my head warm.
6. We will eat lunch at **noon**.
7. The kitchen is a very busy **room** at my house.
8. Where can we get more **wood** for the fire?
9. Jenna's **boot** is covered with mud.
10. Manuel has a loose **tooth**.

Spelling Practice   *Pages 126–127*
Introduce the spelling rule and have students read the **list words** aloud. Encourage students to look back at their **Warm-Up Tests** and apply the spelling rule to any misspelled words.

As students work through the **Spelling Practice** exercises, remind them to look back at their **list words** or in their dictionaries if they need help. For **Word Groups**, you may want to explain how students can figure out the answers by modeling some examples (*swim, fish, ocean* or *time, clock, watch*).

 See Tape Recording, page 15

Spelling Words in Action

How does a starfish move?

Stars of the Sea

The starfish got its name because most starfish are shaped like stars.

Starfish live in the ocean. The bottom of each starfish arm is covered with tiny, tube-shaped feet. Each **foot** has a tiny suction pad on the end. The starfish uses these for crawling along the ocean floor.

Clams and oysters make a **good** meal for a starfish. The starfish wraps itself around the clam or oyster. **Soon** it pulls the shells apart. A starfish doesn't have a single **tooth**. It turns its **food** into a liquid and drinks it.

A starfish can do some amazing things. It can drop an arm if it is attacked. Then it grows a new one back. If a starfish is cut in two, each piece can grow into a new starfish. Now that's a pretty neat trick!

> Look back at the words in dark print. Say each word. What vowel sound do you hear? What do you notice about the spelling for each word?

125

Spelling Practice

 TIP
Two letters can stand for the o͞o sound, as in <u>noon</u>, or the o͝o sound, as in <u>foot</u>. Listen for the two sounds that are spelled **oo** in the **list words**.

LIST WORDS
1. foot *foot*
2. food *food*
3. soon *soon*
4. good *good*
5. hood *hood*
6. noon *noon*
7. room *room*
8. wood *wood*
9. boot *boot*
10. tooth *tooth*

Grouping Vowel Pairs
Write **list words** under the heading that shows the sound that **oo** stands for in each one.

oo as in <u>moon</u>

1. food   2. soon
3. noon   4. room
5. boot   6. tooth

oo as in <u>book</u>

7. foot   8. good
9. hood   10. wood

Word Groups

Write the **list word** that belongs with each group.

1. arm, leg,

    foot

2. shoe, sneaker,

    boot

3. hat, cap,

    hood

4. great, OK,

    good

5. morning, night,

    noon

6. fang, tusk,

    tooth

Story

Write **list words** to finish the story.

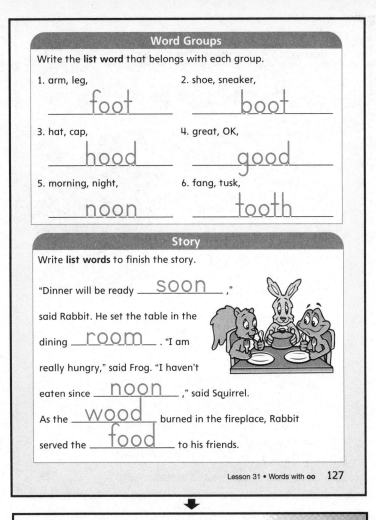

"Dinner will be ready _____soon_____,"
said Rabbit. He set the table in the
dining _____room_____ . "I am
really hungry," said Frog. "I haven't
eaten since _____noon_____," said Squirrel.
As the _____wood_____ burned in the fireplace, Rabbit
served the _____food_____ to his friends.

Spelling and Writing

Proofreading

The paragraph has six mistakes. Use the
proofreading marks to fix each mistake.
Write the misspelled **list words** correctly
on the lines.

   A shark's touth is very sharp. They are
are gud swimmers. Sharks will eat almost
anything. Even an old boot could be fude
for a a shark.

Proofreading Marks

◯ spelling mistake
⊙ add period
ℓ take something out

1. tooth
2. good
3. food

Writing a Narrative Paragraph

What is your favorite sea animal? Write a
paragraph about it. Tell why you like it. Tell what
it looks like.

_____

_____

_____

_____

BONUS WORDS

brook
pool
wool
cool
loose

Spelling Strategy

Write each **list word** on the board, leaving a
blank for *oo*. Then ask the class to name the
missing letters and the sound they stand for.
Call on a volunteer to fill in the missing letters
and say the complete word, stressing the $\overline{oo}$
or oo sound.

BONUS WORDS Have students write a story using all
the bonus words, then trade papers with a
partner to read aloud.

Spelling and Writing   Page 128

The **Proofreading** exercise will help students
prepare to proofread their paragraphs. As students
complete the writing activity, encourage them to
brainstorm ideas, write a first draft, revise, and
proofread their work. To publish their writing

- students may want to make a book of
  underwater animals
- research photos in books or on Web sites to
  match the animals they described

Writer's Corner You may want to show and read
a picture book about a fantastic sea creature, such
as *The Rainbow Fish* by Marcus Pfister. Then
encourage students to write their own stories
about a made-up sea creature.

Final Test

1. I found Al's **boot** under a chair.
2. That muffin was so **good**, I could eat four
   more!
3. I read a story about a girl who wore a red
   hood.
4. Luis lost his front **tooth** today.
5. Is your desk made out of metal or **wood**?
6. Another way to say 12 p.m. is **noon**.
7. Cinderella's **foot** fit into the tiny glass slipper.
8. **Soon** it will be time to go home.
9. The **room** is large and sunny.
10. Have you learned about the **food** pyramid?

Words with the <u>oi</u> and <u>ou</u> Sound

Words with the <u>oi</u> and <u>ou</u> Sound | Lesson 32

Objective
To spell words that contain diphthongs *oi* or *ou*

Phonics | Correlated Phonics Lessons *MCP Phonics*, Level B, Lessons 95, 97

Spelling Words in Action   Page 129

In this selection, students learn how to make a flowerpot craft called Ms. Claypot—complete with growing green "hair." Ask students why they would or wouldn't like to make Ms. Claypot and what other names they could give her.

Encourage students to look back at the words in dark print. Ask volunteers to say each word and tell which ones have the *oi* sound and which ones have the *ou* sound.

Warm-Up Test
1. I love the happy **sound** of robins singing!
2. Why do you have a **frown** on your face?
3. The **soil** in Aunt Beth's garden is very rich.
4. The dentist looked into my **mouth**.
5. You get down from that tree right **now**!
6. Uncle Steve went to the **toy** store to buy a gift.
7. Big wells pump **oil** out of the ground.
8. I hope the rain doesn't **spoil** our picnic.
9. What made that terrible **noise**?
10. A big white **owl** lives in Grandpa's barn.

Spelling Practice   Pages 130–131

Introduce the spelling rule and have students read the **list words** aloud. Encourage students to look back at their **Warm-Up Tests** and apply the spelling rule to any misspelled words.

As students work through the **Spelling Practice** exercises, remind them to look back at their **list words** or in their dictionaries if they need help. To make sure everyone understands the riddle in the **Word Puzzle** exercise, ask a volunteer to explain the pun on the word *eye* and the letter *i*.

for ESL students See Letter Cards, page 15

100

Spelling Words in Action

What color is Ms. Claypot's hair?

Ms. Claypot

Who is Ms. Claypot? She never makes any **noise**, not one little **sound**. She never wears a **frown**, but always has a big smile. She has green hair! Ms. Claypot is not a **toy**. She is a flower pot.

To make Ms. Claypot you will need: a clay pot, a dish, some **soil**, grass seeds, paper, glue, and scissors.

Turn the pot upside-down. Cut eyes, a nose, and a **mouth** out of paper. Glue them on the side of the pot to make her face. **Now** put the soil on top of her head. Scatter the seeds on top of the soil. Then put Ms. Claypot on a dish filled with water. Set her in a sunny place.

Always keep water in her dish. It will soak up through the clay pot and feed the seeds at the top. In a few weeks, Ms. Claypot will grow green "hair." Don't be surprised if she soon needs a haircut!

> Look back at the words in dark print. Say each word. What words have the <u>oi</u> sound you hear in <u>noise</u>? Which words have the <u>ou</u> sound you hear in <u>sound</u>?

129

Spelling Practice

TIP
The sound oi can be spelled **oy** or **oi**, as in <u>toy</u> and <u>oil</u>. The sound ou can be spelled **ow** or **ou**, as in <u>now</u> and <u>sound</u>. Listen for the **oi** and **ou** sounds in the **list words**.

LIST WORDS
1. sound *sound*
2. frown *frown*
3. soil *soil*
4. mouth *mouth*
5. now *now*
6. toy *toy*
7. oil *oil*
8. spoil *spoil*
9. noise *noise*
10. owl *owl*

Spelling with oi and ou

Write each **list word** under the heading that shows the spelling of its **oi** or **ou** sound.

oi as in <u>coin</u>
1. soil   2. oil
3. spoil   4. noise

ow as in <u>how</u>
5. frown   6. now
7. owl

ou as in <u>loud</u>
8. sound   9. mouth

oy as in <u>boy</u>
10. toy

130   Lesson 32 • Words with the **oi** and **ou** Sound

Word Meaning

Write a **list word** to match each meaning.

1. a noise

   sound

2. something to play with

   toy

3. an opening in the face

   mouth

4. a night bird that hoots

   owl

5. at this time

   now

6. dirt

   soil

Word Puzzle

Write **list words** to fill in the puzzle. Then read down the shaded boxes to answer the riddle.

1. a sad look on someone's face
2. dirt
3. a liquid used for cooking
4. to ruin or break something
5. a bad or loud sound

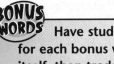

1. F R O W N
2. S O I L
3. O I L
4. S P O I L
5. N O I S E

Riddle: If I lose an eye, I'll still have a nose. What am I?

Answer: _noise_

Lesson 32 • Words with the **oi** and **ou** Sound   **131**

Spelling and Writing

Proofreading

The paragraph has six mistakes. Use the proofreading marks to fix each mistake. Write the misspelled **list words** correctly on the lines.

An owl lives in the woods. It says,

"Whoo, whoo" when it opens its mowth.

Can you make a noyse that sounds

like an owl?

Proofreading Marks

⬭ spelling mistake
⊙ add period
⌃ add something

1. _owl_

2. _mouth_

3. _noise_

Writing a Make-Believe Story

What if you found a magic bean like Jack in the Beanstalk? What if you planted a penny and grew a money tree? Write a make-believe story.

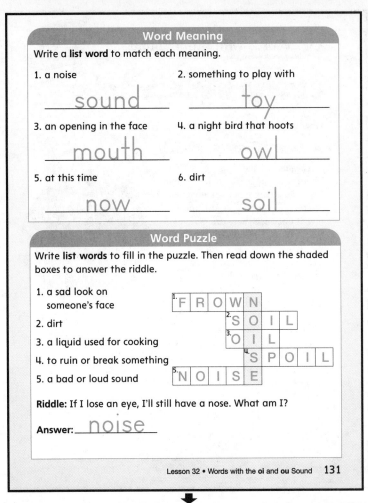

BONUS WORDS

crowd
tower
around
pound
boil

132   Lesson 32 • Words with the **oi** and **ou** Sound

Spelling Strategy

Divide the class into four groups and assign each group the letters *oy*, *oi*, *ow*, or *ou*. Then call out each **list word** and have the group whose letters are in the word stand up. Ask volunteers from the group to

- write the **list word** on the board
- point to *oy*, *oi*, *ow*, or *ou*
- say the word, stressing the *oi* or *ou* sound that the letters stand for.

BONUS WORDS Have students write a definition for each bonus word but not the word itself, then trade papers with a partner to write the bonus word that matches each definition.

Spelling and Writing   *Page 132*

The **Proofreading** exercise will help students prepare to proofread their stories. As students complete the writing activity, encourage them to brainstorm ideas, write a first draft, revise, and proofread their work. To publish their writing, students may want to

- combine their stories into a collection
- illustrate their work for a bulletin-board display.

Writer's Corner Students might enjoy listening to you read a poem about a plant or a flower. Invite them to write the title of the poem and to draw a picture to go with it.

Final Test

1. I hear the **sound** of a parade marching by.
2. That crocodile has such sharp teeth in its **mouth**!
3. My favorite **toy** is my doll house.
4. We are **now** working on our spelling test.
5. Does that buzzing **noise** bother you?
6. The food will **spoil** if you leave it in the sun.
7. Sometimes babies **frown** when they are tired.
8. Is **oil** used to heat our school?
9. The **owl** sleeps all day and hunts at night.
10. First put some **soil** in each pot, then plant the seed.

Objective
To spell words with the ô sound

 Correlated Phonics Lesson
MCP Phonics, Level B, Lesson 91

Spelling Words in Action   *Page 133*

In this selection, students read about Space Camp—a place where children can take an exciting "ride" in a spaceship. Ask students what they would like to do if they visited Space Camp.

Encourage students to look back at the words in dark print. Ask volunteers to say each word and name the vowel sound they hear.

Warm-Up Test
1. I'll **call** my mother to tell her I'll be late.
2. Please hang this poster on the **wall**.
3. I will **draw** a picture of my pet turtle.
4. Most basketball players are very **tall**.
5. Throw the **ball** to Rosa.
6. This poor dog has hurt his **paw**!
7. Do all babies **crawl** before they walk?
8. Mr. Bell wants to **talk** to my parents.
9. The umpire ended the game **because** of rain.
10. It would be fun to take a **walk** in space.

Spelling Practice   *Pages 134–135*

Introduce the spelling rule and have students read the **list words** aloud. Call students' attention to the silent *l* in *walk* and *talk*, and the *all* spelling pattern at the end of *call, ball, wall,* and *tall.* Then encourage students to look back at their **Warm-Up Tests** and apply the spelling rule to any misspelled words.

As students work through the **Spelling Practice** exercises, remind them to look back at their **list words** or in their dictionaries if they need help.

 See Variant Spellings, page 14

Spelling Words in Action

What is the name of the camp in this story?

A Camp That's "A-OK!"

They **call** it the "U.S. Space Camp." There is one near Huntsville, Alabama. Children go there to learn about space.

The camp lasts a week. Children love it **because** there are many things to do. You can **talk** to people who know about space travel. You get to see some really **tall** rockets that once took people into space. You can help **draw** a plan for a spaceship. You do your drawing on a computer. Then build a rocket of your own. Watch it zoom into the sky.

There is more fun when you take a make-believe trip into space. It feels just like the real thing! Your trip might be to the moon. You'll learn what it's like to **walk** on the moon.

Look back at the words in dark print. Say each word. What vowel sound do you hear?

133

Spelling Practice

TIP
The ô sound can be spelled three different ways: *au*, as in **because**, *aw*, as in **draw**, and *a*, as in **call**.

LIST WORDS
1. call	*call*
2. wall	*wall*
3. draw	*draw*
4. tall	*tall*
5. ball	*ball*
6. paw	*paw*
7. crawl	*crawl*
8. talk	*talk*
9. because	*because*
10. walk	*walk*

Spelling with the ô Sound

Write each **list word** under the heading that spells its ô sound.

aw as in <u>claw</u>
1. draw   2. paw
3. crawl

a as in <u>all</u>
4. call   5. wall
6. tall   7. ball
8. talk   9. walk

au as in <u>haul</u>
10. because

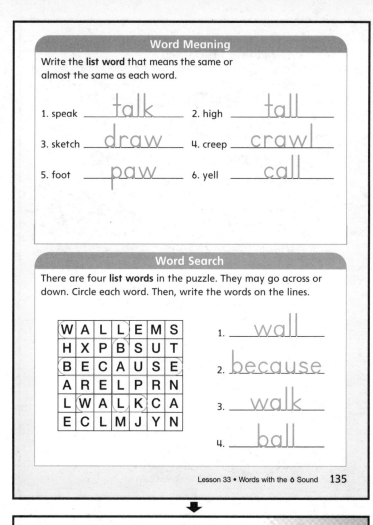

Word Meaning

Write the **list word** that means the same or almost the same as each word.

1. speak _talk_
2. high _tall_
3. sketch _draw_
4. creep _crawl_
5. foot _paw_
6. yell _call_

Word Search

There are four **list words** in the puzzle. They may go across or down. Circle each word. Then, write the words on the lines.

W	A	L	L	E	M	S
H	X	P	B	S	U	T
B	E	C	A	U	S	E
A	R	E	L	P	R	N
L	W	A	L	K	C	A
E	C	L	M	J	Y	N

1. _wall_
2. _because_
3. _walk_
4. _ball_

Spelling and Writing

Proofreading

The paragraph has six mistakes. Use the proofreading marks to fix each mistake. Write the misspelled **list words** correctly on the lines.

Proofreading Marks
- ⬭ spelling mistake
- ⊙ add period
- ≡ capital letter

Imagine getting a phone (cawl) from space, maybe you'll (tauk) to a friend who lives on a space station. That's a long distance call (becuz) space is a lot of miles away⊙

1. _call_
2. _talk_
3. _because_

Writing Questions

What would you like to know about space travel? Write some questions you have about space travel. Proofread your questions and fix any mistakes.

BONUS WORDS

straw
hall
dawn
salt
automobile

_____

_____

Spelling Strategy

Say the ô sound for students, then ask them to close their eyes and listen carefully as you call out each **list word**. Encourage them to picture the word, focusing on the letters that spell ô (*au*, *aw*, or *a*). After students open their eyes, ask the class to name the letters that spell the vowel sound. Call on a volunteer to write the word on the board and circle the *au*, *aw*, or *a*.

BONUS WORDS Have students write a sentence for each bonus word, but leave the bonus word blank. Then ask them to trade papers with a partner to fill in the missing word in each sentence.

Spelling and Writing   *Page 136*

The **Proofreading** exercise will help students prepare to proofread their questions. As students complete the writing activity, encourage them to brainstorm ideas, write a first draft, revise, and proofread their work. To publish their writing, students may want to ask the class their questions. Help students answer them, referring to a Web site, an encyclopedia, and other books when necessary.

Writer's Corner Students might enjoy looking at illustrations or diagrams of various kinds of spacecraft. Encourage students to invent their own spaceship, draw a picture of it, and write a few sentences telling about it.

Final Test

1. The **ball** rolled into the street.
2. I can't play hockey today **because** I'm sick.
3. Will you please **call** me when you get home?
4. Jamie had to **crawl** under the bed to get his shoe.
5. Liz likes to **draw** pictures of birds.
6. The kitten is cleaning its **paw**.
7. Julie's house has a stone **wall** next to it.
8. Dad wants to **talk** to us about our chores.
9. Jerry is six feet **tall** and he's still growing!
10. Would you like to **walk** in the park?

Objective
To spell words that contain the prefix *un* or *re*

Phonics Correlated Phonics Lessons
MCP Phonics, Level B,
Lessons 103–104

Spelling Words in Action   *Page 137*

In this selection, students learn how to recycle a plastic bottle into a birdfeeder. Afterward, invite students to talk about birds they have seen and ask if any have a birdfeeder at home.

Encourage students to look back at the words in dark print. Ask volunteers to say each word and tell how the first part of it is spelled.

Warm-Up Test
1. It is better to be kind than **unkind**.
2. This dress is **unlike** any I've ever seen!
3. Rob has **retold** that joke a hundred times.
4. Let's **reread** the poem together.
5. I was **unhappy** when I lost my new ball.
6. Please **recheck** the oven temperature for me.
7. We will **remake** the toast that burned.
8. May I **return** the shoes that don't fit me?
9. The guard will **unlock** the museum gate.
10. Why did you **untie** the knot?

Spelling Practice   *Pages 138–139*

Introduce the spelling rule and explain that prefixes change the meanings of the base words, using *tie/untie* and *told/retold* as examples. Then have students read the **list words** aloud. Encourage them to look back at their **Warm-Up Tests** and apply the spelling rule to any misspelled words.

As students work through the **Spelling Practice** exercises, remind them to look back at their **list words** or in their dictionaries if they need help.

 See Questions/Answers, page 15

104

Spelling Words in Action

What can you make with a plastic bottle?

Recycling Is for the Birds

Don't **untie** that garbage bag to throw away an empty plastic bottle! Recycle the bottle. **Remake** it into a birdfeeder.

First, wash out the bottle. Then, cut a large hole in the side. The hole should be about two inches from the bottom of the bottle.

Next, decorate the bottle with markers. Then, tie a string around the neck of the bottle. Replace the bottle cap if you have it.

Fill the bottom of the bottle with bird seed. Then, hang it from the branch of a tree.

Remember to check and **recheck** your birdfeeder. Make sure it always has some food in it. The birds will be **unhappy** if it is empty. It would be **unkind** not to keep it full.

Now sit back and enjoy watching the birds!

Look back at the words in dark print. Say each word. What do you notice about the beginning of each word?

137

Spelling Practice

 TIP
A **prefix** is a word part that is added to the beginning of a base word. The prefix **un** means <u>not</u> or <u>the opposite</u>, as in <u>unkind</u>. The prefix **re** means <u>back</u> or <u>do again</u>, as in <u>reread</u>.

LIST WORDS
1. unkind *unkind*
2. unlike *unlike*
3. retold *retold*
4. reread *reread*
5. unhappy *unhappy*
6. recheck *recheck*
7. remake *remake*
8. return *return*
9. unlock *unlock*
10. untie *untie*

Spelling with Prefixes
Write each **list word** next to its number. Circle the prefix in each word.

1. unkind   2. unlike
3. retold   4. reread
5. unhappy   6. recheck
7. remake   8. return
9. unlock   10. untie

138 Lesson 34 • Adding **un** and **re**

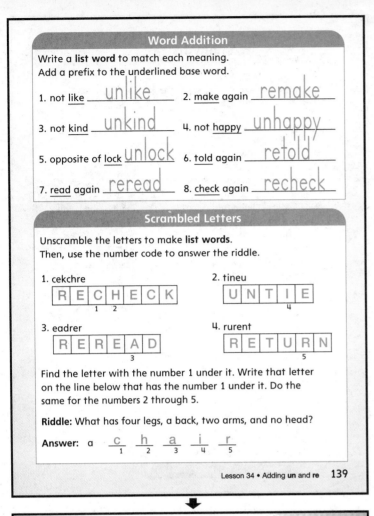

Word Addition

Write a **list word** to match each meaning.
Add a prefix to the underlined base word.

1. not <u>like</u> _unlike_
2. <u>make</u> again _remake_
3. not <u>kind</u> _unkind_
4. not <u>happy</u> _unhappy_
5. opposite of <u>lock</u> _unlock_
6. <u>told</u> again _retold_
7. <u>read</u> again _reread_
8. <u>check</u> again _recheck_

Scrambled Letters

Unscramble the letters to make **list words**.
Then, use the number code to answer the riddle.

1. cekchre

R	E	C	H	E	C	K
	1	2				

2. tineu

U	N	T	I	E
			4	

3. eadrer

R	E	R	E	A	D
		3			

4. rurent

R	E	T	U	R	N
				5	

Find the letter with the number 1 under it. Write that letter
on the line below that has the number 1 under it. Do the
same for the numbers 2 through 5.

Riddle: What has four legs, a back, two arms, and no head?

Answer: a <u>c</u> <u>h</u> <u>a</u> <u>i</u> <u>r</u>
       1 2 3 4 5

Lesson 34 • Adding **un** and **re**   139

⬇

Spelling and Writing

Proofreading

The paragraph has six mistakes. Use the
proofreading marks to fix each mistake.
Write the misspelled **list words** correctly
on the lines.

You can never be be ⟨unhapie⟩ when
you recycle things. It's so much fun to
⟨remaik⟩ something into something
different⊙ What you make will be ⟨unlyke⟩
anything made by by someone else.

Proofreading Marks
- ◯ spelling mistake
- ⊙ add period
- ℮ take out something

1. _unhappy_
2. _remake_
3. _unlike_

Writing Directions

Do you know how to make something
by recycling? Write directions telling
how to make it.

BONUS WORDS

rebuild
restart
redo
unhook
unsafe

_____

_____

_____

_____

140   Lesson 34 • Adding **un** and **re**

Spelling Strategy

Write each **list word** on the board as an
incomplete word equation (*re + turn =*). Then ask a
volunteer to come to the board and write the
complete word, giving its meaning. After all the **list
words** have been written, ask students to suggest
other words that begin with the prefixes *un* and *re*.
If students have trouble thinking of words, you
might suggest *rewrite*, *refill*, *unlucky*, and *uneven*.

BONUS WORDS Have students use each bonus word
in a sentence, then trade papers with a
partner to circle the prefix for each bonus
word in the sentences.

Spelling and Writing   **Page 140**

The **Proofreading** exercise will help students
prepare to proofread their directions. As students
complete the writing activity, encourage them to
brainstorm ideas, write a first draft, revise, and
proofread their work. To publish their writing,
students may want to

- write their ideas and directions to send to
  a local newspaper, either for a Letter to
  the Editor or for a Recycling/Household
  Hints column
- make a class book titled "Recycling."

Writer's Corner Students might enjoy looking in
books about pioneer life to learn how everyday
objects were recycled then. Invite students to
choose their favorite pioneer recycling idea and
write a few sentences about why they like it.

Final Test

1. I want my party to be **unlike** other parties.
2. Listen carefully as I **reread** the directions.
3. May we **untie** our shoes and take them off?
4. Did Erica **return** your book to the library?
5. The captain will **recheck** the map.
6. Jenny was **unhappy** when it was time to
   go home.
7. Oh no! Now I have to **remake** the bed!
8. Sometimes the rules of nature seem **unkind**.
9. Jorge lost his key and couldn't **unlock** the door.
10. Grandpa **retold** our favorite ghost stories.

Homonyms

Objective
To spell homonyms

 Correlated Phonics Lesson
MCP Phonics, Level B, Lesson 109

Spelling Words in Action   *Page 141*

In "Putt-Putt Golf," students learn about a miniature version of a popular game as well as what it means to get a "hole-in-one." Ask students whether they have ever played miniature golf and invite them to discuss their favorite games or sports.

Encourage students to look back at the words in dark print. Ask volunteers to say the words and tell which words have the same sound, but different spellings.

Warm-Up Test
1. What made that **hole** in the screen?
2. I didn't stay for the **whole** movie.
3. There is **no** excuse for your bad mood.
4. Does anyone **know** how to play the drums?
5. Do **not** throw your clothes on the floor.
6. I can't get this **knot** untied.
7. I **ate** early because I was hungry.
8. The **eight** players divided into four teams.
9. Is this the path **to** the camp?
10. Bring us some tape and some pencils, **too**.
11. He has **two** brothers who look just like him.
12. My **right** hand hurts.
13. I have to **write** a poem for class.
14. My baby sister is **one** year old.
15. I heard you **won** your skating contest.

Spelling Practice   *Pages 142–143*

Introduce the spelling rule and have students read the **list words** aloud. Encourage students to look back at their **Warm-Up Tests** and apply the spelling rule to any misspelled words.

As students work through the **Spelling Practice** exercises, remind them to look back at their list words or in their dictionaries if they need help. Point out that the **Spelling Practice** differs from those in previous lessons. Then read the directions with students and ask which word the first clue suggests (*hole*). Tell students that they should write 1 in the first blank.

 See Words in Context, page 14

106

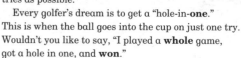

What do you think a "hole in one" is?

Putt-Putt Golf

Some people call it miniature golf. It's called putt-putt golf, **too**. Whatever it's called, it's a lot of fun.

There's **no** secret to playing mini golf. If you **know** how to swing a golf club, you can play.

Putt-putt golf is like real golf, but the course is much smaller. You play with a real golf ball and golf club. You use the club to hit the ball. You try to get the ball into a **hole** called a cup. The idea is **to** get the ball into every hole with as few tries as possible.

Every golfer's dream is to get a "hole-in-**one**." This is when the ball goes into the cup on just one try. Wouldn't you like to say, "I played a **whole** game, got a hole in one, and **won**."

Look back at the words in dark print. Say each word. Which words have the same sound but different spellings?

141

Spelling Practice

TIP

Homonyms are words that sound alike but have different spellings and different meanings, such as **to**, **too**, and **two**.

LIST WORDS
1. hole   *hole*
2. whole   *whole*
3. no   *no*
4. know   *know*
5. not   *not*
6. knot   *knot*
7. ate   *ate*
8. eight   *eight*
9. to   *to*
10. too   *too*
11. two   *two*
12. right *right*
13. write *write*
14. one   *one*
15. won   *won*

Spelling Homonyms
Match each **list word** with its clue. Write the word's number in the space.

1. an opening	1	2. complete	2
3. did eat	7	4. did not lose	15
5. to tie tightly	6	6. also	10
7. understand	4	8. in no way	5
9. not wrong	12	10. not yes	3
11. move toward	9	12. before two	14
13. a pair	11	14. four plus four	8
15. form letters	13		

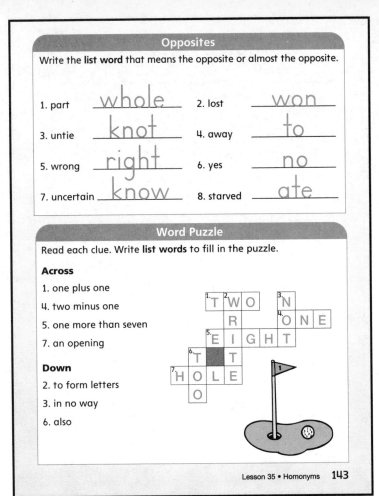

Opposites

Write the **list word** that means the opposite or almost the opposite.

1. part ___whole___   2. lost ___won___

3. untie ___knot___   4. away ___to___

5. wrong ___right___   6. yes ___no___

7. uncertain ___know___   8. starved ___ate___

Word Puzzle

Read each clue. Write **list words** to fill in the puzzle.

Across

1. one plus one
4. two minus one
5. one more than seven
7. an opening

Down

2. to form letters
3. in no way
6. also

```
T W O   N
      R   O N E
    E I G H T
    T   T
  H O L E
    O
```

Lesson 35 • Homonyms   **143**

Spelling and Writing

Proofreading

The paragraph below has six mistakes. Use the proofreading marks to fix each mistake. Write the misspelled **list words** correctly on the lines.

Proofreading Marks

- ◯ spelling mistake
- ≡ capital letter
- ℒ take something out

   I put a a (hole) puzzle together by myself. I put all the (write) pieces together. I have (too) more puzzles to go. the next one has a thousand pieces. I'm not sure if i can do that one alone.

1. ___whole___

2. ___right___

3. ___two___

Writing a List

Many games use a ball. How many can you think of? Make a list of them.

_____

_____

_____

_____

BONUS WORDS

aunt
ant
for
four
deer
dear

144   Lesson 35 • Homonyms

Spelling Strategy

Write each **list word** on a separate card and hold up the cards one at a time. Ask a volunteer to say each word and use it in a sentence. If a student uses a word correctly, give the card to him or her. After all the cards have been distributed, students with cards can say their words, give the meanings, and call on volunteers to spell them.

BONUS WORDS Have students write a sentence using each pair of bonus word homonyms but leaving the actual words blank. Then have them trade papers with a partner to fill in the missing words.

Spelling and Writing   *Page 144*

   The **Proofreading** exercise will help students prepare to proofread their lists. As students complete the writing activity, encourage them to brainstorm ideas, write a first draft, revise, and proofread their work. To publish their writing, students may want to read their lists aloud and demonstrate how to play one of their favorite ball games.

Writer's Corner   You may want to bring in the sports section of your local newspaper and read the headlines and the first few paragraphs of some of the stories. Afterward, invite students to write a few sentences about their favorite team or sports figure.

Final Test

1. The **whole** field is covered with wildflowers.
2. We **ate** sandwiches for lunch today.
3. You can't play outside now. It's **too** dark!
4. Which table has **eight** chairs?
5. Only **one** person at a time can be president.
6. **Write** a story about your favorite memory.
7. The workers put up a fence around the **hole**.
8. The **two** children each had a good idea.
9. Let me **know** what time the show begins.
10. Should we take a **right** turn at the corner?
11. Which team **won** the game?
12. **No**, I am not hungry yet.
13. This **knot** is impossible to untie!
14. My family went **to** California on vacation.
15. Joe's name was **not** on the list.

Lesson 36

Review Lessons 31–35

Objective

To review spelling words with vowel pairs; with *oo*; with the *oi* or *ou* sound; with the *ô* sound; with prefixes: adding *un* or *re*; and homonyms

Check Your Spelling Notebook
Pages 145–148

Based on your observations, note which words are giving students the most difficulty and offer assistance for spelling them correctly. Here are some frequently misspelled words to watch for: *soon, because, whole, know, too, two, write,* and *right*.

To give students extra help and practice in taking standardized tests, you may want to have them take the **Warm-Up Test** for this lesson on pages 110–111. After scoring the tests, return them to students so that they can record their misspelled words in their spelling notebooks.

Suggest that students practice their troublesome words by writing them with crayons or markers. They can use black or blue, but switch to a bright color to write the letters that are giving them trouble. After practicing their words, students can work through the exercises for lessons 31–35 and the cumulative review, **Show What You Know.** Before they begin each exercise, you may want to go over the spelling rule.

 Take It Home

Invite students to use the **list words** in lessons 31–35 at home to write "loaded sentences." With a family member, students can make up sentences, trying to use as many **list words** in each one as possible. For a complete list of the words, encourage students to take their *Spelling Workout* books home. Students can also use **Take It Home Master 6** on pages 112–113 to help them do the activity. Invite students to share their sentences with the class.

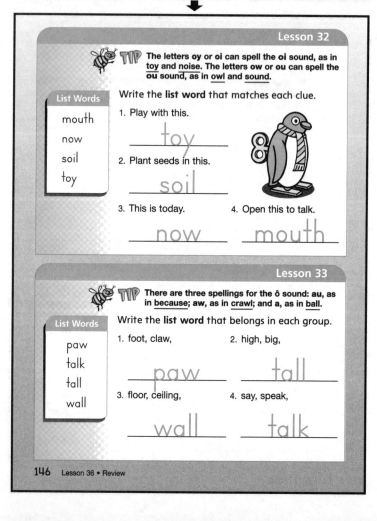

Lessons 31–35 · Review

Lesson 36

In Lessons 31–35 you learned how to spell words with the oo, oo, ou, oi, and ô sounds. You also learned about prefixes and homonyms.

Check Your Spelling Notebook

Look at the words in your spelling notebook. Which words for Lessons 31 through 35 did you have the most trouble with? Write them here.

_____

_____

Lesson 31

TIP Words with oo can have two sounds. Listen to the oo sound, as in <u>soon</u>, and the oo sound, as in <u>hood</u>.

List Words
food
good
boot
noon

Write the **list word** that belongs in each group.

1. morning, evening,

   noon

2. eggs, bread,

   food

3. nice, kind,

   good

4. shoe, sneaker,

   boot

145

Lesson 32

TIP The letters oy or oi can spell the oi sound, as in <u>toy</u> and <u>noise</u>. The letters ow or ou can spell the ou sound, as in <u>owl</u> and <u>sound</u>.

List Words
mouth
now
soil
toy

Write the **list word** that matches each clue.

1. Play with this.

   toy

2. Plant seeds in this.

   soil

3. This is today.

   now

4. Open this to talk.

   mouth

Lesson 33

TIP There are three spellings for the ô sound: au, as in <u>because</u>; aw, as in <u>crawl</u>; and a, as in <u>ball</u>.

List Words
paw
talk
tall
wall

Write the **list word** that belongs in each group.

1. foot, claw,

   paw

2. high, big,

   tall

3. floor, ceiling,

   wall

4. say, speak,

   talk

146   Lesson 36 • Review

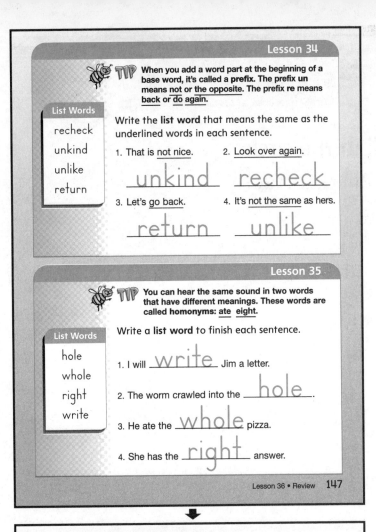

Lesson 34

TIP When you add a word part at the beginning of a base word, it's called a prefix. The prefix **un** means not or the opposite. The prefix **re** means back or do again.

List Words
recheck
unkind
unlike
return

Write the **list word** that means the same as the underlined words in each sentence.

1. That is not nice. _unkind_
2. Look over again. _recheck_
3. Let's go back. _return_
4. It's not the same as hers. _unlike_

Lesson 35

TIP You can hear the same sound in two words that have different meanings. These words are called homonyms: ate eight.

List Words
hole
whole
right
write

Write a **list word** to finish each sentence.

1. I will _write_ Jim a letter.
2. The worm crawled into the _hole_.
3. He ate the _whole_ pizza.
4. She has the _right_ answer.

Lesson 36 • Review 147

Show What You Know

Lessons 31–35 Review

One word is misspelled in each set of **list words**. Fill in the circle next to the **list word** that is spelled incorrectly.

1. ● fut	○ toy	○ call	○ untie
2. ○ unlike	○ paw	● knowe	○ to
3. ○ owl	○ ate	○ good	● spoyl
4. ○ tall	● rechek	○ wood	○ no
5. ● unloc	○ oil	○ boot	○ food
6. ○ not	○ too	● craul	○ now
7. ○ soil	○ ball	○ noon	● wholl
8. ○ return	● becaus	○ wall	○ draw
9. ● frawn	○ room	○ talk	○ two
10. ○ soon	○ one	○ hole	● hod
11. ○ won	○ remake	● wright	○ walk
12. ○ knot	● unhappey	○ tooth	○ unkind
13. ○ call	○ boot	● rereed	○ right
14. ● noyse	○ tall	○ wood	○ hole
15. ○ good	○ not	○ untie	● mauth
16. ○ one	● sownd	○ unlike	○ room
17. ○ soon	○ right	● tauk	○ owl
18. ○ won	○ return	○ draw	● aight
19. ● retolde	○ noon	○ paw	○ wall
20. ○ walk	○ ball	● soyl	○ remake

148 Lesson 36 • Review

Final Test

1. My favorite jeans have a big **hole** in the knee.
2. Check and **recheck** your answers on the test.
3. How did the puppy get a splinter in its **paw**?
4. The lion opened its **mouth** wide and roared.
5. We brought lots of **food** to the picnic.
6. This glass of juice tastes so **good**!
7. We have to go home **now**.
8. Do you think she'll grow up to be **tall**?
9. You can **return** the sweater if it doesn't fit.
10. Your **whole** family is so talented!
11. Did Susan get the **right** answer?
12. Calling people names is very **unkind**.
13. Mom wants to **talk** to me about my report card.
14. The gardener scattered flower seeds in the **soil**.
15. Has anyone found my other **boot** yet?
16. Chris made his sailboat out of **wood**.
17. That old rag doll is Christina's favorite **toy**.
18. Mr. Washington tacked a map on the **wall**.
19. Tanya is **unlike** her twin sister in many ways.
20. When did you learn how to **write** your name?

Check Your Spelling Notebook

After writing each word, students can circle the letters in the vowel pair; the letters that spell the ô, oi, or ou sound; the prefix un or re; or they can tell whether the word is a homonym and name the word or words it sounds like.

Name _____

Read each set of words. Fill in the circle next to the word that is spelled correctly.

1. ⓐ mowth   ⓑ muth
   ⓒ mouthe   ⓓ mouth

2. ⓐ unkinde   ⓑ unkind
   ⓒ unkined   ⓓ unkaind

3. ⓐ fude   ⓑ foode
   ⓒ food   ⓓ fud

4. ⓐ tawl   ⓑ tall
   ⓒ tal   ⓓ taul

5. ⓐ righte   ⓑ rihgte
   ⓒ right   ⓓ rit

6. ⓐ soil   ⓑ soyle
   ⓒ soyl   ⓓ soile

7. ⓐ hoal   ⓑ whoal
   ⓒ hole   ⓓ hoel

8. ⓐ good   ⓑ goode
   ⓒ gud   ⓓ gude

9. ⓐ boot   ⓑ boote
   ⓒ buut   ⓓ boott

Lesson Review Test (Side B)

Read each set of words. Fill in the circle next to the word that is spelled correctly.

10. ⓐ tawlk ⓑ talke
    ⓒ talk ⓓ tawlke

11. ⓐ wood ⓑ wud
    ⓒ woode ⓓ wude

12. ⓐ unliek ⓑ unlik
    ⓒ unlaik ⓓ unlike

13. ⓐ pau ⓑ pawe
    ⓒ paue ⓓ paw

14. ⓐ toi ⓑ toy
    ⓒ toey ⓓ tyo

15. ⓐ write ⓑ wrighte
    ⓒ wriet ⓓ wrait

16. ⓐ woll ⓑ wol
    ⓒ wall ⓓ wal

17. ⓐ rechek ⓑ richeck
    ⓒ richek ⓓ recheck

18. ⓐ return ⓑ retern
    ⓒ returne ⓓ riturn

Take It Home 6

Your child has learned to spell many new words in Lessons 31–35 and would enjoy sharing them with you and your family. Read on for some ideas that will make reviewing those spelling words as easy as A-B-C!

Load 'em Up!

This activity is just loaded with spelling words—but it couldn't be easier! Simply help your child write sentences loaded with as many spelling words as possible—the longer and wackier the better!

Lesson 31
1. boot
2. food
3. foot
4. good
5. hood
6. noon
7. room
8. soon
9. tooth
10. wood

Lesson 32
1. frown
2. mouth
3. noise
4. now
5. oil
6. owl
7. soil
8. sound
9. spoil
10. toy

Lesson 33
1. ball
2. because
3. call
4. crawl
5. draw
6. paw
7. talk
8. tall
9. walk
10. wall

Lesson 34
1. recheck
2. remake
3. reread
4. retold
5. return
6. unhappy
7. unkind
8. unlike
9. unlock
10. untie

Lesson 35
1. ate
2. eight
3. hole
4. knot
5. know
6. no
7. not
8. one
9. right
10. to
11. too
12. two
13. whole
14. won
15. write

Show and Spell

With your child, take turns acting out the spelling word that each picture represents. Remember, you can't just guess a word—you have to spell it, too!

_____   _____

_____   _____

_____   _____

_____   _____

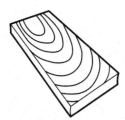

_____   _____

Writing and Proofreading Guide

1. Choose something to write about.

2. Write your ideas. Don't worry about making mistakes.

3. Now proofread your work.
   Use these proofreading marks to check your work.

Proofreading Marks

- ⬯ spelling mistake
- ≡ capital letter
- ⊙ add period
- ⌃ add something
- ⌄ add apostrophe
- ℮ take out something
- ¶ indent paragraph

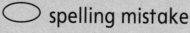

the elephant has a a long trunke

4. Make your final copy.

   The elephant has a long trunk.

5. Share your writing.

Using Your Dictionary

The *Spelling Workout* Dictionary shows you many things about your spelling words.

The **entry word** listed in ABC order is the word you are looking up.

The **sound-spelling** or **respelling** tells how to say the word.

The **definition** tells what the word means.

hop (häp) to move by making short jumps [The bunny will <u>hop</u> into our garden.] **hops, hopped, hopping**

The **sample sentence** shows how to use the word.

Other **forms** of the word are listed.

Pronunciation Key

SYMBOL	KEY WORDS	SYMBOL	KEY WORDS	SYMBOL	KEY WORDS	SYMBOL	KEY WORDS
a	ask, fat	͝o͝o	look, pull	b	bed, dub	t	top, hat
ā	ape, date	o͞o	ooze, tool	d	did, had	v	vat, have
ä	car, lot	ou	out, crowd	f	fall, off	w	will, always
				g	get, dog	y	yet, yard
e	elf, ten	u	up, cut	h	he, ahead	z	zebra, haze
ē	even, meet	ʉ	fur, fern	j	joy, jump		
				k	kill, bake	ch	chin, arch
i	is, hit	ə	a in ago	l	let, ball	ŋ	ring, singer
ī	ice, fire		e in agent	m	met, trim	sh	she, dash
			e in father	n	not, ton	th	thin, truth
ō	open, go		i in unity	p	put, tap	*th*	then, father
ô	law, horn		o in collect	r	red, dear	zh	s in pleasure
oi	oil, point		u in focus	s	sell, pass		

able (ā bəl) can do something [He is <u>able</u> to tell jokes.]

afraid (ə frād) feeling scared [Jan is not <u>afraid</u> of anything.]

ago (ə gō) in the past [We met a year <u>ago</u>.]

alarm (ə lärm) the bell or buzzer on an alarm clock [I set my <u>alarm</u> for 6 a.m.] —**alarms**

all (ôl) **1** the whole thing [I can eat <u>all</u> my vegetables.] **2** every one [<u>All</u> my socks are blue.]

also (ôl so) too [Maria is my sister and <u>also</u> my friend.]

always (ôl wāz) every time [Lisa <u>always</u> does her homework.]

ant (ant) a small insect that lives in or on the ground [An <u>ant</u> crawled across the picnic table.] —**ants**

anything (en ē thiŋ) any object or event [There could be <u>anything</u> in that box!]

apple (ap əl) a red, green, or yellow fruit that is firm and juicy and grows on trees [Sam ate the red <u>apple</u>.] —**apples**

arch (ärch) **1** the curved part of something [There was an <u>arch</u> over the door.] **2** to curve or bend [My cat will often <u>arch</u> its back.] —**arches, arched, arching**

aren't (ärent) are not [I hope you <u>aren't</u> going to wear your new shoes in the mud!]

around (ə round) in a circle [The wheel turned <u>around</u>.]

ask (ask) **1** to use words to find out or get something [Let's <u>ask</u> Mom for a ride to the game.] **2** to invite [I will <u>ask</u> Jeff to my party.] —**asks, asked, asking**

ate (āt) did eat [Louisa <u>ate</u> her peas.]

a	ask, fat
ā	ape, date
ä	car, lot
e	elf, ten
ē	even, meet
i	is, hit
ī	ice, fire
ō	open, go
ô	law, horn
oi	oil, point
o͝o	look, pull
o͞o	ooze, tool
ou	out, crowd
u	up, cut
ʉ	fur, fern
ə	a in ago
	e in agent
	e in father
	i in unity
	o in collect
	u in focus
ch	chin, arch
ŋ	ring, singer
sh	she, dash
th	thin, truth
th	then, father
zh	s in pleasure

aunt (ant *or* änt) a sister of one's mother or father [My <u>aunt</u> is my father's little sister.] —**aunts**

automobile (ôt ə mə bēl) a car moved by an engine [Dad drives a red <u>automobile</u>.] —**automobiles**

away (ə wā) **1** to some other place [Billy moved <u>away</u> from here.] **2** in the proper place [Please put the rabbit <u>away</u>.] **3** not here [Our teacher is <u>away</u> this week.]

back (bak) **1** the part of the body on the other side of one's chest [The runner had a number on her <u>back</u>.] **2** the opposite of the front [Ellie sat in the <u>back</u> of the room.] **3** to move toward the rear [Can you <u>back</u> your bike into the garage?] **4** in the opposite direction [Seth ran there and <u>back</u>.] **5** in return [You do not have to pay <u>back</u> this money.] —**backs, backed, backing**

bad (bad) not pleasant [The <u>bad</u> weather kept everybody indoors.] —**worse, worst**

bait (bāt) food put on a hook or trap to catch fish or animals [She used a worm as <u>bait</u> when she fished.]

bake (bāk) to cook by dry heat [We will <u>bake</u> the bread for one hour.] —**bakes, baked, baking**

ball (bôl) anything with a round shape [Mo's <u>ball</u> of string rolled across the floor.] —**balls**

band (band) **1** a strip of some material used to wrap around or hold something together [The rubber <u>band</u> held the lid on the box.] **2** a group of musicians [The <u>band</u> played our favorite song.] —**bands**

beach (bēch) the sand or ground at the edge of an ocean or lake [Nate found pretty shells on the beach.] —**beaches**

beast (bēst) any large, four-footed animal [An elephant is a very large beast.] —**beasts**

beat (bēt) **1** to hit or strike again and again [I like to hear the rain beat against the roof.] **2** to win over [Our team will beat your team in basketball.] —**beats, beat, beaten, beating**

beaver (bē vər) an animal that can live on land and in water [The beaver built a dam across the stream.] —**beavers**

became (bē kām) did become [Gwen became ill after eating too much food.]

because (bē kôz) the reason for [I am happy today because it is my birthday.]

bed (bed) **1** a piece of furniture used for resting or sleeping [I changed the sheets on my bed.] **2** sleep [It is time for me to go to bed.] **3** a piece of ground where flowers grow [Dad planted tulips in the flower bed.] —**beds**

beg (beg) to ask for as charity or as a gift [I need to beg for a dollar from my mom.] —**begs, begged, begging**

behind (bē hīnd) **1** late or slow [We fell behind in our work.] **2** in back of [The man was sitting behind my seat.]

belt (belt) a strip of leather or cloth that goes around the waist [Rose wore a belt with her new dress.] —**belts**

bit (bit) a small piece or amount [He got a bit of dirt on his pants.] —**bits**

bite (bīt) to cut with the teeth [Don't bite off such a big piece.] —**bites, bit, biting**

a	ask, fat
ā	ape, date
ä	car, lot
e	elf, ten
ē	even, meet
i	is, hit
ī	ice, fire
ō	open, go
ô	law, horn
oi	oil, point
o͞o	look, pull
o͞o	ooze, tool
ou	out, crowd
u	up, cut
ʉ	fur, fern
ə	a in ago
	e in agent
	e in father
	i in unity
	o in collect
	u in focus
ch	chin, arch
ŋ	ring, singer
sh	she, dash
th	thin, truth
th	then, father
zh	s in pleasure

blanket (blaŋ kət) a warm covering used on a bed [A wool <u>blanket</u> will keep you warm at night.] —**blankets**

blow (blō) to force air out from the mouth [<u>Blow</u> out the candles.] —**blows, blew, blowing**

blue (blo͞o) having the color of the clear sky or the deep sea [My cat has <u>blue</u> eyes.] —**bluer, bluest**

blueberry (blo͞o ber ē) a small, round, dark blue berry that is eaten [Amy made a <u>blueberry</u> pie.] —**blueberries**

boat (bōt) a small vessel for traveling on water [We rode in a <u>boat</u> to the island.] —**boats**

body (bäd ē) the whole part of a person or animal [You should eat foods that are good for your <u>body</u>.] —**bodies**

boil (boil) to bubble up and become steam by being heated [<u>Boil</u> the water to make tea.] —**boils, boiled, boiling**

boot (bo͞ot) a covering of leather or rubber for the foot and part of the leg [My <u>boot</u> fell off my foot into the sticky mud.] —**boots**

born (bôrn) brought into life or being [Mario was <u>born</u> in July.]

bottle (bät l) a glass or plastic container for water, milk, or juice [The baby drank juice from a <u>bottle</u>.] —**bottles**

bowl (bōl) a deep, rounded dish [Susan ate a <u>bowl</u> of soup.] —**bowls**

box¹ (bäks) a cardboard or wooden container [The <u>box</u> had a lid.] —**boxes**

box² (bäks) to hit with the fist [Ed will <u>box</u> the champ tonight.] —**boxes, boxed, boxing**

a	ask, fat
ā	ape, date
ä	car, lot
e	elf, ten
ē	even, meet
i	is, hit
ī	ice, fire
ō	open, go
ô	law, horn
oi	oil, point
o͝o	look, pull
o͞o	ooze, tool
ou	out, crowd
u	up, cut
ʉ	fur, fern
ə	a in ago
	e in agent
	e in father
	i in unity
	o in collect
	u in focus
ch	chin, arch
ŋ	ring, singer
sh	she, dash
th	thin, truth
th	then, father
zh	s in pleasure

boy (bȯi) a child who will grow up to be a man [The <u>boy</u> loved his father.] —**boys**

brave (brāv) full of courage [The <u>brave</u> firefighter saved the baby.] —**braver, bravest**

bread (bred) a loaf baked from dough made of flour and other things [We sliced the <u>bread</u> to make wheat toast.] —**breads**

bread

brook (bro͝ok) a small stream [Freddy jumped across the <u>brook</u>.] —**brooks**

bunny (bun ē) a rabbit [The <u>bunny</u> hopped away.] —**bunnies**

burn (bʉrn) **1** to be on fire [The logs will <u>burn</u> for a few hours.] **2** to injure by heat [The hot stove will <u>burn</u> your hand.] **3** to feel hot [Your face will <u>burn</u> if you have a fever.] —**burns, burned, burning**

by (bī) near [The child is <u>by</u> her mother.]

---

call (kôl) **1** to shout or yell [I heard you <u>call</u> for your brother.] **2** to telephone [I need your phone number to <u>call</u> you.] —**calls, called, calling**

Cc

camera (kam ər ə *or* kam rə) a closed box for taking photographs [Judy took a photograph of her dog with a <u>camera</u>.] —**cameras**

canary (kə ner ē) a small, yellow songbird kept as a pet in a cage [The <u>canary</u> sang all morning.] —**canaries**

candle (kan dəl) a piece of wax with a wick that gives off light when burned [We lit a <u>candle</u> in the dark room.] —**candles**

can't (kant) cannot [Willie <u>can't</u> find his shoes.]

carry (ker ē) to take from one place to another [Jenny will <u>carry</u> Ben's books from school.] —**carries, carried, carrying**

cart (kärt) a small wagon [He put the lettuce in a grocery <u>cart</u>.] —**carts**

cent (sent) one penny [Maggie spent every <u>cent</u> she had on her sister's present.] —**cents**

cheese (chēz) a solid food made by pressing together curds of soured milk [Shirley made a ham and <u>cheese</u> sandwich.] —**cheeses**

cherry (cher ē) a small, round, sweet fruit [I like <u>cherry</u> ice cream the best.] —**cherries**

child (child) a young boy or girl [The <u>child</u> ran to her mother.] —**children**

circle (sur kel) **1** anything round [The children formed a <u>circle</u> around their teacher.] **2** to move around [The planets <u>circle</u> the sun.] —**circles, circled, circling**

city (sit ē) a very large town [Juan lives in a <u>city</u> with many tall buildings.] —**cities**

class (klas) one group or room of students in a school [Each <u>class</u> went on a field trip.] —**classes**

clean (klēn) **1** without dirt [The dishes were <u>clean</u>.] **2** to make neat and tidy [Please <u>clean</u> your desk.] —**cleaner, cleanest; cleans, cleaned, cleaning**

clue (klo͞o) a thing that helps to solve a puzzle [The <u>clue</u> helped the police find the robber.] —**clues**

coach (kōch) **1** a large, closed cart pulled by horses [The queen got out of the <u>coach</u>.] **2** a person who helps people play sports [My baseball <u>coach</u> said I played well.] **3** to help people play sports [Fred will <u>coach</u> the football team this year.] —**coaches, coached, coaching**

cherries

coat (kōt) something with sleeves that opens down the front and is worn over clothing to keep one warm or dry [Bonnie's new winter coat is made of wool.] —**coats**

coconut (kō kə nut) the large, round fruit of a coconut palm [I ate a coconut at the beach.] —**coconuts**

cold (kōld) very chilly [The weather was too cold for swimming.] —**colder, coldest**

color (kul ər) **1** the different shades of things, such as crayons or paints [Joan's favorite color is red.] —**colors 2** to use crayons or paints to fill in a picture [It is fun to color pictures with a friend.] —**colored, coloring**

cool (ko͞ol) not warm but not very cold [When the sun went down, the air became cool.] —**cooler, coolest**

corn (kôrn) a grain that grows in kernels on large cobs [Nell loves to eat corn on the cob.]

crash (krash) to fall, hit, or break with a very loud sound [Steve hoped that his sled would not crash into a tree.] —**crashes, crashed, crashing**

crater (krāt ər) a hollow that is shaped like a bowl [There is a crater at the mouth of the volcano.] —**craters**

crawl (krôl) to creep slowly on the ground [Alonzo's baby brother learned to crawl very early.] —**crawls, crawled, crawling**

crowd (kroud) a large group of people gathered together [A crowd filled the movie theater.] —**crowds**

crown (kroun) a headdress of gold and jewels worn by a king or queen [The queen's crown had diamonds and rubies in it.] —**crowns**

a	ask, fat
ā	ape, date
ä	car, lot
e	elf, ten
ē	even, meet
i	is, hit
ī	ice, fire
ō	open, go
ô	law, horn
oi	oil, point
o͝o	look, pull
o͞o	ooze, tool
ou	out, crowd
u	up, cut
ʉ	fur, fern
ə	a in ago
	e in agent
	e in father
	i in unity
	o in collect
	u in focus
ch	chin, arch
ŋ	ring, singer
sh	she, dash
th	thin, truth
th	then, father
zh	s in pleasure

crown

cub (kub) babies of certain animals such as bears or lions [The mother bear kept her <u>cub</u> close to her.] —**cubs**

curtain (kʉrt n) a piece of cloth hung at a window or in front of a stage [When the <u>curtain</u> was raised, the play began.] —**curtains**

cut (kut) to make an opening in with a knife or other sharp tool [Mike <u>cut</u> his chin while he was shaving.] —**cuts, cut, cutting**

cute (kyo͞ot) pretty or pleasing [Everyone thought that the baby monkeys were <u>cute</u>.] —**cuter, cutest**

dawn (dôn) the beginning of day [The rooster crowed at <u>dawn</u>.] —**dawns**

dear (dir) **1** much loved [Reza is my <u>dear</u> friend.] **2** a polite form of address in a letter [He began the letter with "<u>Dear</u> Aunt Betty."] —**dearer, dearest**

deep (dēp) far down, far in, or far back [The water in the lake was very <u>deep</u>.] —**deeper, deepest**

deer (dir) a swift-running, hoofed animal [We saw a <u>deer</u> in the forest.] —**deer**

dirt (dʉrt) matter that makes things unclean [Roy got <u>dirt</u> on his clean shirt.]

doesn't (duz ənt) does not [Marsha <u>doesn't</u> have a pet.]

draw (drô) to make a picture with pencils, pens, or crayons [Alice likes to <u>draw</u> horses.] —**draws, drew, drawn, drawing**

due (do͞o) owed or expected [My library book is <u>due</u> today.]

dust (dust) **1** fine, powdery material in the air [The <u>dust</u> from the dirt road made me cough.] **2** to wipe the <u>dust</u> from [Please <u>dust</u> the table.] —**dusts, dusted, dusting**

---

eagle (ē gəl) a large, strong bird [The <u>eagle</u> soared above the hills.] —**eagles**

ear (ir) either one of the two organs in the head through which sound is heard [The cute dog had one <u>ear</u> up and one <u>ear</u> down.] —**ears**

easy (ē zē) not hard to do [It was <u>easy</u> for Tom to learn to ride the bike.] —**easier, easiest**

eight (āt) the next number after seven [This cup holds <u>eight</u> ounces of water.]

enjoy (en joi) to get pleasure from [I <u>enjoy</u> reading books.] —**enjoys, enjoyed, enjoying**

---

face (fās) **1** the front of the head [Our teacher had a big smile on her <u>face</u>.] —**faces 2** to turn toward something [Please <u>face</u> the class.] —**faces, faced, facing**

faint (fānt) **1** weak [I heard a <u>faint</u> whisper.] **2** to fall into a sleep-like state [He will <u>faint</u> at the sight of blood.] —**faints, fainted, fainting**

far (fär) not near [My grandparents live <u>far</u> from our house.] —**farther, farthest**

farm (färm) a piece of land with buildings where crops and animals are raised [Tony's uncle has many cows on his <u>farm</u>.] —**farms**

feed (fēd) to give food to [Ryan will <u>feed</u> the fish.] —**feeds, fed, feeding**

fell (fel) dropped to a lower place [It hurt when I <u>fell</u> out of the tree.]

few (fyo͞o) not many [Yes, I'll have a <u>few</u> raisins.]

find (fīnd) to get something by looking for it [I hope I <u>find</u> my dime.] —**finds, found, finding**

fine¹ (fīn) **1** very good [You did a <u>fine</u> job on your homework!] **2** having very small parts [The beach has very <u>fine</u> sand.] —**finer, finest**

fine² (fīn) money paid for a mistake [Kiyo paid a <u>fine</u> for her late library books.] —**fines**

fire (fīr) **1** burning flames [We told stories by the <u>fire</u>.] **2** to shoot off something [He will <u>fire</u> the starting gun.] **3** to tell someone to leave a job [He had to <u>fire</u> the worker who was late every day.] —**fires, fired, firing**

first (fu̇rst) the number-one thing [Paul was the <u>first</u> runner to cross the finish line.]

fit (fit) to be the right size [You need skates that <u>fit</u> your feet.] —**fits, fitted, fitting**

fix (fiks) to repair or mend [Can you <u>fix</u> the broken chair?] —**fixes, fixed, fixing**

flat (flat) smooth and level [The top of the table is <u>flat</u>.] —**flatter, flattest**

flew (flo͞o) moved through the air, usually with wings [The plane <u>flew</u> above the clouds.]

floor (flôr) the bottom part of a room on which one walks [We put a rug on the <u>floor</u>.] —**floors**

fog (fôg) a thick mist that is hard to see through [We couldn't see the road in the <u>fog</u>.]

fold (fōld) to bend something over upon itself so that one part is on top of another [Please <u>fold</u> the napkins.] —**folds, folded, folding**

food (fo͞od) a thing we eat to live and grow [We cooked the <u>food</u> in the oven.] —**foods**

a	ask, fat
ā	ape, date
ä	car, lot
e	elf, ten
ē	even, meet
i	is, hit
ī	ice, fire
ō	open, go
ô	law, horn
oi	oil, point
o͝o	look, pull
o͞o	ooze, tool
ou	out, crowd
u	up, cut
u̇	fur, fern
ə	a in ago
	e in agent
	e in father
	i in unity
	o in collect
	u in focus
ch	chin, arch
ŋ	ring, singer
sh	she, dash
th	thin, truth
th	then, father
zh	s in pleasure

foot (foŏt) **1** the part of the body on which people or animals stand [Mick rested his foot on the stool.] **2** a twelve-inch measure [The snow was more than a foot deep.] —**feet**

for (fôr) in order to be, keep, have, get, or read [He swims for exercise.]

forest (fôr əst) a thick growth of trees [Deer live in the forest.] —**forests**

four (fôr) the cardinal number between three and five [Two plus two equals four.]

fox (fäks) a wild animal of the dog family with reddish fur and a long, bushy tail [The red fox cared for her young ones.] —**foxes**

fresh (fresh) newly made, got, or grown [A fresh tomato tastes delicious.] —**fresher, freshest**

fried (frīd) cooked over heat in oil or fat [Herman loves fried eggs.]

friend (frend) someone a person knows well and likes [I like to play with my friend Sara.] —**friends**

frog (frôg) a small, croaking pond animal that jumps [The tadpole will grow up to be a frog.] —**frogs**

from (frum) **1** starting at [Dad works from nine until five.] **2** out of [Take your book from the desk.] **3** made or sent by [Simon got a gift from his aunt.]

frown (froun) a sad look on a person's face [Gina's frown became a smile when she saw the funny clown.] —**frowns**

fry (frī) to cook over heat in oil or fat [I will fry the egg in butter.] —**fries, fried, frying**

funny (fun ē) causes laughter [The clown's baggy pants looked funny.] —**funnier, funniest**

frog

Gg

gate (gāt) a swinging door in a fence [Dean opened the <u>gate</u> to let me in.] —**gates**

gather (ga*th* ər) to bring or come together in one place or group [<u>Gather</u> your books.] —**gathers, gathered, gathering**

gentle (jent l) mild, soft, or easy [A <u>gentle</u> breeze cooled my face.] —**gentler, gentlest**

get (get) **1** to come to own [Mom said we could <u>get</u> a puppy.] **2** to arrive somewhere [We may <u>get</u> to Texas by noon.] **3** to go and bring [Please <u>get</u> me an apple.] —**gets, got, gotten, getting**

gift (gift) a present [I bought a <u>gift</u> for my mother.] —**gifts**

girl (gʉrl) a female child [Maria is the <u>girl</u> with the red bow in her hair.] —**girls**

glad (glad) happy [I am <u>glad</u> that you came to see me.] —**gladder, gladdest**

glass (glas) **1** a hard substance that breaks easily and lets light through [The window pane is made of <u>glass</u>.] **2** a lens people use to help them see [I will look through the <u>glass</u> to read the small print.] **3** a thing to drink out of that is often clear and does not have a handle [Pour milk into the <u>glass</u>.] —**glasses**

glove (gluv) a covering for the hands to keep them warm or protect them [Lance lost his golf <u>glove</u>.] —**gloves**

go (gō) to move from one place to another [Bea will <u>go</u> to your house at noon.] —**goes, went, gone, going**

goat (gōt) an animal like a sheep that has horns [The <u>goat</u> chews its cud.] —**goats**

good (go͝od) pleasing [The apples taste very <u>good</u>.] —**better, best**

grass (gras) green plants with narrow, pointed leaves that cover lawns and meadows [We mow the <u>grass</u> every week in the summer.]

gray (grā) a color between black and white [The sky was <u>gray</u> and full of dark clouds.]

greedy (grēd ē) wanting or taking all that one can get [The <u>greedy</u> boy ate all the cookies.] —**greedier, greediest**

grew (grōo) **1** became large or older [Nina <u>grew</u> four inches in one year.] **2** raised [The farmer <u>grew</u> beans last year.]

growl (grou̇l) to make a low, rumbling, threatening sound in the throat [Dogs <u>growl</u> when they are angry.] —**growls, growled, growling**

gum[1] (gum) something sticky to chew [We do not chew <u>gum</u> in school.]

gum[2] (gum) the part of the mouth that holds the teeth [Melissa felt a new tooth in the baby's <u>gum</u>.] —**gums**

had (had) owned or held [The cat <u>had</u> a bell around its neck.]

half (haf) either of two equal parts of something [Five is <u>half</u> of ten.] —**halves**

hall (hôl) a passageway from which doors open into rooms [My room is at the end of the <u>hall</u>.] —**halls**

handle (han dəl) **1** the part by which something is lifted, held, or turned [Lana picked up the mug by the <u>handle</u>.] **2** to hold or touch [You must <u>handle</u> the kittens gently.] —**handles, handled, handling**

hard (härd) **1** not soft [Luke likes <u>hard</u>, crunchy crackers.] **2** not easy [It's <u>hard</u> to do outdoor work on a hot day.] —**harder, hardest**

have (hav) own or hold [I <u>have</u> a bowl of grapes.] —**has, had, having**

head (hed) **1** the part of the body above the neck [Diane wore a hat on her <u>head</u>.] **2** the front or top of something [Wait for me at the <u>head</u> of the line.] —**heads**

healthy (hel thē) well [Exercise to keep <u>healthy</u>.] —**healthier, healthiest**

heat (hēt) **1** great warmth [The <u>heat</u> made me sleepy.] **2** to make or become warm or hot [The fire will <u>heat</u> the room.] —**heats, heated, heating**

heavy (hev ē) weighing very much [That piano is very <u>heavy</u>.] —**heavier, heaviest**

heel (hēl) the back part of the foot [I have a blister on my <u>heel</u>.] —**heels**

help (help) to do something to make a thing easier for someone [I like to <u>help</u> Dad dry the dishes.] —**helps, helped, helping**

her (hʉr) having to do with a girl or a woman [Mom had a smile on <u>her</u> face.]

hide (hīd) to put or keep out of sight [I will <u>hide</u> the gift in my closet.] —**hides, hid, hidden, hiding**

hill (hil) ground that is a little higher than the land around it [We could see far from the top of the <u>hill</u>.] —**hills**

him (him) having to do with a boy or man [Ivan asked me to help <u>him</u>.]

his (hiz) belonging to him [<u>His</u> book is on the desk.]

a	ask, fat
ā	ape, date
ä	car, lot
e	elf, ten
ē	even, meet
i	is, hit
ī	ice, fire
ō	open, go
ô	law, horn
oi	oil, point
o͝o	look, pull
o͞o	ooze, tool
ou	out, crowd
u	up, cut
ʉ	fur, fern
ə	a in ago
	e in agent
	e in father
	i in unity
	o in collect
	u in focus
ch	chin, arch
ŋ	ring, singer
sh	she, dash
th	thin, truth
th	then, father
zh	s in pleasure

hole (hōl) an opening in something [There is a hole in my sock.] —**holes**

holiday (häl ə dā) a day on which most people do not have to work [We have a holiday next Monday.] —**holidays**

hood (hood) **1** a covering for the head [Jerry had a blue coat with a hood.] **2** the lid that covers the engine of a car [Brenda lifted the hood of the car.] —**hoods**

hop (häp) to move by making short jumps [The bunny will hop into our garden.] —**hops, hopped, hopping**

hope (hōp) to wish for or want very much [We hope that we can use our sleds today.] —**hopes, hoped, hoping**

horse (hôrs) a large animal with four legs, hoofs, a long tail, and a mane [Sweet Pea was a fine racing horse.] —**horses**

hour (our) sixty minutes [Dinner will be ready in one hour.] —**hours**

hug (hug) to clasp in the arms and hold close [The baby likes to hug her teddy bear.] —**hugs, hugged, hugging**

huge (hyōōj) very large [The horse seemed huge to the little girl.]

I'd (īd) **1** I had **2** I would **3** I should [I'd like an apple.]

I'm (īm) I am [I'm tired.]

inch (inch) a unit used to measure things [A quarter is about one inch wide.] —**inches**

isn't (iz ənt) is not [Scooter isn't his real name.]

it's (its) **1** it is [It's time to go.] **2** it has [It's been a fun day.]

joey (jō ē) a young kangaroo [The mother kangaroo cared for her joey.] —**joeys**

jog (jäg) to run at a slow, even pace [Pat will jog in the park each day.] —**jogs, jogged, jogging**

joy (joi) a very happy feeling [You could see the joy on his face when he won.]

just (just) exactly [Angela was just on time for class.]

keep (kēp) **1** to hold or save [Alex will keep his report card.] **2** to write down a record of something [Do you keep a diary?] **3** to continue [Keep calling until you get an answer.] —**keeps, kept, keeping**

key (kē) **1** a small metal piece that opens a lock [Lara uses a key to start her car.] **2** one of the flat parts that is pressed down on a typewriter or a piano [That key on the piano is broken.] —**keys**

kick (kik) to hit with the foot [Brian can kick the ball far.] —**kicks, kicked, kicking**

kind[1] (kīnd) sort or variety [What kind of ice cream do you like?] —**kinds**

kind[2] (kīnd) friendly, generous [My aunt is a kind person.] —**kinder, kindest**

knew (no͞o) was sure of [Quan knew what time it was.]

knot (nät) a loop in a string or ribbon that is pulled tight [The shoelaces were tied in a knot.] —**knots**

know (nō) **1** be sure of [Did you know the answer?] **2** to hear, feel, or see something [Susie says that she does not know Lee.] —**knows, knew, known, knowing**

lake (lāk) a large body of water with land all around [There are many fish in the lake.] —**lakes**

lamb (lam) a young sheep [The wool of the little lamb was soft and white.] —**lambs**

lay (lā) **1** to put or place [Lay your books on the table.] **2** to give an egg, as a chicken does [A hen will lay an egg in the nest.] —**lays, laid, laying**

led (led) showed the way [The guide led them along the path.]

let (let) to allow [They let me help.] —**lets, let, letting**

let's (lets) let us [Let's hurry to get to the show on time.]

lettuce (let əs) a plant with crisp, green leaves that is often used in salads [Do you like lettuce and tomato sandwiches?]

lie¹ (lī) to stretch one's body in a flat position [Lie down on the bed.] —**lies, lay, lying**

lie² (lī) **1** something said that is not true [What he said was a lie.] **2** to say what is not true [Do not lie to me.] —**lies, lied, lying**

line (līn) **1** a cord, rope, or string [She will hang the sheets on the line to dry.] **2** a long, thin mark [Draw a line under the best answer.] **3** a straight row [We stood in line at the bank.] —**lines**

list (list) **1** a set of words or numbers set down in order [Mom made a list of items she needed.] **2** to make a list [Please list the names of your friends for me.] —**lists, listed, listing**

lobster (läb stər) a large shellfish with big claws [Many people like to eat lobster.] —**lobsters**

lamb

a	ask, fat
ā	ape, date
ä	car, lot
e	elf, ten
ē	even, meet
i	is, hit
ī	ice, fire
ō	open, go
ô	law, horn
oi	oil, point
�	look, pull
o͞o	ooze, tool
ou	out, crowd
u	up, cut
ʉ	fur, fern
ə	a in ago
	e in agent
	e in father
	i in unity
	o in collect
	u in focus
ch	chin, arch
ŋ	ring, singer
sh	she, dash
th	thin, truth
th	then, father
zh	s in pleasure

lock (läk) to fasten a door or safe [Please <u>lock</u> the door.] —**locks, locked, locking**

look (look) to turn one's eyes in order to see [<u>Look</u> at your book.] —**looks, looked, looking**

loose (lo͞os) not firmly fastened [My front tooth is <u>loose</u>.] —**looser, loosest**

love (luv) **1** to have a deep and tender feeling for [My mother and father <u>love</u> me.] **2** to like very much [Al and Rita <u>love</u> Swiss cheese.] —**loves, loved, loving**

low (lō) **1** not high or tall [The batter swung at the <u>low</u> pitch.] **2** below others or less than usual [The hat was for sale at a <u>low</u> price.] —**lower, lowest**

lucky (luk ē) having good things happen by chance [Jim was <u>lucky</u> to have found a dime.] —**luckier, luckiest**

mad (mad) angry [My mother is <u>mad</u> at me for being late.] —**madder, maddest**

main (mān) the most important [A baby's <u>main</u> food is milk.]

many (men ē) a large number of [<u>Many</u> people go to the bank on payday.]

maple (mā pəl) a shade tree grown for its hard wood or sap, which is used to make syrup [I love <u>maple</u> syrup.] —**maples**

march (märch) to walk with regular, steady steps as soldiers do [I am going to <u>march</u> in the parade.] —**marches, marched, marching**

mare (mer) a female horse [My horse is a brown <u>mare</u>.] —**mares**

mask (mask) something worn over the face [Donna wore a scary Halloween mask.] —**masks**

math (math) a subject dealing with numbers and symbols [We learned how to add in math class today.]

may (mā) **1** might [This may be the wrong road.] **2** to be allowed [Yes, you may go out to play.]

mean¹ (mēn) to be a sign of [What does this letter mean?] —**means, meant, meaning**

mean² (mēn) unkind or not nice [Never be mean to your sister.] —**meaner, meanest**

meet (mēt) **1** to see someone for the first time [It's been very nice to meet you!] **2** to plan to be at a place where someone else plans to be, too [Let's meet in the gym after school.] **3** to be joined [The two rivers meet ahead.] —**meets, met, meeting**

met (met) saw someone for the first time [I met my neighbor yesterday.]

midnight (mid nīt) twelve o'clock at night [A new day begins after midnight.]

mile (mīl) a distance of 5,280 feet or 1.609 kilometers [We live a mile away.] —**miles**

mind (mīnd) **1** the thinking part of a person [Jason has a good mind for math.] **2** to care about [Would you mind helping me?] —**minds, minded, minding**

minute (min it) any of the sixty equal parts of an hour [There are sixty seconds in one minute.] —**minutes**

a	ask, fat
ā	ape, date
ä	car, lot
e	elf, ten
ē	even, meet
i	is, hit
ī	ice, fire
ō	open, go
ô	law, horn
oi	oil, point
o͞o	look, pull
o͞o	ooze, tool
ou	out, crowd
u	up, cut
ʉ	fur, fern
ə	a in ago
	e in agent
	e in father
	i in unity
	o in collect
	u in focus
ch	chin, arch
ŋ	ring, singer
sh	she, dash
th	thin, truth
th	then, father
zh	s in pleasure

mitt (mit) a padded glove worn by baseball players [Sheila brought her catcher's mitt.] —**mitts**

mix (miks) to stir together [You can mix the flour and eggs.] —**mixes, mixed, mixing**

Monday (mun dā) the second day of the week [School begins on Monday.] —**Mondays**

month (munth) about a thirty-day period [Summer vacation begins in the month of June.] —**months**

moon (mo͞on) the largest heavenly body that can be seen in the night sky [A full moon can be quite bright.] —**moons**

more (môr) greater or larger [May I have more bread, please?]

most (mōst) almost all [Most children like to visit the zoo.]

mouth (mouth) the opening in the head used for eating and talking [She chews with her mouth closed.] —**mouths**

much (much) a large amount [We liked the movie very much.]

mule (myo͞ol) an animal that is a cross between a horse and a donkey [A mule can be a great help to a farmer.] —**mules**

must (must) has to [This hat must be Meg's.]

mustn't (mus ənt) must not [You musn't talk to strangers.]

mitt

nap (nap) **1** to sleep for a short time [Do you nap in the afternoon?] **2** a short sleep [The baby takes a nap twice a day.] —**naps, napped, napping**

neck (nek) the part of a man or animal that joins the head to the body [The man wore a tie around his neck.] —**necks**

new (no͞o) here for the first time [Pete's mom bought a <u>new</u> car.] —**newer, newest**

nibble (nib əl) to eat with quick, small bites [Mice like to <u>nibble</u> cheese.] —**nibbles, nibbled, nibbling**

nice (nīs) good, pleasant, or polite [Miss Lee is a <u>nice</u> teacher.] —**nicer, nicest**

no (nō) not so; opposite of yes [<u>No</u>, I did not call you.]

noise (nȯiz) a sound [The car's horn made a loud <u>noise</u>.] —**noises**

noon (no͞on) twelve o'clock in the daytime [We eat lunch at <u>noon</u>.]

nose (nōz) the part of the face that has two openings for breathing and smelling [Breathe through your <u>nose</u>, not your mouth.] —**noses**

not (nät) in no way [Let's <u>not</u> forget our manners.]

nothing (nuth iŋ) not a thing; zero [There was <u>nothing</u> left on the dish.]

now (nȯu) at this time [Please come over <u>now</u> for lunch.]

oak (ōk) the tree on which acorns grow and that is used for lumber [Aunt Lil sat down under the <u>oak</u> tree.] —**oaks**

ocean (ō shən) a large body of salt water that covers much of the Earth [Whales live in the <u>ocean</u>.] —**oceans**

oil (ȯil) **1** a greasy liquid used for cooking [Gary likes <u>oil</u> on his salad.] **2** a greasy liquid used for fuel [Some people use <u>oil</u> in lamps.] —**oils**

old (ōld) having been around for a long time [These are my <u>old</u> tennis shoes.]

one (wun) the number before two [You may take only <u>one</u> cookie.]

only (ōn lē) without any others [My friends were the <u>only</u> ones who knew the secret.]

opening (ō pən iŋ) **1** the act of making open [He is <u>opening</u> the door for us.] **2** an open place or hole [We fixed the <u>opening</u> in the wall with plaster.] —**openings**

orbit (ôr bit) the path of a heavenly body or satellite around another [The Earth will make an <u>orbit</u> around the Sun once every 365 days.] —**orbits**

oven (uv ən) an enclosed space for baking or roasting food [Mom put a turkey in the <u>oven</u>.] —**ovens**

over (ō vər) **1** above [The sky <u>over</u> us is blue.] **2** so that the other side is up [Flip the pancake <u>over</u>.] **3** again [Would you please read that story <u>over</u>?] **4** finished [At last, the trip was <u>over</u>.]

owl (oul) a bird with a large head, large eyes, a hooked beak, and sharp claws [The <u>owl</u> sleeps during the day.] —**owls**

own (ōn) **1** belonging to or having to do with oneself [I have my <u>own</u> toy.] **2** to have for oneself [We <u>own</u> two cars.] —**owns, owned, owning**

oyster (ois tər) a shellfish with a soft body that lives inside two rough shells joined together [A pearl grows inside an <u>oyster</u>.] —**oysters**

a	ask, fat
ā	ape, date
ä	car, lot
e	elf, ten
ē	even, meet
i	is, hit
ī	ice, fire
ō	open, go
ô	law, horn
oi	oil, point
oo	look, pull
o͞o	ooze, tool
ou	out, crowd
u	up, cut
ʉ	fur, fern
ə	a in ago
	e in agent
	e in father
	i in unity
	o in collect
	u in focus
ch	chin, arch
ŋ	ring, singer
sh	she, dash
th	thin, truth
th	then, father
zh	s in pleasure

pack (pak) to put things together in something for carrying or storing [I will <u>pack</u> my suitcase tonight.] —**packs, packed, packing**

pad (pad) a number of sheets of paper fastened together along one edge [She wrote a story on a <u>pad</u>.] —**pads**

paint (pānt) **1** liquid color put on with a brush [The fresh <u>paint</u> gave the room a new look.] **2** to put color on with a brush [The boys began to <u>paint</u> the fence.] —**paints, painted, painting**

pale (pāl) having little color in the face or skin [He was very <u>pale</u> after his illness.] —**paler, palest**

park (pärk) **1** a place to rest or play [We flew kites in the <u>park</u>.] **2** to leave a car or truck in one place for a time [Did you <u>park</u> in the driveway?]

part (pärt) **1** a piece of something [Here's a <u>part</u> of my apple.] **2** a role in a play [Who will play the king's <u>part</u>?] **3** the line where one's hair is combed two ways [The <u>part</u> in Ted's hair is straight.] **4** to go away from each other [The twins wanted to stay together and never <u>part</u>.] —**parts, parted, parting**

paw (pô) the foot of an animal that has claws [The dog lifted its front <u>paw</u>.] —**paws**

peach (pēch) a pinkish-yellow fruit with fuzzy skin and a rough pit [I love to eat <u>peach</u> pie with ice cream.] —**peaches**

penny (pen ē) a coin worth one cent [Cora put the shiny new <u>penny</u> in her bank.] —**pennies**

people (pē pəl) persons [The streets were full of <u>people</u>.]

piano

a	ask, fat
ā	ape, date
ä	car, lot
e	elf, ten
ē	even, meet
i	is, hit
ī	ice, fire
ō	open, go
ô	law, horn
oi	oil, point
o͞o	look, pull
o͞o	ooze, tool
ou	out, crowd
u	up, cut
ʉ	fur, fern
ə	a in ago
	e in agent
	e in father
	i in unity
	o in collect
	u in focus
ch	chin, arch
ŋ	ring, singer
sh	she, dash
th	thin, truth
th	then, father
zh	s in pleasure

pet (pet) **1** an animal that is tamed and kept as a companion [That dog is our <u>pet</u>.] —**pets 2** to stroke or pat gently [I want to <u>pet</u> the horse.] —**pets, petted, petting**

piano (pē an ō) a large instrument with many wire strings in a case with a keyboard [Small hammers hit the <u>piano</u> strings when you press the keys.] —**pianos**

pie (pī) a dish with filling in a crust [The pumpkin <u>pie</u> was still warm.] —**pies**

pillow (pil ō) a bag filled with feathers or foam used to rest the head on [I like to sleep on a soft <u>pillow</u>.] —**pillows**

pine (pīn) an evergreen tree with needles for leaves [It is fun to collect <u>pine</u> cones.] —**pines**

pint (pīnt) a measure of volume equal to one-half quart [I drank a <u>pint</u> of milk at lunch.] —**pints**

pipe (pīp) a long tube through which water, gas, or oil can flow [The water spilled out of the <u>pipe</u>.] —**pipes**

plan (plan) a way of doing something that has been thought out ahead of time [Dad has a <u>plan</u> for our summer vacation.] —**plans**

plane (plān) a short form of **airplane** [We took a <u>plane</u> to New York.] —**planes**

plate (plāt) a flat dish for food [Raul ate all the food on his <u>plate</u>.] —**plates**

play (plā) **1** to have fun [It is fun to <u>play</u> games.] **2** to make music [Helen is learning to <u>play</u> the flute.] —**plays, played, playing 3** a story acted out on a stage [Amal had a small part in the <u>play</u> at school.] —**plays**

plus   (plus) added to [Two <u>plus</u> two equals four.]
   —**pluses**

pocket   (päk ət) a small pouch sewed into
   clothing for carrying things [Diane kept a
   comb in her <u>pocket</u>.] —**pockets**

pond   (pänd) a small lake [A frog jumped into the
   <u>pond</u>.] —**ponds**

pool   (po͞ol) a small pond [Many frogs live in that
   <u>pool</u>.] —**pools**

porcupine   (pôr kyo͞o pīn) a wild animal having
   long, sharp spines [The spines of a <u>porcupine</u>
   are called quills.] —**porcupines**

pot

pot   (pät) a round pan for cooking [Gus cooked a
   whole <u>pot</u> of soup.] —**pots**

pound   (pound) a unit of weight [I bought a
   <u>pound</u> of potatoes.] —**pounds**

pup   (pup) a young dog [The little <u>pup</u> chewed on
   my slipper.] —**pups**

purple   (pur pəl) a color that is a mixture of red
   and blue [The king has a <u>purple</u> robe.]

push   (po͞osh) to press against so as to move
   [I like to <u>push</u> my little sister on the swing.]
   —**pushes, pushed, pushing**

pup

put   (po͝ot) to set in a place [Please <u>put</u> your
   shoes away.] —**puts, put, putting**

quick (kwik) fast [We had time for a quick snack.] —**quicker, quickest**

quilt (kwilt) a bed covering made of layers of cloth and filling that are stitched together to form patterns [The top layer of the quilt was made of carefully sewn pieces.] —**quilts**

raccoon (ra ko͞on) a furry animal with black rings on its tail and a black mask over its eyes [The raccoon is active at night.] —**raccoons**

race (rās) **1** a contest of speed [Tanya won the race.] —**races 2** to go very fast [I will race you to the corner.] —**races, raced, racing**

rack (rak) a framework or stand for holding or displaying things [Choose a magazine from the rack.] —**racks**

rake (rāk) **1** a tool with a long handle that has a set of teeth at one end [A rake can be used to smooth the soil.] —**rakes 2** to gather or smooth with a rake [We will rake the leaves into a pile.] —**rakes, raked, raking**

reach (rēch) **1** to stretch out one's arm [Bess could not reach the top shelf.] **2** to arrive somewhere [The train will reach New York in one hour.] —**reaches, reached, reaching**

read[1] (rēd) to get the meaning of words that are written [Most people learn to read in first grade.] —**reads, read, reading**

read[2] (red) got the meaning of words that were written [Walt liked the book so much that he read it twice!]

real (rēl) true or not fake [Are those real pearls?]

rebuild (rē bild) to build again [They will <u>rebuild</u> the old house.] —**rebuilds, rebuilt, rebuilding**

recheck (rē chek) look again to see if something is all right [I must <u>recheck</u> my homework.] —**rechecks, rechecked, rechecking**

redo (rē doo͞) to do again or do over [I like to <u>redo</u> my favorite puzzle.] —**redoes, redid, redoing**

remake (rē māk) to make again [Tish will <u>remake</u> this old fur coat into a new jacket.] —**remakes, remade, remaking**

reread (rē rēd) to read again [Mark will <u>reread</u> his favorite book.] —**rereads, reread, rereading**

restart (rē stärt) to start again [Mom had to <u>restart</u> the motor.] —**restarts, restarted, restarting**

retold (rē tōld) said again [Grandpa <u>retold</u> the story to each of his seven grandchildren.]

return (ri tʉrn) **1** to go or come back [When will you <u>return</u> from your trip?] **2** to bring or put back [Do not forget to <u>return</u> your library book.] —**returns, returned, returning**

right (rīt) **1** correct; not wrong [Greg was <u>right</u> about the weather.] **2** the hand or side that is not the left [Give me your <u>right</u> hand.]

river (riv ər) a large stream of water that flows into an ocean, lake, or other river [A long bridge was built over the <u>river</u>.] —**rivers**

road (rōd) a way for cars and trucks to go from one place to another [The <u>road</u> was very bumpy.] —**roads**

room (ro͞om) **1** a space in a building set off by walls [Every <u>room</u> in the house had a large window.] **2** enough space [Does your desk have enough <u>room</u> for another book?] —**rooms**

road

a	ask, fat
ā	ape, date
ä	car, lot
e	elf, ten
ē	even, meet
i	is, hit
ī	ice, fire
ō	open, go
ô	law, horn
oi	oil, point
o͝o	look, pull
o͞o	ooze, tool
ou	out, crowd
u	up, cut
ʉ	fur, fern
ə	a in ago
	e in agent
	e in father
	i in unity
	o in collect
	u in focus
ch	chin, arch
ŋ	ring, singer
sh	she, dash
th	thin, truth
th	then, father
zh	s in pleasure

rule (r$\overline{oo}$l) **1** a law [We have a rule at our house about no jumping on beds!] **2** to have power over [A new king was chosen to rule over the country.] —**rules, ruled, ruling**

run (run) to go by moving the legs very fast [Ashley will have to run to catch the bus.] —**runs, ran, run, running**

rush (rush) to move with great speed [Fatima had to rush to swim practice.] —**rushes, rushed, rushing**

Ss

sad (sad) unhappy [The sad children missed their old house.] —**sadder, saddest**

said (sed) used words to tell something [We all heard what Nancy said.]

sail (sāl) **1** a big sheet of canvas or cloth used on a boat or ship to catch the wind to make it move [We raised the sail on the boat.] —**sails 2** to travel in a boat or ship [They planned to sail around the world.] —**sails, sailed, sailing**

salt (sôlt) a white substance used to flavor and preserve foods [Add a little salt to the soup.] —**salts**

same (sām) just like another; alike [Your bike is the same as mine.]

sandwich (san dwich) two or more slices of bread with a filling between them [I'd like a cheese sandwich.] —**sandwiches**

sat (sat) rested on one's bottom by bending at the waist [The lady sat on the park bench all day.]

satisfy (sat is fī) to meet the needs or wishes of; to make content; to please [Only first prize will satisfy him.] —**satisfies, satisfied, satisfying**

Saturn (sat ərn) the sixth planet away from the Sun [Saturn is known for its many rings.]

save (sāv) **1** to keep until later [Some people save their money in a bank.] **2** to keep someone or something from harm [The doctor tries to save lives.] —**saves, saved, saving**

saw¹ (sô) **1** a tool used to cut wood [Frank used a saw to cut the logs.] —**saws 2** to cut wood with this tool [Can you help me saw these boards?] —**saws, sawed, sawing**

saw² (sô) did see [I saw Bob yesterday.]

say (sā) to use words to tell something [Did you say your name was Margo?] —**says, said, saying**

scarlet (skär lət) very bright red [Mike's face turned scarlet from his sunburn.]

sea (sē) an ocean [Dave dreamed of sailing on the sea.] —**seas**

second (sek ənd) a part of a minute; an instant [Please, wait just a second.] —**seconds**

see (sē) **1** to look at [You can see the tall building from here.] **2** to understand [Now I see what you mean.] **3** to go to someone for help [When will you see a doctor about that foot?] —**sees, saw, seen, seeing**

seed (sēd) the part of a flowering plant that will grow into a new plant [The bean seed needs soil and water to grow.] —**seeds**

sell (sel) to give in return for money [Will you sell me this book for one dollar?] —**sells, sold, selling**

send (send) **1** to cause to go [I will send you home for lunch.] **2** to mail [She will send a letter to you soon.] —**sends, sent, sending**

a	ask, fat
ā	ape, date
ä	car, lot
e	elf, ten
ē	even, meet
i	is, hit
ī	ice, fire
ō	open, go
ô	law, horn
σi	oil, point
σο	look, pull
o͞o	ooze, tool
ou	out, crowd
u	up, cut
ʉ	fur, fern
ə	a in ago
	e in agent
	e in father
	i in unity
	o in collect
	u in focus
ch	chin, arch
ŋ	ring, singer
sh	she, dash
th	thin, truth
th	then, father
zh	s in pleasure

serve/shot

serve (surv) **1** to do work for someone [Mona will <u>serve</u> as their maid.] **2** to offer food or drink [Mother will <u>serve</u> us a hot meal.] —**serves, served, serving**

set (set) **1** to put [You may <u>set</u> the plant over here.] **2** to make or become firm [Is the pudding <u>set</u> yet?] **3** to fix a date, time, or place [Julie <u>set</u> the date for her party.] **4** to sink [The Sun will <u>set</u> in the west.] —**sets, set, setting 5** a group of things [Max has a brand-new <u>set</u> of drums.] —**sets**

shape (shāp) the outer form [The cloud had the <u>shape</u> of a lamb.] —**shapes**

sheep (shēp) an animal related to the goat whose body is covered with heavy wool [I pet a <u>sheep</u> in the zoo.] —**sheep**

shell (shel) a hard outer covering [The turtle peeped out of its <u>shell</u>.] —**shells**

ship (ship) any vessel, larger than a boat, for traveling on deep water [They traveled by <u>ship</u> to Europe.] —**ships**

shirt (shurt) a garment worn on the upper part of the body, usually having a collar and a buttoned opening [Peter wore a plaid <u>shirt</u>.] —**shirts**

shop (shäp) to go to a store to buy something [Toya likes to <u>shop</u> in the fabric store.] —**shops, shopped, shopping**

shore (shôr) land at the edge of a sea or lake [The boat was pulled up on the <u>shore</u> of the lake.] —**shores**

shot (shät) **1** the act or sound of shooting a gun [I heard the <u>shot</u>.] **2** a throw [José took a <u>shot</u> at the basket.] **3** the forcing of fluid into a person's body with a needle [The doctor gave me a <u>shot</u>.] —**shots**

shout (shout) **1** a loud call [We could hear Ted's shout for more nails.] **2** to call loudly [I had to shout because I was so far away.] —**shouts, shouted**

shrimp (shrimp) a small shellfish with a long tail used for food [We peeled the shrimp before we boiled it.] —**shrimp**

shut (shut) **1** to close [Please shut the windows if it rains.] —**shuts, shut, shutting 2** closed [Make sure the door is shut.]

shy (shī) timid [The puppy was too shy to play.] —**shyer, shyest**

sight (sīt) **1** something that is seen [The Grand Canyon is a pretty sight.] **2** the sense of seeing with one's eye [Jeff lost the sight in one eye.] —**sights**

silver (sil vər) **1** a white precious metal [She wore a silver necklace.] **2** a grayish-white color [Their car had silver trim.]

sir (sur) a polite way to speak to a man [No, sir, I did not see your dog.] —**sirs**

siren (sī rən) a thing that makes a loud, warning sound [The firefighter turned on the siren.] —**sirens**

skate (skāt) **1** to move along on ice [We like to skate in the winter.] —**skates, skated, skating 2** a shoe with a blade fastened on it for gliding on ice or rollers fastened for gliding on floors [Ben left the rink to lace his skate.] —**skates**

skin (skin) **1** the covering of the body of a person or animal [Franz scraped his skin when he fell.] **2** the outer covering of some fruits or vegetables [I peeled off the skin of the orange.] —**skins**

a	ask, fat
ā	ape, date
ä	car, lot
e	elf, ten
ē	even, meet
i	is, hit
ī	ice, fire
ō	open, go
ô	law, horn
oi	oil, point
oo	look, pull
ōō	ooze, tool
ou	out, crowd
u	up, cut
u	fur, fern
ə	a in ago
	e in agent
	e in father
	i in unity
	o in collect
	u in focus
ch	chin, arch
ŋ	ring, singer
sh	she, dash
th	thin, truth
th	then, father
zh	s in pleasure

socks

skip (skip) **1** to move by hopping on one foot and then the other [Lucy will <u>skip</u> down the path.] **2** to pass over something [Since it is late, we will <u>skip</u> a few stories.] —**skips, skipped, skipping**

skirt (skʉrt) a piece of clothing that hangs from the waist of a woman or girl [Paula's <u>skirt</u> is made of wool.] —**skirts**

sleep (slēp) to be in the condition of rest with the eyes closed [Sometimes I dream when I <u>sleep</u>.] —**sleeps, slept, sleeping**

sleepy (slē pē) ready to fall asleep [Do you get <u>sleepy</u> at night?] —**sleepier, sleepiest**

slice (slīs) **1** a thin, broad piece of something [I will eat one <u>slice</u> of pizza.] —**slices 2** to cut [Tina will <u>slice</u> the melon for us.] —**slices, sliced, slicing**

smell (sməl) **1** to breathe in the odor of something [I <u>smell</u> fresh bread.] —**smells, smelled, smelling 2** an odor [That flower has a wonderful <u>smell</u>!]

smoke (smōk) the cloud that rises from something burning [We saw the <u>smoke</u> from their campfire.]

snake (snāk) a long, thin reptile with no legs [A <u>snake</u> will eat unwanted insects in your garden.] —**snakes**

so (sō) to such a degree or amount [Why are you <u>so</u> late?]

sock (säk) a warm covering for the foot that is worn inside a shoe [This <u>sock</u> does not match the other one.] —**socks**

soft (sôft) not hard [A baby's skin is <u>soft</u>.] —**softer, softest**

soil (soil) **1** the top layer of the Earth [This <u>soil</u> is good for plants.] **2** to make dirty [Please do not <u>soil</u> your new tennis shoes.] —**soils, soiled, soiling**

sold (sōld) gave something in return for money [Carl <u>sold</u> two baseball cards for ten dollars.]

soon (so͞on) in a short time [<u>Soon</u> it will be time for the flowers to bloom.] —**sooner, soonest**

sound (sound) a noise [The <u>sound</u> of the train was loud.] —**sounds**

space (spās) the area that stretches in all directions, has no limits, and contains all things in the universe [The Earth, the Sun, and all the stars exist in <u>space</u>.]

sparkle (spär kəl) to give off sparks or flashes of light [The waves <u>sparkle</u> in the sunlight.] —**sparkles, sparkled, sparkling**

spell (spel) to say the letters in a word [Les could <u>spell</u> many words.] —**spells, spelled, spelling**

splash (splash) to make a liquid scatter and fall in drops [Don't <u>splash</u> water on the floor.] —**splashes, splashed, splashing**

spoil (spoil) **1** to ruin [If you tell anyone, you'll <u>spoil</u> the surprise.] **2** to rot [The fruit will <u>spoil</u> in a few days.] **3** to cause someone to want too much from others [I wish Grandma would not <u>spoil</u> you.] —**spoils, spoiled, spoiling**

spread (spred) to open out or stretch out, in space or time [The duck <u>spread</u> its wings.] —**spreads, spread, spreading**

sprout (sprout) to begin to grow [The seed will <u>sprout</u> in a few days.] —**sprouts, sprouted, sprouting**

stamp (stamp) to bring one's foot down with force [Please don't <u>stamp</u> in the puddle.] —**stamps, stamped, stamping**

a	ask, fat
ā	ape, date
ä	car, lot
e	elf, ten
ē	even, meet
i	is, hit
ī	ice, fire
ō	open, go
ô	law, horn
oi	oil, point
o͞o	look, pull
o͞o	ooze, tool
ou	out, crowd
u	up, cut
ʉ	fur, fern
ə	**a** in ago
	e in agent
	e in father
	i in unity
	o in collect
	u in focus
ch	chin, arch
ŋ	ring, singer
sh	she, dash
th	thin, truth
th	then, father
zh	**s** in pleasure

stand (stand) to be or get into an upright position on one's feet [<u>Stand</u> by your desk.] —**stands, stood, standing**

start (stärt) to begin to go, do, act, or be [The show will <u>start</u> at 8:30.] —**starts, started, starting**

stick (stik) **1** a small branch or twig [We picked up every <u>stick</u> in the yard.] —**sticks 2** to press a sharp point into something [<u>Stick</u> this toothpick into the sandwich.] **3** to fasten, as with glue [The stamp will not <u>stick</u> to my letter.] **4** to stay close [<u>Stick</u> with me at the zoo.] —**sticks, stuck, sticking**

still (stil) **1** quiet [The woods were very <u>still</u>.] **2** until now [Are you <u>still</u> playing the same game?]

stop (stäp) to keep from going on, moving, or acting [<u>Stop</u> the car.] —**stops, stopped, stopping**

story¹ (stôr ē) a telling of something; a tale [We all loved the <u>story</u> about the dancing bear.] —**stories**

story² (stôr ē) a floor in a building [The elevator stops at the ninth <u>story</u>.] —**stories**

straw (strô) **1** hollow stalks of wheat, rye, or other cereal plants [The hat was woven out of <u>straw</u>.] **2** a slender tube of paper or plastic, used for drinking [She drank her milk through a <u>straw</u>.] —**straws**

stray (strā) to wander from a certain place [Cats may <u>stray</u> from home.] —**strays, strayed, straying**

stream (strēm) a body of flowing water [We crossed the <u>stream</u> on stepping stones.] —**streams**

a	ask, fat
ā	ape, date
ä	car, lot
e	elf, ten
ē	even, meet
i	is, hit
ī	ice, fire
ō	open, go
ô	law, horn
oi	oil, point
oo	look, pull
o͞o	ooze, tool
ou	out, crowd
u	up, cut
ʉ	fur, fern
ə	a in ago
	e in agent
	e in father
	i in unity
	o in collect
	u in focus
ch	chin, arch
ŋ	ring, singer
sh	she, dash
th	thin, truth
th	then, father
zh	s in pleasure

strike (strīk) **1** to hit [Strike the ball when it comes to you.] **2** to stop working to get something [The workers will strike on Monday.] —**strikes, struck, striking**

stuck (stuk) pressed a sharp point into [He stuck his finger with a needle.]

such (such) so much [I had such fun at school!]

sweep (swēp) to clean, usually by brushing with a broom [Please sweep the floor.] —**sweeps, swept, sweeping**

swim (swim) to move in the water by moving arms, legs, fins, or tail [Dan is learning to swim in the pool.] —**swims, swam, swum, swimming**

table (tā bəl) a piece of furniture with a flat top and legs [We ate at the kitchen table.] —**tables**

tack (tak) **1** a short nail with a flat head and sharp point [This tack fell off the bulletin board.] —**tacks 2** to fasten with tacks [Tack this sign to the post.] —**tacks, tacked, tacking**

talk (tôk) **1** to say words [That parrot can really talk!] —**talks, talked, talking 2** the act of saying words [We need to have a talk.] —**talks**

tall (tôl) not low or short [That tower is so tall that I cannot see the top of it.] —**taller, tallest**

tame (tām) no longer wild [The man kept a tame wolf.] —**tamer, tamest**

tape (tāp) **1** a sticky, narrow piece of cloth or plastic [Use this tape to wrap the gift.] **2** a narrow strip of plastic used to record sounds [Let's play the tape that has our favorite songs.] —**tapes 3** to wrap with tape [We will tape the box shut.] **4** to record on tape [Did you tape Steve's song?] —**tapes, taped, taping**

teach (tēch) to show or help to learn how to do something [Will you <u>teach</u> me to skate?] —**teaches, taught, teaching**

team (tēm) a group of people playing together against another group [Tina is on the swim <u>team</u>.] —**teams**

tell (tel) **1** to say [<u>Tell</u> me your name.] **2** to give the story [That book will <u>tell</u> you about the Pilgrims' first Thanksgiving.] —**tells, told, telling**

tent

tent (tent) a canvas shelter [Linda's <u>tent</u> had room for six campers.] —**tents**

then (then) the time after; next [The show ended, and <u>then</u> we went home.]

they (thā) the people or animals being talked about [Joel's parents did not say when <u>they</u> would be home.]

they're (ther) they are [<u>They're</u> going to be surprised.]

thick (thik) great in width or depth from side to side [A <u>thick</u> wall surrounded the garden.] —**thicker, thickest**

thin (thin) not wide or deep; not thick [Norm did not skate on the <u>thin</u> ice.] —**thinner, thinnest**

think (thiŋk) to use the mind [We must <u>think</u> of a plan.] —**thinks, thought, thinking**

those (thōz) people or things mentioned [Are <u>those</u> your books?]

threw (throo) sent through the air by a fast motion of the arm [Mike <u>threw</u> the ball to Ed.]

tie (tī) **1** to bind with string, rope, or cord [You may <u>tie</u> the tire swing to this tree.] **2** a piece of cloth men wear around their neck [John's <u>tie</u> is red with black dots.] **3** when the scores of two teams are the same [Beth hopes her team will be able to break the <u>tie</u>.] —**ties, tied, tying**

tiny (tī nē) very small [A <u>tiny</u> ant ran under the leaf.] —**tinier, tiniest**

tired (tīrd) worn out [Lee was <u>tired</u> after the game.]

to (to͞o) **1** in the direction of [Lean <u>to</u> the left.] **2** onto [Paste the stamp <u>to</u> the envelope.]

toast (tōst) bread that has been heated and browned [I like eggs and <u>toast</u> for breakfast.] —**toast**

today (tə dā) on this day [<u>Today</u> is my birthday.]

toe (tō) one of the five parts at the end of a foot [I have a blister on my <u>toe</u>.] —**toes**

together (to͞o ge*th* ər) with one another [Let's walk to the store <u>together</u>.]

too (to͞o) **1** also [Todd laughed and Fran did, <u>too</u>.] **2** more than enough [These boxes are <u>too</u> heavy to carry.]

took (to͝ok) **1** got by force [The bigger girl <u>took</u> the toy away.] **2** called for; needed [This recipe <u>took</u> all the flour we had.] **3** carried [Jake <u>took</u> his book with him.]

tooth (to͞oth) any of the bony, white parts in the mouth used for biting and chewing [Toya lost her <u>tooth</u> in school.] —**teeth**

tower (tou ər) a building that is much higher than it is wide or long [The castle had a <u>tower</u>.] —**towers**

a	ask, fat
ā	ape, date
ä	car, lot
e	elf, ten
ē	even, meet
i	is, hit
ī	ice, fire
ō	open, go
ô	law, horn
oi	oil, point
o͝o	look, pull
o͞o	ooze, tool
ou	out, crowd
u	up, cut
ʉ	fur, fern
ə	a in ago
	e in agent
	e in father
	i in unity
	o in collect
	u in focus
ch	chin, arch
ŋ	ring, singer
sh	she, dash
th	thin, truth
th	then, father
zh	s in pleasure

tray

a	ask, fat
ā	ape, date
ä	car, lot
e	elf, ten
ē	even, meet
i	is, hit
ī	ice, fire
ō	open, go
ô	law, horn
oi	oil, point
o͞o	look, pull
o͞o	ooze, tool
ou	out, crowd
u	up, cut
ʉ	fur, fern
ə	a in ago
	e in agent
	e in father
	i in unity
	o in collect
	u in focus
ch	chin, arch
ŋ	ring, singer
sh	she, dash
th	thin, truth
th	then, father
zh	s in pleasure

toy (toi) a plaything [That rattle is the baby's favorite <u>toy</u>.] —**toys**

trade (trād) to give one thing for another [Neil will <u>trade</u> baseball cards with you.] —**trades, traded, trading**

trail (trāl) a path formed when people or animals pass [We formed a <u>trail</u> up the mountain.] —**trails**

tray (trā) a flat item used for carrying food or other things [The dentist keeps his tools on a metal <u>tray</u>.] —**trays**

trim (trim) **1** to cut or clip [Keesha will <u>trim</u> the dead branches off the tree.] **2** to decorate [Will you help us <u>trim</u> the Christmas tree?] —**trims, trimmed, trimming**

trip (trip) **1** to stumble or cause to stumble [Do not <u>trip</u> over the log.] **2** a journey, especially a short one [We took a <u>trip</u> to the zoo.] —**trips, tripped, tripping**

truck (truk) a large vehicle used to carry loads [Pedro will load the <u>truck</u>.] —**trucks**

true (tro͞o) **1** correct; not false [We know that her story was <u>true</u>.] **2** loyal [James is a <u>true</u> friend.] —**truer, truest**

trunk (trunk) **1** the main stem of a tree [An oak tree has a long, straight <u>trunk</u>.] **2** an elephant's snout [The elephant picked up the peanut with his <u>trunk</u>.] **3** a large box for storing things [I found this old hat in the <u>trunk</u>.] **4** the space in the rear of the car [I locked the groceries in the <u>trunk</u>.] —**trunks**

tube (to͞ob) a long, slender container [She bought a <u>tube</u> of toothpaste.] —**tubes**

tug (tug) **1** pull with force [Watch that the baby does not <u>tug</u> the tablecloth.] **2** to tow with a tugboat [Did you see them <u>tug</u> the barge?] —**tugs, tugged, tugging**

tumble (tum bəl) to do somersaults, handsprings, or other tricks of an acrobat [The children <u>tumble</u> on the mat.] —**tumbles, tumbled, tumbling**

tune (to͞on) a song [The old man hummed my favorite <u>tune</u>.] —**tunes**

turn (tʉrn) **1** to move something around [<u>Turn</u> the key toward the left.] **2** to change [The rain may <u>turn</u> to snow.] —**turns, turned, turning** **3** chance to do something [Everyone will have a <u>turn</u> to ride the horse.] —**turns**

turtle (tʉrt l) a slow-moving animal that has a hard outer shell [Mark keeps the <u>turtle</u> in the box.] —**turtles**

two (to͞o) the number after one [There are <u>two</u> shoes in a pair.]

---

uncle (uŋ kəl) the brother of one's father or mother [My <u>uncle</u> is Mom's big brother.] —**uncles**

unhappy (un hap ē) sad [Pam is <u>unhappy</u> about the weather.] —**unhappier, unhappiest**

unhook (un ho͝ok) to unfasten a hook [He had to <u>unhook</u> the gate to enter the yard.] —**unhooks, unhooked, unhooking**

unkind (un kīnd) hurting someone's feelings [Rosa has never said an <u>unkind</u> word to anyone.]

unlike (un līk) different [This new car is <u>unlike</u> our old one.]

unlock (un läk) to open with a key [Please <u>unlock</u> the door.] —**unlocks, unlocked, unlocking**

Uu

unsafe (un sāf) dangerous [That broken ladder is unsafe to climb.]

untie (un tī) to take apart a knot or bow [He likes to untie his shoes.] —**unties, untied, untying**

use (yo͞oz) **1** to put into action [You may use my radio.] **2** do away with [Try not to use up all of the toothpaste.] —**uses, used, using**

walk (wôk) **1** to move along on foot [Walk on the sidewalk.] **2** the act of walking [Norman went for a long walk.] —**walks, walked, walking**

wall (wôl) the flat side of a room or a building [Linda hung her painting on a wall.] —**walls**

want (wänt) to wish or long for [I want dessert.] —**wants, wanted, wanting**

warm (wôrm) **1** feeling a little heat [This blanket keeps me warm.] **2** showing strong feeling [Her smile was warm and friendly.] —**warmer, warmest**

waterfall (wôt ər fôl) a steep fall of water [Niagara Falls is a large waterfall on the Niagara River.] —**waterfalls**

week (wēk) seven days [It will take a week to do this job.] —**weeks**

were (wur) had been [The birds were singing.]

we're (wir *or* wē ər) we are [Here's the tree house that we're building.]

weren't (wurnt) were not [They weren't home when we arrived.]

we've (wēv) we have [We've been roller skating all morning.]

whale (hwāl) a very large sea mammal [The whale swam close to our boat.] —**whales**

whale

what (hwut) **1** which thing [What is your name?] **2** so much [What a big mess this is!]

wheat (hwēt) the cereal grass whose grain is used in making the most common type of flour [The fields of wheat stretched for miles.]

when (hwen) at what time [When did you eat breakfast?]

where (hwer) at what place [Where are my glasses?]

whip (hwip) **1** a rod with a strip of leather at one end [The lion tamer carried a whip.] —**whips** **2** to beat into a froth [I helped Mom whip the cream for the dessert.] —**whips, whipped, whipping**

who (hoō) what person or persons [Who made this big mess?]

whole (hōl) in one piece; entire [Wanda ate a whole box of cereal.]

why (hwī) for what reason [Why did he go home?]

wide (wīd) long from side to side [The box was too wide to fit through the door.] —**wider, widest**

will (wil) a word that shows that something is yet to be done [Darla will call you soon.]

win (win) to get by work or skill [Tom wants to win the award.] —**wins, won, winning**

wind¹ (wīnd) to turn or coil something around itself [George will wind the kite string.] —**winds, wound, winding**

wind² (wind) air that is moving [The wind blew my hat away.] —**winds**

wire (wīr) metal that has been pulled into a very long, thin thread [A fence of barbed wire kept the cattle in.] —**wires**

wish (wish) to want [I wish I could see you soon.] —**wishes, wished, wishing**

a	ask, fat
ā	ape, date
ä	car, lot
e	elf, ten
ē	even, meet
i	is, hit
ī	ice, fire
ō	open, go
ô	law, horn
oi	oil, point
oo	look, pull
o͞o	ooze, tool
ou	out, crowd
u	up, cut
ʉ	fur, fern
ə	a in ago
	e in agent
	e in father
	i in unity
	o in collect
	u in focus
ch	chin, arch
ŋ	ring, singer
sh	she, dash
th	thin, truth
th	then, father
zh	s in pleasure

won   (wun) gotten by work or skill [Do you know who <u>won</u> first prize?]

wood   (wood) **1** the hard material of a tree [We need <u>wood</u> for the fire.] **2** lumber [We used <u>wood</u> and nails to build the fort.] —**woods**

wool   (wool) yarn, cloth, or clothing made from the hair of sheep, goats, or llamas [That sweater is made of very soft <u>wool</u>.]

word   (wurd) a group of letters that mean something [Can you read that <u>word</u>?] —**words**

work   (wurk) **1** using energy or skill to make or do something [Farming is hard <u>work</u>.] **2** one's job [Mom left for <u>work</u>.] **3** to do what something is supposed to do [This old radio does not <u>work</u>.] —**works, worked, working**

world   (wurld) the Earth [Sonja wants to travel around the <u>world</u>.] —**worlds**

worm   (wurm) a small, creeping animal with a soft, slender body, no legs, and no backbone [There is a <u>worm</u> under the leaf.] —**worms**

worth   (wurth) the value of something [That vase is <u>worth</u> a lot of money.]

write   (rīt) to form letters or words with a pencil or a pen [Rick will <u>write</u> his name down on paper for you.] —**writes, wrote, written, writing**

yet   (yet) up to now [He is not gone <u>yet</u>.]

you   (yoo) the person or people talked to [<u>You</u> are my best friend.]

you'll   (yool) you will or you shall [<u>You'll</u> be the first to know.]

you've   (yoov) you have [<u>You've</u> got to do your homework.]

Level B Student Record Chart

Name _____

			Pretest	Final Test
Lesson	1	Consonants		
Lesson	2	Consonants		
Lesson	3	Short-Vowels **a** and **i**		
Lesson	4	Short-Vowels **u** and **o**		
Lesson	5	Short-Vowel **e**		
Lesson	6	Lessons 1–5 • Review	■	
Lesson	7	Long-Vowel **a**		
Lesson	8	Long-Vowel **i**		
Lesson	9	Long-Vowel **u**		
Lesson	10	Long-Vowel **o**		
Lesson	11	Long-Vowel **e**		
Lesson	12	Lessons 7–11 • Review	■	
Lesson	13	Blends with **l** and **r**		
Lesson	14	Blends with **s**		
Lesson	15	**y** with a Vowel		
Lesson	16	**y** as a Vowel		
Lesson	17	Words with **le**		
Lesson	18	Lessons 13–17 • Review	■	
Lesson	19	Words with **sh** and **th**		
Lesson	20	Words with **ch** and **wh**		
Lesson	21	Words with **c** and **ck**		
Lesson	22	Vowels with **r**		
Lesson	23	Contractions		
Lesson	24	Lessons 19–23 • Review	■	
Lesson	25	Vowels with **r**		
Lesson	26	Adding Endings		
Lesson	27	Adding Endings		
Lesson	28	Adding Endings		
Lesson	29	Words with Vowel Pairs		
Lesson	30	Lessons 25–29 • Review	■	
Lesson	31	Words with **oo**		
Lesson	32	Words with the **oi** and **ou** Sound		
Lesson	33	Words with the **ô** Sound		
Lesson	34	Adding **un** and **re**		
Lesson	35	Homonyms		
Lesson	36	Lessons 31–35 • Review	■	

Lesson	6	12	18	24	30	36
Standardized Review Test						

Review Test
Answer Key

Lesson 6

1. d	10. b
2. a	11. d
3. d	12. b
4. c	13. c
5. a	14. c
6. d	15. a
7. b	16. c
8. b	17. d
9. c	18. a

Lesson 12

1. c	10. d
2. b	11. c
3. a	12. b
4. b	13. d
5. d	14. c
6. c	15. d
7. a	16. b
8. a	17. a
9. b	18. a

Lesson 18

1. b	10. c
2. d	11. a
3. c	12. d
4. d	13. b
5. b	14. d
6. c	15. b
7. a	16. a
8. d	17. d
9. a	18. a

Lesson 24

1. c	10. b
2. b	11. b
3. d	12. c
4. a	13. c
5. d	14. a
6. b	15. d
7. c	16. b
8. b	17. a
9. c	18. d

Lesson 30

1. b	10. b
2. a	11. d
3. d	12. a
4. d	13. b
5. d	14. d
6. a	15. c
7. c	16. c
8. c	17. d
9. c	18. b

Lesson 36

1. d	10. c
2. b	11. a
3. c	12. d
4. b	13. d
5. c	14. b
6. a	15. a
7. c	16. c
8. a	17. d
9. a	18. a

List Words

Word	Lesson
able	17
afraid	7
ago	10
all	1
also	2
anything	19
apple	17
arch	20
aren't	23
ask	2
ate	35
away	15
back	21
baked	28
ball	33
band	3
beach	11
beat	29
became	21
because	33
bed	5
behind	8
belt	5
bodies	28
boot	31
bottle	17
boxes	26
boys	15
bread	5
bunny	16
burning	26
by	16
call	33
candle	17
can't	23
carries	28
cent	21
city	21
class	13
clean	11
coach	20
coat	10
color	21
corn	22
crash	19

Word	Lesson
crawl	33
cut	1
cute	9
deep	11
draw	33
due	9
dust	4
easy	11
eight	35
face	7
far	22
farm	22
feed	11
fell	2
few	9
find	8
fine	8
fire	8
first	25
fit	3
flat	13
flew	13
floor	22
food	31
foot	31
fox	1
fried	28
friend	13
frog	4
from	13
frown	32
fry	16
funniest	28
gate	7
get	2
girl	25
gladdest	27
glasses	26
glove	13
go	10
goat	10
good	31
grass	13
gray	15
grew	9

Word	Lesson
gum	4
had	2
handle	17
hard	22
have	3
having	28
head	5
help	5
her	25
hide	8
hill	1
him	3
his	2
hole	35
hood	31
hope	10
hopped	27
horse	22
I'm	23
isn't	23
it's	23
jogging	27
joy	15
keep	11
key	16
kick	21
knot	35
know	35
lake	7
lay	29
let	2
let's	23
line	8
list	3
loves	28
low	10
lower	29
luckier	28
lucky	16
main	29
many	16
math	19
may	15
mean	29
meet	11

Word	Lesson
mile	8
mind	8
mitt	3
mixed	27
moon	1
more	22
most	14
mouth	32
much	20
mule	9
must	4
neck	21
new	1
nice	8
no	35
noise	32
noon	31
not	35
nothing	19
now	32
oil	32
old	2
one	35
only	16
opening	26
over	10
owl	32
own	10
paint	7
park	22
part	22
paw	33
peach	20
penny	16
people	17
pie	29
plate	13
plays	15
pot	4
pup	4
purple	17
put	1
quick	21
race	21
rake	7

160

List Words

Word	Lesson	Word	Lesson	Word	Lesson	Word	Lesson
reached	26	sir	25	thin	19	wall	33
read	29	skin	3	think	19	wants	26
real	11	skipping	27	those	10	warm	22
recheck	34	skirt	25	tie	29	week	11
remake	34	slice	14	tiny	16	were	25
reread	34	smell	14	to	35	we're	23
retold	34	smoke	14	today	15	we've	23
return	34	snake	14	toes	29	what	20
right	35	sock	4	together	19	when	20
roads	29	soft	4	too	35	where	20
room	31	soil	32	took	2	whip	20
rule	9	sold	10	tooth	31	who	20
running	27	soon	31	toy	32	whole	35
sad	3	sound	32	trades	28	why	16
sadder	27	spell	14	tray	15	wide	8
said	5	spoil	32	trimming	27	will	3
sail	7	stick	21	truck	13	wind	1
same	7	still	14	true	9	winning	27
sat	2	story	14	trunk	13	wishes	26
save	7	strike	14	tug	4	won	35
saw	1	such	20	tune	9	wood	31
say	15	swim	14	turn	25	word	25
sea	11	table	17	turtle	17	worked	26
sees	26	tack	3	two	35	world	25
sell	5	talk	33	uncle	17	worth	25
sending	26	tall	33	unhappy	34	write	35
serving	28	tape	7	unkind	34	yet	5
set	5	tell	1	unlike	34	you	9
shopped	27	tent	5	unlock	34	you'll	23
shot	4	then	19	untie	34		
shout	19	they	15	use	9		
shut	19	they're	23	walk	33		

Bonus Words

Word	Lesson	Word	Lesson	Word	Lesson	Word	Lesson
alarm	22	curtain	25	loose	31	sleepy	14
always	15	dawn	33	madder	27	so	10
ant	35	dear	35	marching	26	space	21
around	32	deer	35	mask	2	sparkle	17
aunt	35	dirt	25	met	5	splash	14
automobile	33	doesn't	23	Monday	15	spread	5
bad	1	eagle	17	mustn't	23	stamp	14
bait	7	ear	1	napped	27	stand	3
ball	1	enjoy	15	nibble	17	start	22
beast	14	faint	29	nose	10	stop	4
beaver	25	fix	1	pack	21	straw	33
begged	27	fog	4	pad	3	stray	15
bit	3	fold	10	palest	28	stream	14
bite	8	for	35	pet	5	stuck	4
blanket	13	forest	22	pint	8	sweeps	26
blow	10	four	35	pipe	8	tame	7
blue	2	fresh	13	plan	13	teach	11
blueberries	28	gather	28	plane	7	team	29
boat	10	gentle	17	pool	31	thick	28
boil	32	gift	3	pound	32	thinnest	27
born	22	greedy	16	pushed	26	threw	9
bowl	29	growl	13	rack	3	tired	28
brave	7	hall	33	rebuild	34	toast	29
brook	31	healthier	28	redo	34	tower	32
camera	21	heat	11	restart	34	trail	7
canary	16	heavy	5	rushes	26	trip	1
cart	22	heel	11	salt	33	tube	9
cheese	20	holiday	15	sandwich	20	tumble	17
cherry	16	huge	9	satisfy	16	unhook	34
child	20	hugging	27	shape	28	unsafe	34
circle	21	I'd	23	sheep	11	weren't	23
clue	9	just	4	shell	28	whale	20
coconut	21	kind	8	ship	2	wheat	20
cold	2	knew	9	shirt	25	wire	8
cool	31	led	5	shore	28	wool	31
crashes	26	lie	29	shy	16	worm	25
crowd	32	lock	4	sleep	11	you've	23
crown	13	look	2	sleepiest	28		

Spelling Enrichment

Bulletin Board Suggestion

Good Spellers Don't Monkey Around Prepare a bulletin board that shows a monkey hanging from a tree. Use yellow construction paper to make paper bananas. Write a list word on each banana and post the bananas on the bulletin board. Dictate a few list words each day as a mini-test. Have students self-correct their tests. Remove any banana from the board containing a word that everyone in the class was able to spell correctly.

Awards titled "I've Gone Bananas Over Spelling" can be given to students at the end of any week during which all the bananas were removed from the bulletin board.

Group Practice

Fill-In Write spelling words on the board. Omit some of the letters and replace them with dashes. Have the first student in Row One come to the board to fill in one of the missing letters in any of the words. Then, have the first student in Row Two continue the procedure. Continue having students in each row take turns coming up to the board to fill in letters until all the words are completed. Any student who is able to correctly fill in a word earns a point for his or her row. The row with the most points at the end of the game wins.

Erase Write list words on the board. Then, ask the class to put their heads down while you call on a student to come to the board and erase one of the words. This student then calls on a class member to identify the erased word. The identified word is then restored and the student who correctly identified the erasure can be the person who erases next.

Crossword Relay First draw a large grid on the board. Then, divide the class into several teams. Teams compete against each other to form separate crossword puzzles on the board. Individuals on each team take turns racing against members of the other teams to join list words until all possibilities have been exhausted. A list word may appear on each crossword puzzle only once. The winning team is the team whose crossword puzzle contains the greatest number of correctly spelled list words or the team who finishes first.

Scramble Prepare letter cards sufficient to spell all the list words. Distribute letter cards to all students. Some students may be given more than one letter card. The teacher then calls out a list word. Students holding the letters contained in the word race to the front of the class to form the word by standing in the appropriate sequence with their letter cards.

Proofreading Relay Write two columns of misspelled list words on the board. Although the errors can differ, be sure that each list has the same number of errors. Divide the class into two teams and assign each team to a different column. Teams then compete against each other to correct their assigned lists by team members taking turns erasing and replacing an appropriate letter. Each member may correct only one letter per turn. The team that corrects its entire word list first wins.

Detective Call on a student to be a detective. The detective must choose a spelling word from the list and think of a structural clue, definition, or synonym that will help classmates identify it. The detective then states the clue using the format, "I spy a word that. . . ." Students are called on to guess and spell the mystery word. Whoever answers correctly gets to take a turn being the detective.

Spelling Tic-Tac-Toe Draw a tic-tac-toe square on the board. Divide the class into X and O teams. Take turns dictating spelling words to members of each team. If the word is spelled correctly, allow the team member to place an X or O on the square. The first team to place three X's or O's in a row wins.

Words of Fortune Have students put their heads down while you write a spelling word on the board in large letters. Then, cover each letter with a sheet of sturdy paper. The paper can be fastened to the board with magnets. Call on a student to guess any letter of the alphabet the student thinks may be hidden. If that particular letter is hidden, then reveal the letter in every place where it appears in the word by removing the paper.

The student continues to guess letters until an incorrect guess is made or the word is revealed. In the event that an incorrect guess is made, a different student continues the game. Continue the game until every list word has been hidden and then revealed.

Spelling Enrichment

Dictionary Activities

Around the World Designate the first person in the first row to be the traveler. The traveler must stand next to the student seated behind him or her. Then, dictate any letter of the alphabet at random. Instruct the two students to quickly name the letter of the alphabet that precedes the given letter. The student who is first to respond with the correct answer becomes the traveler while the other student sits at that desk. The traveler then moves to compete with the next person in the row. The game continues with the traveler moving up and down the rows as the teacher dictates various alphabet letters. See who can be the traveler who has moved the farthest around the classroom. For variety, you may want to require students to state the letter that follows the given letter. You may also want to dictate pairs of list words and have students name which word comes first.

Stand-Up While the teacher pronounces a word from the spelling dictionary, students look up the entry word and point to it. Tell students to stand up when they have located the entry. See who is the first student to stand up.

This game can be played using the following variations:

1. Have students stand when they have located the guide words for a given word.

2. Have students stand when they are able to tell on what page a given list word appears in the dictionary.

Alphabetical Scramble Prepare tagboard cards with spelling words written on them in large letters. Distribute the cards to students. Call on three students to come to the front of the room and arrange themselves so that their word cards are in alphabetical order.

Cut-Off Distribute a strip of paper to each student. Instruct students to write any four spelling words on the strip. All but one of the words should be in alphabetical order. Then have students exchange their strip with a partner. Students use scissors to cut off the word that is not in alphabetical sequence and tape the remaining word strips together. If students find this activity too difficult, you might have them cut all four words off the strip and arrange them alphabetically on their desks.

Applied Spelling

Journal Allow time each day for students to write in a journal. A spiral bound notebook can be used for this purpose. Encourage students to express their feelings about events that are happening in their lives at home or at school, or they could write about what their plans are for the day. To get them started, you may have to provide starter phrases. Allow them to use "invented" spelling for words they can't spell.

Collect the journals periodically to write comments that echo what the student has written. For example, a student's entry might read, "I'm hape I gt to plae bazball todae." The teacher's response could be "Baseball is my favorite game, too. I'd be happy to watch you play baseball today at recess." This method allows students to learn correct spelling and sentence structure without emphasizing their errors in a negative way.

Letter to the Teacher On a regular basis, invite students to write a note to you. At first you may have to suggest topics or provide a starter sentence. It may be possible to suggest a topic that includes words from the spelling list. Write a response at the bottom of each letter that provides the student with a model of any spelling or sentence structure that apparently needs improvement.

Daily Edit Each day, provide a brief writing sample on the board that contains errors in spelling, capitalization, or punctuation. Have students rewrite the sample correctly. Provide time later in the day to have the class correct the errors on the board. Discuss why the spelling is as it is while students self-correct their work.

Acrostic Poems Have students write a word from the spelling list vertically. Then instruct them to join a word horizontally to each letter of the list word. The horizontal words must begin with the letters in the list word. They also should be words that describe or relate feelings about the list word. Encourage students to refer to a dictionary for help in finding appropriate words. Here is a sample acrostic poem:

Zebras
Otters
Ostriches

Spelling Enrichment

Words-in-a-Row Distribute strips of writing paper to each student. Ask students to write three spelling words in a row. Tell them to misspell two of the words. Then have students take turns writing their row of words on the board. They can call on a classmate to identify and underline the correctly spelled word in the row. Continue until all students have had a chance to write their row of words.

Nursery Rhyme Exchange Provide students with copies of a familiar nursery rhyme. Discuss how some of the words can be exchanged for other words that have similar meanings. Ask students to rewrite the nursery rhyme exchanging some of the words. You may want to encourage students to try this technique with nursery rhymes of their choice. Be sure to give students the opportunity to read their rhymes to the class.

Partner Spelling Assign spelling buddies. Allow partners to alternate dictating or writing sentences that contain words from the spelling list. The sentences can be provided by the teacher or generated by students. Have students check their own work as their partner provides the correct spelling for each sentence.

Scrap Words Provide each student with several sheets of tagboard, scraps of fabric or wallpaper, and some glue. Ask students to cut letters out of the scrap materials and glue them to the tagboard to form words from the spelling list. Display the colorful scrap words around the classroom.

Punch Words Set up a work center in the classroom with a supply of construction paper strips, a hole puncher, sheets of thin paper, and crayons. Demonstrate to students how the hole puncher can be used to create spelling words out of the construction paper. Permit students to take turns working at the center in their free time. Students may also enjoy placing a thin sheet of paper over the punch words and rubbing them with a crayon to make colorful word designs. You can then display their punch word and crayon creations.

Word Cut-Outs Distribute scissors, glue, a sheet of dark-colored construction paper, and a supply of old newspapers and magazines to the class. Have students look through the papers and magazines for list words. Tell them to cut out any list words they find and glue them on the sheet of construction paper. See who can find the most list words. This technique may also be used to have students construct sentences or cut out individual letters to form words.

Word Sorts Invite students to write each list word on a separate card. Then, ask them how many different ways the words can be organized (such as animate vs. inanimate, past-tense or vowel patterns, similarity or contrast in meaning). As students sort the words into each category, have them put words that don't belong in a category into an exception pile.

Spelling Notebook

Definitions and Rules

The alphabet has two kinds of letters—**vowels** and **consonants**. The **vowels** are **a**, **e**, **i**, **o**, and **u** (and sometimes **y**). All the rest of the letters are **consonants**.

Each **syllable** in a word must have a vowel sound. If a word or syllable has only one vowel and it comes at the beginning or between two consonants, the vowel usually stands for a **short-vowel** sound.

        c**a**t   s**i**t   c**u**p

A **long-vowel** sound usually has the same sound as its letter name.

When **y** comes at the end of a word with one syllable, the **y** at the end usually has the sound of long **i**, as in *dry* and *try*. When **y** comes at the end of a word with more than one syllable, it usually has the sound of long **e**, as in *city* and *funny*.

When two or more **consonants** come together in a word, their sounds may blend together. In a **consonant blend**, you can hear the sound of each letter.

        smile   **sl**ide   f**ri**end

A **consonant digraph** consists of two consonants that go together to make one sound.

        sharp   four**th**   ea**ch**

A **consonant cluster** consists of three consonants together in one syllable.

        thrills   pa**tch**   **spl**ash

A **vowel pair** consists of two vowels together where the first vowel stands for the long sound and the second vowel is silent.

        t**ea**cher   f**ai**l   s**oa**k

A **vowel digraph** consists of two vowels that together make a long-vowel sound, a short-vowel sound or a special sound of their own.

        br**ea**d   s**oo**ner   **au**to

A **diphthong** consists of two vowels that blend together to make one sound.

        b**oy**   **oi**l   cl**ou**d

A **base word** is a word to which a prefix or suffix may be added to change its meaning.

        un**law**ful   re**place**   **shy**ness

A **root** is a word part to which a prefix or suffix may be added to change its meaning.

        in**duct**ion   re**pel**   con**duct**

An **ending** is a letter or group of letters added to the end of a base word to make the word singular or plural or to tell when an action happened.

        hat**s**   fox**es**   run**s**   rain**ed**   help**ing**

A **prefix** is a word part that is added to the beginning of a base word or a root. A prefix changes the meaning of the base word.

        unhappy   **dis**trust   **re**pel   **con**duct

A **suffix** is a word part that is added to the end of a base word or root to make a new word.

        cheer**ful**   agree**able**   dic**tion**   port**able**

When you write words in **alphabetical order**, use these rules:

1. If the *first letter* of two words is the same, use the second letter.
2. If the *first two letters* are the same, use the third letter.

There are two **guide words** at the top of each page in the dictionary. The word on the left tells you the first word on the page. The word on the right tells you the last word on the page. All the words in between are in alphabetical order.

The dictionary puts an **accent mark** (′) *after* the syllable with the strong sound.

        pʉr′sən

There is a vowel sound that can be spelled by any of the vowels. It is often found in a syllable that is not accented, or stressed, in a word. This vowel sound has the sound-symbol /ə/. It is called the **schwa**.

The word *I* is always a **capital** letter.

A **contraction** is a short way of writing two words. It is formed by writing two words together and leaving out one or more letters. Use an **apostrophe** (′) to show where something is left out.

        it is = it's   we will = we'll

A **compound word** is a word made by joining two or more words.

        cannot   anyway   maybe   firehouse